JAMES JOYCE AND THE POLITICS OF EGOISM

In *James Joyce and the politics of egoism* a leading scholar approaches the entire Joycean canon through the concept of "egoism." This concept, Jean-Michel Rabaté argues, runs throughout Joyce's work, and involves and incorporates its opposite, "hospitality," a term Rabaté understands as meaning an ethical and linguistic opening to "the other." For Rabaté, both concepts emerge from the fact that Joyce published crucial texts in the London-based review *The Egoist* and later moved on to forge strong ties with the international Paris avant-garde. Rabaté examines the theoretical debates surrounding these connections, linking Joyce's engagement with Irish politics with the aesthetic aspects of his texts. Through egoism, he shows, Joyce defined a literary sensibility founded on negation; through hospitality, Joyce postulated the creation of a new, utopian readership. Rabaté explores Joyce's complex negotiation between these two poles in a study of interest to all Joyceans and scholars of modernism.

JEAN-MICHEL RABATÉ is Professor of English at the University of Pennsylvania. He is the author of *Writing the Image after Roland Barthes* (1997), *The Ghosts of Modernity* (1996), and *Joyce Upon the Void: the Genesis of Doubt* (1991). He has also written and edited many books and articles on modernism and literary theory.

D1722220

JAMES JOYCE AND THE POLITICS OF EGOISM

JEAN-MICHEL RABATÉ

CAMBRIDGE
UNIVERSITY PRESS

PUBLISHED BY THE PRESS SYNDICATE OF THE UNIVERSITY OF CAMBRIDGE
The Pitt Building, Trumpington Street, Cambridge, United Kingdom

CAMBRIDGE UNIVERSITY PRESS
The Edinburgh Building, Cambridge CB2 2RU, UK
40 West 20th Street, New York, NY 10011–4211, USA
10 Stamford Road, Oakleigh, VIC 3166, Australia
Ruiz de Alarcón 13, 28014 Madrid, Spain
Dock House, The Waterfront, Cape Town 8001, South Africa

http://www.cambridge.org

First published 2001

Printed in the United Kingdom at the University Press, Cambridge

Typeface Baskerville MT 11/12.5 pt.   *System* QuarkXPress™   [SE]

A catalogue record for this book is available from the British Library

Library of Congress Cataloguing in Publication data

James Joyce and the politics of egoism / Jean-Michel Rabaté.
p.   cm.
Includes bibliographical references (p.) and index.
ISBN 0 521 80425 6 – ISBN 0 521 00958 8 (pbk.)
1. Joyce, James, 1882–1941 – Political and social views.   2. Politics and
literature – Ireland – History – 20th century.   3. Joyce, James, 1882–1941 – Views on
egoism.   4. Difference (Psychology) in literature.   5. Joyce, James, 1882–1941 – Ethics.   6.
Modernism (Literature) – Ireland.   7. Hospitality in literature.   8. Egoism in literature.   9.
Self in literature.   I. Title.
PR6019.09Z78384   2001
823'.912–dc21   2001016170

ISBN 0 521 80425 6 hardback
ISBN 0 521 00958 8 paperback

Contents

Preface

This is a book without an Introduction or a Conclusion. Just twelve chapters in an order which, although not random, will not be immediately perceptible. It should look like a dodecaphonic series harping on a handful of key motifs – the ego as symptom of literary modernity; the pervasive tension between egoism and hospitality; late Modernism defined less by formal innovation than by an emphasis on a new reader; the curious interactions, antagonistic and yet parallel, between Joyce's esthetic program and the emergence of Irish nationalism, to name but a few.

Thanks to the old rhetorical rule of *post hoc, propter hoc*, and also to excellent editorial advice provided by the anonymous readers who considered an earlier version of these chapters, they now follow each other in some kind of narrative. The foundations for this book were laid in the summer of 1996, when I was asked simultaneously to give two plenary addresses at different Joyce conferences. First, I opened the Zurich James Joyce Symposium at Fritz Senn's kind invitation (as I read "Joyce the egoist" with a bottle of Chanel's *Egoïste* after-shave on my lectern, this gave rise to entirely unfounded rumors that I was being sponsored by the French brand). Then I was asked by Julian Wolfreys to close the International Conference on Joyce and Theory at Dundee (at which I spoke on lice and fleas, and as this time I had refrained from bringing along any toiletries, when people in the audience started scratching their heads, pensively I hope, I was pleased to think that they were distracted from previous heated controversies on Irish politics). In between, I had gone to Dublin to give a talk at the James Joyce Summer School, and I presented on Joyce's concept of hospitality. I had three major concepts to work from, first egoism, then hospitality, and finally the concept of a self-generating and organic language that found in lice a perfect emblem.

It was only after another conference at Yale University in September

1998 on Eugène Jolas and *transition* that I saw another axis emerge: the shift from *The Egoist* (a review which captures very well all the excitement of early and high modernism in London) to *transition* (an international magazine based in Paris that condenses the eclectic verve of later Modernism) seemed to allegorize the entire trajectory of what we call Modernism.

The narrative which links all these chapters is nevertheless not totally linear (and above all not chronological), and aims at leaving a degree of autonomy to each chapter. All the essays that have been already published have been significantly rewritten. Here is the list of the chapters that use texts published in journals or collections. They have been substantially modified for this volume. I would like to thank the editors for permission to reproduce these pages:

Chapter 3, "Joyce the egoist," was published in *Modernism/Modernity*, vol. 4, no. 3, September 1997, pp. 45–65. Chapter 5, "Theory's slice of life," was published in *Re:Joyce. Text, Culture, Politics*, edited by John Brannigan, Geoff Ward and Julian Wolfreys (London: Macmillan, 1998), pp. 121–45. Part of chapter 6, "Joyce vs. the king," was published in *Seeing Double: Revisioning Edwardian and Modernist Literature*, edited by Carola M. Kaplan and Anne B. Simpson (New York: Saint Martin's Press, 1996), pp. 99–109. Chapter 8, "Joyce's transitional revolution," was published in *The Journal of Modern Literature*, Special Issue "Joyce and the Joyceans," winter 1998/99, vol. 22, no. 2, pp. 245–52. Sections of chapter 9, "Hospitality and Sodomy," were published in *Quare Joyce*, edited by Joseph Valente (Ann Arbor: Michigan University Press, 1999), pp. 35–44, and in *Collideorscape of Joyce: Festschrift for Fritz Senn*, edited by Ruth Frehner and Ursula Zeller (Dublin: Lilliput Press, 1998), pp. 341–52. Chapter 10, "Hospitality in the capital city" was published in *The Romanic Review*, vol. 86, no. 3, May 1995, pp. 485–500 and *European James Joyce Studies, Genetic Probes*, edited by David Hayman (Rodolpi, Amsterdam, 1996), pp. 65–83. I have published a different version of the analysis of Luke: 16 from chapter 12 in "The 'Mujic of the Footure': Future, Ancient, Fugitive," forthcoming in a collection of essays devoted to Jacques Derrida, *Futures*.

Abbreviations

Joyce, James, *Letters*, vol. I, ed. S. Gilbert (London: Faber, 1957); vols. II and III, ed. R. Ellmann (London: Faber, 1966): respectively *LI*, *LII* and *LIII*, followed by page number.

Joyce, James, *Selected Letters*, ed. Richard Ellmann (London: Faber, 1975): *LIV*, followed by page number.

Joyce, James, *Ulysses*, ed. H. W. Gabler (London: Penguin, 1986): *U*, followed by number of chapter and line.

Joyce, James, *Critical Writings*, ed. Ellsworth Mason and Richard Ellmann (New York: Viking, 1964): *CW*, followed by page number.

Joyce, James, *Dubliners*, ed. Terence Brown (London: Penguin, 1992): *D*, followed by page number.

Joyce, James, *Finnegans Wake* (London: Faber, 1939): *FW*, followed by page and line number.

Joyce, James, *A Portrait of the Artist as a Young Man*, ed. Chester Anderson (New York: Viking, 1968): *APA*, followed by page number.

Joyce, James, *A Portrait of the Artist as a Young Man*, ed. Seamus Deane (London: Penguin, 1993): *P*, followed by page number.

Joyce, James, *Stephen Hero*, ed. Theodore Spencer, revised edn by John H. Slocum and Herbert Cahoon (London: Jonathan Cape, 1956): *SH*, followed by page number.

The James Joyce Archive, ed. Michael Groden *et al.* (New York and London: Garland, 1977–79), *JJA*, followed by volume and page number.

Joyce, Stanislaus, *The Complete Dublin Diary*, ed. George H. Healey (Ithaca: Cornell University Press, 1971): *DD*, followed by page number.

Ellmann, Richard, *James Joyce*, 2nd revised edn (Oxford: Oxford University Press, 1983): *JJII*, followed by page number.

Power, Arthur, *Conversations with James Joyce*, ed. Clive Hart (London: Millington, 1974): *CJJ*, followed by page number.

Note: double slashes (oblique lines) in quotations indicate paragraph breaks.

CHAPTER ONE

Après mot, le déluge: *the ego as symptom*

On July 20, 1998, the editorial board of the Modern Library, a division of Random House – a jury made up of ten writers, critics and editors, among whom were A. S. Byatt, William Styron, Gore Vidal, Shelby Foote and Christopher Cerf – revealed to the public the list they had drawn up of the hundred best novels of the twentieth century. Joyceans from all over the word could rejoice: *Ulysses* came up first, soon followed by *A Portrait of the Artist as a Young Man* in the third position. More unexpected but quite as heartening for fans was the fact that *Finnegans Wake* had found its way into the list as number seventy-seven. No doubt Joyce would have loved the elegant numerological progression: 1 – 3 – 77. As a new century begins, perhaps the time has come for another assessment: will Joyce's stature still tower above the English-speaking world in the twenty-first century, or was this critical acclaim just a way of leaving behind us an embarrassing literary monument? In 1998, moreover, the backlash was immediate, the ten jury members were denounced as elitist and sexist by disgruntled cavilers. Had they been twelve, they might have been identified with the apostles of a new Joycean creed – as the famous collective study *Our Exagmination Round His Factification For Incamination of Work in Progress* launched the ironical concept as early as 1929, just before the world economy collapsed and Joyce's personal life became fraught with difficulties.

Readers of the American press, for the majority of whom the best novel of the twentieth century would obviously not be *Ulysses* but *The Great Gatsby*, perhaps *The Fountainhead* if not *Atlas Shrugged* (I have not referred to Ayn Rand at random, as will become clear in the second part of this chapter), had been prepared for Joyce's triumph by the issue of *Time* magazine date June 8, 1998. There, under the general heading of "Hundred Artists and Entertainers of the Century" one observed the figure of Joyce looming large among "geniuses" like Pablo Picasso, Charlie Chaplin, Igor Stravinsky, Bob Dylan, and Elvis Presley. In this issue, Joyce was the only novelist to whom four pages of text and several photographs were devoted. The presentation by Paul Gray[1] wryly concluded on the obscurity of the *Wake*: "Today, only dedicated Joyceans regularly attend the *Wake*. A century from now, his readers may catch up with him." This echoed, consciously or not, the famous opening of Richard Ellmann's 1959 biography, that was to enshrine Joyce's life for so long: "We are still learning to be James Joyce's contemporaries." (*JJII*, 3) – while confirming the hope expressed by its author that *Finnegans Wake* was in advance of its times. When he had to defend the seeming madness of his project, Joyce defiantly stated: "Perhaps it is insanity. One will be able to judge in a century" (*JJII*, 590).

The current tendency, however, would be to consider *Finnegans Wake* less *sub specie aeternitatis* than as a product of its own times, to see it as a book that is typical of the thirties, of a moment when experimental writing in an international and multilinguistic context could appear as the only logical outcome of Modernism. Before the term Post-Modernism had even been invented, most Modernist writers felt caught up in a sweeping movement that led to a rejection of parochialism and pushed to a generalized "Revolution of the Word." Like most revolutions of this century, this too would fail – or at least be met with incomprehension from the audience, while attracting cult-like followers enamored with obscurity itself. *Work in Progress*, in spite of the numerous allusions to contemporary events scattered by Joyce in his literary maze until the completion of the book in the late 1938, has still today the reputation of being isolated from politics, ethics, and broader cultural concerns that ought to dominate in dark times of war, crisis, and dire survival. This has been triggered by the undeniable difficulty of deciphering the topical echoes and allusions in the obscurely punning polyglottic prose of *Finnegans Wake*.

Was this a writer's blindness which could be blamed on the spirit of the times, or should one recall Joyce's gnawing awareness that he had to publish his last novel before another world war started, otherwise it would simply disappear? I would like to suggest here that Joyce's ultimate literary gamble, a gamble that might have to be left to this century's close to be assessed fully, has to do with a collective utopia blending language and politics, a radical utopia with avant-gardist and anarchistic overtones shared by the *transition* group led by Eugène Jolas. This is why I have chosen as an epigraph for this first chapter a limerick written in honor of *transition*'s editor, a homage to the publication of Jolas's polyglottic poems entitled *Mots Déluge*. In "Versailles 1933," Joyce also puns on his own name that he uses as a verb:

> So the jeunes joy with Jolas
> Book your berths: Après mot, le déluge!

Joyce's witty re-writing of the cynical motto of France's *ancien régime* – as King Louis XV allegedly stated, offhandedly brushing aside importunate criticism of his extravagant spending, and also probably aware of the impending storm that would erupt with the 1789 Revolution: *Après moi, le déluge!* ("After me, the deluge!") – into "After (the) word, the deluge" shows very clearly the multiple links between an embattled ego, the ongoing "Revolution of the Word" and an apocalyptic consciousness of time's end. Some of the difficulties Joyce faced when he attempted to create not only a new language but also a new reader, as I will show in the last chapters, had to do with his having completed his last book at a time when Modernist beliefs in progress were being rapidly replaced by a more cynical awareness that history (in the sense of a meta-narrative, or of "universal history") only progresses from catastrophe to catastrophe. Joyce was still creating his *A la Recherche de l'histoire perdue* just when real history seemed to confirm Walter Benjamin's apocalyptic vision.

In the limerick that gleefully associates Joyce with *les jeunes* (this was the typical Modernist expression that would be used by Pound and Lewis as, with more distance, of course, by Woolf), one sees all the young and happy creators embarking on a super-cruise promising not just "berths" but infinitely new "births" – births interestingly dependent on a "Book!" which replays the Mallarmean dream of *Le livre* as a simple imperative ticket-buying. Meanwhile, the old ego of the patriarchal and doomed king (no more the resplendent *roi soleil*, not yet the beheaded corpse of another decade) figuring "his majesty the *Moi*" has been replaced by a *mot* – less a "word" than "the word," as in French with *le verbe*, in Hebrew with *dabar*, in Greek with *logos*, in Latin with *verbum*. This word/verb condenses – this is my main thesis – all the qualities and properties formerly associated with an egoistic or egocentric subject. The fact that Joyce wrote the limerick at Versailles in 1933 (hence its title) gives it a sense of ominous foreboding – as if the fragile Versailles Treaty has less contained than helped unleash the forces of darkness and destruction that started sweeping across Europe after 1933. The deluge would come, for sure, and it would not be just the wonderful new flood of river-names Joyce had gathered in *Anna Liva Plurabelle*. Joyce's witticism seems to

renew Freud's insight in his most political text, a contribution to a book
published after his death: his decision to debunk President Wilson's character so as to avoid, for another time at least, the mistakes already committed. Freud believed that Wilson's messianic delusions, his religious
phraseology, and his lack of human warmth and perception had played
a key role in the creation of a new Europe in which defeated and humil-
iated nations would seethe with a resentment that would then easily be
exploited by demagogues. This ineluctably led to the collective psychosis that accompanied the rise of the Nazi movement. For Freud, Wilson
could have said "*Après moi le déluge!*" even though his talks were full of
peace projects and schemes about the future Society of Nations.[2]

Freud and Bullitt see as Wilson's main symptom his identification with
"God and Christ," (*TWW*, 170), and his tendency to believe his own
words to the detriment of facts:

Wilson's apparent hypocrisy was nearly always self-deception. He had an enormous ability to ignore facts and an enormous belief in words. His feeling for
facts and phrases was the exact reverse of the feeling of a scientist. He could
not bear to allow a beautiful phrase to be slain by a refractory fact. He delighted
in allowing an unpleasant fact to be annihilated by a beautiful phrase. When he
had invented a beautiful phrase, he began to believe in his phrase whatever the
fact might be" (*TWW*, 193)

As we will see, the Modernist impulse was not only directed at the creation of a new language, but of a new ego who can adapt to new "facts,"
whatever they may be. In this context, it is tempting to see a link between
Wilson's dream of a "War to end all wars" (*TWW*, 171) – a neat phrase
that could be used to justify many things, including the American intervention – and Joyce's *Ulysses*, a novel that was often described as a "novel
to end all novels."

I will examine at some length Joyce's relation to Eugène Jolas in the
Parisian context of the thirties, so as to engage with what could be called
Joyce's late Modernism, to borrow Tyrus Miller's apt expression.[3] Let us
just remember how quickly and easily Jolas became Joyce's confidant,
and an editor who would allow him the luxury that Darantiere's printers and Sylvia Beach's finances had generously granted for *Ulysses*: the
ability to work endlessly on large page proofs, those *placards* Joyce filled
with interpolations and late additions as he would today with a com-
puter. Confirming Joyce's use of his own name as a verb, it is Jolas who
explains in his autobiography that the printers would have learned to
expect Joyce's last minute corrections, but would accompany them with

a peculiar oath. They would then say "Joyce, *alors!*"[4] Joyce was delighted to see that his name could not only be distorted into French speech as *"jouasse"* (a slang term meaning "happiness") but could also turn into a printer's swearword!

After Jolas and his friends of *transition,* the critic (if the term can apply at all) who has done the most to restore the meaning of enjoyment as a verb to Joyce's name is Jacques Lacan. By way of introduction to the problematic of egoism, I will assess briefly a few important features of Lacan's groundbreaking contribution to Joycean scholarship.[5] As a growing number of scholars have begun to realize, following Jacques Aubert's inroads into Lacanian readings,[6] Lacan's terms provide a strong frame of reference allowing for a general assessment of Joyce's works. In France and Latin America, thousands of new readers have discovered the pleasure and hardships of a textual battle with the intricacies of *Finnegans Wake,* spurred on by the influential readings provided by Lacan's seminar in the middle of the seventies. I would like to explore the curious "coincidence" of such a late meeting between the two writers.

When Aubert invited Lacan to open the 1975 International Joyce Symposium he was organizing in Paris, he was forcing the reputed psychoanalyst to return once more to literature (after what I have called Lacan's "literary decade" in the fifties and sixties), but in a way that would durably change his entire theory. Lacan gave his talk, entitled "Joyce the Symptom" at the Sorbonne on June 16, 1975, starting from his own encounter with James Joyce at Adrienne Monnier's bookstore and his having heard the memorable first *Ulysses* reading when he was twenty.[7] Lacan's encounter with the Irish writer in 1921 could be seen as an omen, a fateful coincidence reawakened some fifty years later. The most striking feature in this presentation – in the context of last century's evaluation – was that Joyce did not appear essentially as the author of *Ulysses,* a novel mentioned in passing and merely to dispel the notion that it might based on Homer's *Odyssey* (*JAL,* 27), but as the writer of *Finnegans Wake,* a text described as his "major and final work" (*JAL,* 26). Lacan began by disclosing his central insight immediately – that Joyce embodied the "symptom," a symptom written *sinthome,* to revert to an older form of the word already found in Rabelais. This allowed him to present Joyce not only as a literary saint – a depiction that accords quite well with the way Joyce saw himself and projected himself to his contemporaries – but also to call up at once Aquinas (in French "*saint Thom*-as d'Aquin"), "sin" and literature ("tomes"). He concluded his lecture with the idea that the major "symptom" was contained in Joyce's name, a name embodying *jouissance* (a key Lacanian concept compounding "enjoyment" in all its meanings, along with sexual bliss and property rights).

Even if the focus was on Joyce's ecstatic *jouissance* of language in *Finnegans Wake*, Lacan's reservations were numerous. When Joyce plays with many languages, the dimension of truth risks being lost. He provides a diagram of all symptoms, pointing to their determination by the "Name-of-the-Father." He is busy erecting a literary monument in place of his father's real-life shortcomings, thus making up for failings that he excuses, negates, and sublimates at the same time. No matter how hard Joyce tries to become the *sinthome*, he nevertheless produces a text that cannot engage deeply with his readers, since everyone is only interested in her or his personal symptom. Joyce appears out of touch with the Freudian and Lacanian Unconscious when he flirts with Jung and Mrs. Blavatsky. He is marked by literary megalomania and uses *Finnegans Wake* as a simple "stool" with which he assumes that he will reach immortality. In fact, he will owe this immortality to the toils of thousands of scholars who all labor under the delusion that they will crack the code. Finally, the *jouissance* he ends up bequeathing is the mere hypostasis of his name, a name that becomes a common noun when it translates Freud's name as *jouissance* and as an intransitive verb, *jouir*. Joyce's mastery of style is self-serving, tautological, and finally masturbatory, when he attempts to suture his own knot with his proper name, a name he identifies with universal literature.[8] In this talk, Lacan was sketching the main themes developed in his seminar of the year 1975–76, "The Sinthome." The forceful confrontation with Joyce obliged him to overhaul his theory of the three interlocking circles of the Real, the Imaginary and the Symbolic to show that their knotting depends on the function of a fourth circle, called Sigma for the Symptom.

As the excellent biography written by Elisabeth Roudinesco[9] has noted, Lacan's starting point is unabashedly biographical, which leads him to miss or erase the important distinction between Stephen Dedalus and James Joyce. Lacan explains Joyce's choice of an artistic career as a wish to compensate for a lack on the part of his own father, John Joyce. According to Lacan, James Joyce remains caught up in his father's symptoms even while rejecting him: both are spendthrifts, they drink heavily, seem unable to keep their families sheltered from disaster. Joyce's daughter Lucia's deepening schizophrenia seemed to confirm that Joyce's literary fascination with psychotic discourse was not purely literary.

Lacan's reading is in fact not that far from Jung's interpretation of Joyce; like Jung, he stresses Joyce's wish to defend Lucia against psychoanalysis so as to ward off any suggestion that his own writing could be seen as "schizophrenic" or "psychotic," and like Jung he admits that Lucia drowns in the waters of the unconscious where a more experienced swimmer manages to reach back to the surface.[10]

The last sessions of the Joyce seminar were devoted to discussions of the four knots and Joyce's *jouissance.* In March 1976, Lacan announced new developments on the function of the ego, an ego he contrasted with Joyce's tendency to move toward a Jungian version of the Collective Unconscious, as if Lacan's main insight into the ego had been undissociable from a concept of a "community of Egoists" (to use Max Stirner's phrase).[11] In the last seminar, Joyce's ego was described as occupying the place of the fourth circle: Joyce's ego had become identical with the symptom. The same "mistake" in the knotting of the three circles of the Real, the Imaginary and the Symbolic, was compensated by the ego, in Lacan's drawing not a circle any more, but double square brackets, which then played the role of clamps keeping the circles together; the clamping effect is achieved by a writing which is as much a rewiring as a rewriting. "What I am suggesting is that with Joyce, the ego comes to correct the missing relation. The Borromean knot is reconstituted by such an artifice of writing."[12] Joyce's ego, atoned with the *sinthome*, turns into a literature of supplementary chains, bypasses, ducts, and prosthetic devices.

Why was Lacan's designation of the centrality of the ego in his knot so paradoxical? This can be best appreciated when we remember that Lacan's entire system had been erected as a war machine against "ego-psychology." Since the 1950s, his main polemical thrust had been directed at Anna Freud's legacy in a wholesale critique of the "Americanization of the Unconscious" that occurred when the first generation of Freud's disciples elaborated in his name a practice aiming at increasing ego-defenses. Lacan's first publication in English, "Some Reflections on the Ego,"[13] had postulated that language was constitutive of the ego, and situated in the dimension of hallucination, therefore of delusion. The denunciation of subsequent ego-psychology would be reiterated in countless statements, often quite ironical, as is the following with its revealing English phrases italicized in the original: "A team of *egos* no doubt less equal than autonomous (but by what trade-mark do they recognize in one another the sufficiency of their autonomy?) is offered to the Americans to guide them towards happiness, without upsetting the autonomies, egoistical or otherwise, that pave with their non-conflictual spheres the *American way* of getting there."[14] Here is Lacan's fundamental tenet, and it was therefore a completely unexpected move to see the old ego resurface with Joyce, even if was to introduce the ego as a writerly knot of letters somehow precipitating the symptom as *sinthome*.

When Lacan gave a written version of his talk for the publication of the symposium proceedings,[15] the new text did not explicitly stress the role of the ego in the knot, although its submerged influence was noticeable. This version, completely different from the oral presentation, looked like a pastiche of Joyce's Wakese. Lacan's style in this text published in 1979 is at its most obscure and punning. It jump-starts with a covert reappearance of the *moi*: "*Joyce le Symptôme à entendre comme Jésus la caille: c'est son nom. Pouvait-on s'attendre à autre chose d'emmoi: je nomme*" (*JAL*, 31). ("Joyce the Symptom to be heard as *Jésus la caille*: this is his name. Could one expect anything less from meself: I name.") The reference to Francis Carco's novel portraying Parisian pimps and prostitutes, *Jésus-la-Caille*, ironically replaces Joyce's name in the Montmartre and Pigalle scene of pimps and prostitutes, adding to Joyce's nickname a populist twist (the hero of the novel, Jésus-la-Caille, is a drag queen and a male prostitute who falls in love with the mistress of the most dangerous pimp of the boulevards). With "*emmoi*," Lacan punningly links *de moi* ("of me") with echoes of Emma Bovary through a submerged quote of Flaubert's famous "*Madame Bovary, c'est moi*." By stressing the homophony of "*je nomme*" ("I name") with "*jeune homme*" – the "young man" of Joyce's *Portrait of the Artist*, Lacan follows in the steps of a "young man Joyce" with whom he shares many characteristics – a common religious education, a subsequent revolt against the bourgeois order of their youth, finally the creation of a radically new language allowing them to think originally. The Irish writer acts as Lacan's double, turns into a literary *Doppelgänger* thanks to whom he can justify his own baroque style, while permitting the return of the repressed "ego." Joyce, who consistently refused to be psychoanalyzed, and who duplicates Freud's name translated into English, plays the part of Lacan's lay psychoanalyst, perhaps the only psychoanalyst he could acknowledge, unearthing in him the most stubborn ego-narcissism.

This is why the question of Joyce's madness becomes so crucial. If Joyce was psychotic, was Lacan psychotic too? Lacan wonders thus in February 1976: "After which point is one mad? Was Joyce mad? . . . I began by writing *Inspired Writings*, this is why I should not be astonished to find myself confronting Joyce, and this is why I dare pose the question: Was he mad? By what were his writings inspired to him?"[16] This reference to the 1931 publication of "Ecrits inspirés" in *Annales médicales* sends us back to one of Lacan's earliest articles, when he was trying to understand the logic of psychotic discourse. In this early essay on "Inspired Writings," Lacan had marked his refusal of a medical approach that tended to see the texts of psychotics as "degenerated" or "degraded" by a distortion of affects, and he compared them to the linguistic experiments produced by the Surrealists to point out similar features: "The experiences made by certain writers on a mode of writing they have called Surrealist and whose method they have described very scientifically show the extraordinary degree of autonomy that graphic automatisms can reach, outside any hypnosis."[17] In a bold move for someone who was working within the French psychiatric institution, Lacan refused to distinguish the artful simulation of psychotic delirium such as one finds in *The Immaculate Conception* by Breton and Eluard from "authentic" verbal productions of institutionalized patients: all these texts evince the same structures, are determined by pre-inscribed rhythmic formulas that are subverted and filled with other meanings.

In fact, Lacan was not working in total isolation. More or less at the same time as he was writing "Inspired Writings," Eugène Jolas and Stuart Gilbert were busy collecting and publishing some of these "inspired writings" for *transition*. They were hoping to establish links between Joyce's new language and the language of the mad. This is why in *transition* no. 18 (November 1929), Roger Vitrac devotes a long article in French to "Le Langage à part" ("The language apart") that extensively quotes medical treatises on language trouble in alienated subjects before alluding to poetic texts by Prevert and Desnos as illustrations of the same linguistic process.[18] In his essay, Vitrac quotes not only Seglas but also Baillarger, who worked on aural hallucinations among patients and asserts that "alienated patients fail to recognize their own voices just as one does in dreams" (*ibid.*). Vitrac provides one example:

Unconsciously. – Madame Dubois.
Consciously. – I don't know her. I come from the countryside.
Unconsciously. – Saint Thomas is as white as death.
Consciously. – A saint would have appeared to me? (*ibid.*)

He then generalizes: "What a strange ventriloquism, in which unconscious language has not lost its color and charm. One understands better the lyricism of asides, the occult power of confessions, everything that makes these individualists tick and act, these impulsive egoists of thought, these dreamers entirely possessed by themselves."[19] Vitrac seems to connect these linguistic creations of the insane with an entrenched egoism that has similar roots: madness consists in a linguistic autarchy that can be charming but also betrays an inability to communicate on a social level. However, Vitrac does not suggest a similar derivation for the linguistic experiments of the "Revolution of the Word" launched by Joyce. In the same way, in *transition* no. 26 (1937) Stuart Gilbert publishes an essay on "The Subliminal Tongue" in which he starts with Joyce, then examines a few cases of psychotic language, such as various cases of invented "Martian languages." These include the famous Hélène Smith, observed by Doctor Flournoy, and Patience Worth, whose dissociated personality was the object of psychical research on dissociation of personality by Morton Prince, all quoted in *Finnegans Wake*.

The question of Joyce's potentially psychotic structure remained a haunting one for Lacan, and for the generations of Lacanian psychoanalysts who started reading Joyce in the hope of understanding psychosis. The possible diagnosis of Joyce's psychotic structure can be seen as the result of several related factors: a systematic linguistic deregulation, a re-knotting of the four circles providing a new place for an ego that occupies a crucial but fragile position since it depends entirely upon language to "hold," and more importantly perhaps, the determination of the whole structure by a *jouissance* of language experienced as raw material yielding enjoyment but produced outside the social norms of accepted meanings. It is indeed the "crazy" Joyce of the *Wake* who is given as a model for the new millennium.

THE EGOIST'S DAUGHTER

Lacan's concept of "*jouissance*"[20] – so important to grasp Joyce's new knots – is fundamentally egoistical, since it occupies the opposite pole of a desire marked by the Law of the Other. In a more recent discussion of Lacanian terms, Jacques-Alain Miller confirms this idea: "Lacan took masturbation as an example to show how *jouissance* in itself does not comprise the Other sex . . . When we think of *jouissance*, for instance, of the kind we possess, it is the *jouissance* of the psychical apparatus. It is something which has nothing to do with anyone in the word."[21] This can be brought to bear on Lacan's critique of a residual "Jungism" when he talks about the anonymous dreamer in *Finnegans Wake*. For if we return to the book that marked the first scientific exploration of the world of dreams, a book hailed by Joyce as "an intrepidation of our dreams" (*FW*, 338. 29–30), we will discover that for Freud one essential characteristic of the dreamer is that he or she is totally egoistical. Freud has already demonstrated that every dream is the representation of a wish as fulfilled, and then adds that in one "dream of convenience" in which he thought he could satisfy his thirst by calling up his wife offering him an Etruscan urn, he can conclude that "everything was conveniently arranged": "Since its only purpose was to fulfill a wish, it could be completely egoistical."[22]

This double thesis is reiterated several times in the following sections, as in the section on "typical dreams": "This would not contradict my assertion that dreams are wish-fulfillments, but my other assertion, too, that they are accessible only to egoistic impulses" (*ID*, 303). Freud suggests that the dreamer becomes a child again, and for him "Children are completely egoistic" (*ID*, 283). A humorous footnote was added in 1911, when Freud referred to a lecture given by Ernest Jones in the United States on "the egoism of dreams." Jones met a strong resistance when an American lady stated that the Freudian hypothesis was only valid for Austrians and not for Americans since she was sure that all her dreams were strictly altruistic![23] Joyce knew something about this debate: the notebooks for his *Work in Progress* are full of his own dreams, and the Professor Jones who lectures so pompously on time, space, woman, and man in the *Wake* owes as much to Ernest Jones as to Wyndham Lewis.

The recurrent leitmotif of egoism in dreams throughout the *Interpretation of Dreams* acquires the character of an absolute thesis in the structural account of the "dream-work." Freud keeps the moralistic overtones of "egoism" in his description of a structural function deriving from the position of the "subject of enunciation" or the unconscious Cartesian *cogito* present in the dream:

Dreams are completely egoistical. Whenever my own ego does not appear in the content of the dream, but only some extraneous person, I may safely assume that my own ego lies concealed, by identification, behind the other person; I can insert my ego into the context . . . Thus my ego may be represented in a dream several times over, now directly and now through identification with extraneous persons. By means of a number of such identifications it becomes possible to condense an extraordinary amount of thought material. The fact that the dreamer's own ego appears several times, or in several forms, in a dream is at bottom no more remarkable than that the ego should be contained in a conscious thought several times or in different places or connections – e.g. in the sentence "when *I* think what a healthy child *I* was." (*ID*, 358)[24]

What Freud offers us, in other words, could be called a "grammar of egoism," in which the active and passive voices keep revolving around a mobile subjective center – much as he was to propose later about fantasy in "A Child is Being Beaten."[25]

Freud's commonsensical appeal to a broad notion of egoism can help solve a few interpretive problems about *Finnegans Wake*, since critics continue arguing about the singularity or the multiplicity of Joyce's dreamer. Freud shows that it is not necessary to distinguish between a single dreamer or a series of dreamers: the dreaming self always explodes into a multiplicity, thus creating the paradox of an oneiric egoistic alterity. The notion reverberates in *Finnegans Wake*, as in a passage of the inquest of the Four Masters facing a sleeping and dreaming Yawn: "Or you mean Nolans but Volans, an alibi, do you Mutemalice, suffering unegoistically from the singular but positively enjoying on the plural?" (*FW*, 488. 15–17). Joyce's dreamers *enjoy* in the most rigorous sense, that is intransitively – in a baffling *jouissance* which seduces us into interpreting and eventually perpetuating it – when their collapsible plural allows them to dissolve and become one with the collective dream. Joyce (like Gertrude Stein) would agree that an artist can be a "genius" only if he or she can embody a *jouissance* that keeps all the political, ethical, and esthetic implications of egoism alive – then, indeed, it is impossible "to isolate I from my multiple Mes" (*FW*, 410. 12).

Freud's analysis of egoistic dreams will pave the way for his subsequent description of the writer as a person who is gifted with the paradoxical power of releasing while sharing at the same time this egoism. In the essay entitled "The Poet and Day-Dreaming" written in 1907 and published the following year, he points out the links between children seriously engaged in playing, dreamers deeply ensconced in their private images, and writers of popular fiction ("the less pretentious writers of romances, novels and stories, who are read all the same by the widest circles of men and women"[26]) who know how to create heroes with whom we immediately identify. We identify with the recurrent figure of the hero to whom, despite all the dangers braved, "nothing can happen": "this significant mark of invulnerability very clearly betrays – His Majesty the Ego, the hero of all daydreams, and all novels" (*PDD*, 51). Before returning to Joyce's day-dreams in which a vindication of his rights in front of the King of England figures in good place, I will address the issue of popular fiction. Popular fiction functions at the level of day-dreaming, and panders to our childish fantasies: if all the women fall in love with the hero in a totally unrealistic manner, we are nevertheless as flattered as if this happened to us. The difference between day- or night-dreamers on the one hand and novelists on the other hand lies in a sense of participation. We are often either bored or repulsed by the telling of intimate images or fantasies, so Freud argues, whereas we are kept interested by narratives that provide such great pleasure:

> How the writer accomplishes this is his innermost secret; the essential *ars poetica* lies in the technique by which our feeling of repulsion is overcome, and this has certainly to do with those barriers erected between every individual being and all others [*zwischen jedem einzelnen Ich und den anderen*]. We can guess at two methods used in this technique. The writer softens the egotistical character of the day-dream by changes and disguises, and he bribes us by the offer of a purely formal, that is, aesthetic, pleasure in the presentation of his phantasies. (*PDD*, 54)[27]

Freud's theory of literature has often been called reductive, yet his insight, although almost brutal, is powerful: the function of art is a mere means to an end, which consists in the overcoming of the barriers that separate one ego from other egos with the ultimate aim of releasing a deeper egoism of fantasy that can be shared by all. Art is clearly reduced to a little bribe that will then release even greater pleasure – an "incitement premium" (*Verlockungsprämie*) or a "fore-pleasure" (*Vorlust*) (*PDD*, 54) before a quasi-orgasmic ego-trip can be unleashed. These ideas confirm how Freudian Lacan's reading of Joyce could be, and correspond with surprising exactitude to the arguments put forward by a very popular novelist who also happened to have invented a whole philosophy of egoism, Ayn Rand.

At first sight, no two writers could be more different than Ayn Rand and James Joyce. While Joyce was a fastidious stylist, Ayn Rand's style proceeds through well-worn Hollywoodian clichés (they have been mercilessly and hilariously parodied by Mary Gaitskill in *Two Girls, Fat and Thin*[28]). While Joyce concentrated on his writing almost to the exclusion of everything else, Rand stopped in the middle of the painful writing of her first long novel, *The Fountainhead*, because she felt she had to militate actively in politics, and canvassed without pay in the ill-fated campaign of Wendell Wilkie, the conservative candidate who ran against Roosevelt in 1940.[29] Later, during the worst period of the Cold War, she did not hesitate to participate as a "friendly witness" in the infamous 1947 House Un-American Activities Committee hearings on communism in Hollywood (where she spoke in front of a very young and "friendly" Richard Nixon). And then, of course, comes up the complex issue of how she became the leader of a movement that some compare to a cult, first under the name of "Nathaniel Branden Institute," later rebaptized the "Ayn Rand Institute: the Center for the Advancement of Objectivism." Still today, all of her best-selling novels and essays contain the same little detachable flyer asking reader to make a bold transition between fiction and ethical commitment. Readers who have been interested by the novels should get in touch with the Institute: "Do you share Ayn Rand's view of life? Do you want to fight today's cultural and political trends? If you take the ideas of this book seriously, you will want to find out about . . ." After a list of topics, one finds an address in the name of "Objectivism." This transformation of literature into "philosophy" (if one may use the word) or rather an activist ideology is of course totally foreign to Joyce.

Joyce hated Romanticism with a passion, and *Dubliners* and *Ulysses* contain among many other things a scathing indictment of hero-worship, a systematic debunking of the cult of honor, gallantry, and patriotic sacrifice that afflicted the ideology of Irish revival and culminated in the Easter Rising of 1916. Ayn Rand, on the other hand, was a professed Romantic attached to portraying ideal figures and clinging to hero-worship (she considered, for instance, Howard Roark in *The Fountainhead* not only her type of hero, but the "ideal man," man as he should be). The deliberate idealization provides a basis for a whole vision of life in which raising one's self-esteem implies understanding the rules of radical egoism. Here is how her "philosophy" is sketched in the "Reader's Guide" provided at the end of *The Fountainhead*: "My philosophy, in essence, is the concept of man as a heroic being, with his own happiness as the moral purpose of his life, with productive achievement as his noblest activity, and reason as his only absolute."[30] This is why the habitual flyer condenses this even more pithily: "As an advocate of reason, egoism and capitalism, I seek to reach the men of the intellect – wherever such may be found. – Ayn Rand."

The earliest note for *The Fountainhead* stressed this concept of egoism: "The first purpose of this book is *a defense of egoism in its real meaning*."[31] Indeed, the rather contrived plot culminates when the "genius" architect Howard Roark is led to dynamiting cheap buildings for the poor because his original design has been tampered with, and then has to defend his "egoistic" conception of art and life in court. What the 1949 film adaptation by King Vidor half-heartedly conveys in Gary Cooper's speech works somewhat better at the end of the bulky novel: "I came here to say that I do not recognize anyone's right to one minute of my life . . . I wished to come here and say that I am a man who does not exist for others . . . The world is perishing from an orgy of self-sacrifice"(*F*, 684). Curiously, the term used by Roark to berate the "second-handers" who only exist for or by the others (like Peter Keating, the architect who is ready to compromise in order to succeed, or Ellsworth Toohey, the socialist demagogue, greedy for an impersonal sense of power he taps from the masses by erasing any trace of individualism) is "egotism" not "egoism": "All that which proceeds from man's independent ego is good. All that which proceeds from man's dependence upon men is evil. The egotist in the absolute sense is not the man who sacrifices others . . . He does not exist for any other man – and he asks no other man to exist for him. This is the only form of brotherhood and mutual respect possible between men" (*F*, 680). One compelling idea put forward by Ayn Rand is that the egotist's indifference to the others frees them from their petty delusions, restores their self-esteem by bringing them in closer contact with the drive (the Freudian *Trieb*) hidden beneath their limited desires. This constitutes a sort of inverse pornography, in a contagion of separatedness affirming the solipsistic structure of the drives. In Lacanian terms, the Master first posits his absolute ego by considering only his relationship to drives, which then compels the others to move into a hysterical position of recrimination and theatrical negation, until this is finally overcome when all turn into Masters. The narratological issue in all these texts boils down to an interaction between intolerable demands arising from the subjective entanglements of sexual desire, and a truth to be sought on the side of a solipsistic drive underpinning creativity. This is why egotism cannot be differentiated from egoism: both determine the realm of what *Atlas Shrugged* calls the "Prime Movers," heroic creators who live only for the beauty and perfection of their own achievements, and are autonomous "ends in themselves."

However, Ayn Rand (who mastered English relatively late in her life, as she had arrived from Russia in 1926, to head straight for New York and then Hollywood via Chicago, thus encountering in the flesh her two main fetishes of American culture, skyscrapers and movies) notes in her 1968 Introduction that she was guilty of a semantic slip: wherever she has written "egotism," one should read "egoism," and she blames the mistake on her reliance on a faulty dictionary, *Webster's Daily Use Dictionary* (1933). As a number of critics have pointed out, the issue is less a possible confusion than the paradoxes generated by these terms (Max Stirner encountered similar problems in his *The Ego and His Own*). "Selfishness" in Ayn Rand's later developments of her philosophy comes to mean "pure devotion to an ideal," while "altruism" means a perverted spirit of sacrifice for the masses instilled by any religion of God or humanity. These terms clearly denote more or less the opposite of what they mean in everyday discourse. In the same way, the main reason one can find for her choice of "Objectivism" (a word that had been better illustrated by a poetic movement of the thirties) for her system is that she wishes to avoid any reproach of subjectivism or solipsism. The only "objective" value we have here is in fact the Freudian *Trieb*.

Since one should not take Rand's philosophy too seriously, I would like simply to point out that the weakness of her thinking is compensated by a way of writing that has managed to captivate audiences, decade after decade. She knows how to produce "page-turners" despite the general incoherence of plot and characterization (for instance, one has to believe in *The Fountainhead* that Dominique Francon, the beautiful and clever woman in love with Roark – he has started things very well by raping her in a very original love scene – spends a few years attempting to destroy him because, although she admires his buildings, she thinks that the world is not ready for so much beauty!) and the weakness of the writing itself. The explanation is to be sought in the way Rand blends the allegorical vision of pulp fiction in which everything is good or evil, with a wish to rationalize and demonstrate ideas. Thus when she defines "Objectivist Ethics" in a book called *The Virtue of Selfishness*,[32] she begins by quoting one character from *Atlas Shrugged*. She confirms thereby that she writes "philosophical novels," better and longer versions of the Harlequin genre in which the trick is always to produce a figure of "love at first sight" and then to multiply obstacles until the desired reunion is achieved. In Rand's fictions, it is always the woman who fears the absolutist character of love so that she will want to destroy the object of her passion by killing it. In the end, the pure and uncompromising hero is always reunited with the beautiful woman who loves him despite all attempts from within and without at perverting their bond.

What King Vidor's film adaptation of *The Fountainhead* manages to show quite well is that the ethical issue of egoism corresponds esthetically to the problematic of Modernism in architecture. Roark is partly modeled after Frank Lloyd Wright (who eventually read the novel and appreciated it), and the buildings he designs have one common feature: they show no ornaments, their functionality is obvious in the structure, and the main source of evil in the novel is the wish by lesser architects to add to them silly Beaux-Arts trimmings or classical columns. Roark the quintessential egoist is also a quintessential Modernist, and it is possible that Rand thought of Joyce's famous determination never to alter a line to please his critics or his audience when portraying the architect. As Slavoj Zizek has suggested in a clever analysis of Rand's latent "hysterical lesbianism," she "falls into the line of over-conformist authors who undermine the ruling ideological edifice by their very excessive identification with it."[33] Her over-enthusiastic endorsing of capitalism retains its hysterical force so that somehow the Master's discourse is forced to confront his failure. Capitalism is never pure enough for Rand; it falls prey to the recurrent danger of collectivism, it is too tainted with religiosity.

When I say "capitalism," I mean a full, pure, uncontrolled, unregulated *laissez-faire* capitalism – with a separation of state and economics, in the same way and for the same reasons as the separation of state and church. A pure system of capitalism had never yet existed, not even in America; various degrees of government control had been undercutting and destroying it from the start.[34]

One of the ironies besetting Objectivism in the domain of economics is that one of its most gifted and famous disciples was none other than Alan Greenspan!

This leads to the plot developed in *Atlas Shrugged*: all the "Prime Movers" decide to go on strike in order to protest the dangers of collectivism, and then the whole world grinds to a cataclysmic halt, until they are called back. These autonomous prime movers are embodiments of the Freudian drive in its autotelic affirmation. As Zizek says, Rand's position comes close to a certain feminism when she shows how her fascination for the masculine will leads her to a position of hysteria, but of a hysteria that is surmounted and transcended. This is apparent in the dialectics of giving and not-giving that follow from the novel's premises. Curiously, Ayn Rand's description of the paradoxes involved in giving to others what a single strong ego has made for himself or herself comes very close to Joyce's formulation of the same problem in *Exiles*. When Roark has designed the perfect house for Gail Wynand (the press tycoon who owns everything and who, moreover, has married the woman he loves), he assuages the latter's fears that he will never be able to "own" this house:

What you feel in the presence of a thing you admire is just one word – "Yes." The affirmation, the acceptance, the sign of admittance. And that "Yes" is more than an answer to one thing, it's a kind of "Amen" to life, to the earth that holds this thing, to the thought that created it, to yourself for being able to see it. But the ability to say "Yes" or "No" is the essence of all ownership. It's your ownership of your own ego . . . There is no affirmation without the one who affirms. In this sense, everything to which you grant your love is yours. (*F*, 539)

Then Wynand asks whether this is not equivalent to "sharing," a notion that Ayn Rand clearly abhors. Here is what Roark answers:

No. It's not sharing. When I listen to a symphony I love, I don't get from it what the composer got. His "Yes" was different from mine. He could have no concern for mine and no exact conception of it. That answer is too personal to each man. But in giving himself what he wanted, he gave me a great experience. I'm alone when I design a house, Gail, and you can never know the way in which I own it. But if you said your own "Amen" to it – it's also yours. And I'm glad it's yours. (*F*, 539)

In a very similar manner, Richard Rowan explains to his son Archie why it is better to give precious objects than to keep them, by using an identical logical reversal:

RICHARD: When you have a thing it can be taken from you.
ARCHIE: By robbers? No?
RICHARD: But when you give it you have given it. No robber can take it from you . . . It is yours for ever when you have given it. It will be yours always. That is to give.[35]

One might find in Joyce an older substratum of motives linking egoism and heroism (at least in the not so ironical title of *Stephen Hero*) that can call up Ayn Rand's subversion of her own values. The main fantasy that the creative ego can live and produce just for himself, independently from the gaze of the big Other, is not tantamount to asserting that the self makes up reality. What the comparison between Ayn Rand and Joyce can teach us finally is that solipsism and relativism can be avoided if and only if egoism contains the dialectical means by which it can be surperseded – be it through an almost impossible gift or through an even more paradoxical hospitality to the other.

THE GENIUS OF EGOISM

I will sketch more fully some historical implications of Joyce's involvement in the "philosophy of egoism" and its political consequences in the following chapter. Let me just briefly survey the broad evolution of the concept in Joyce's life and works with a view to answering Lacan's criticism. Joyce made a point of his earlier esthetic never to distinguish art from life, as I will show in chapter 4. In a 1912 essay, he writes of William Blake:

Like many other men of genius, Blake was not attracted to cultured and refined women. Either he preferred to drawing-room graces . . . the simple woman, of hazy and sensual mentality, or, in his unlimited egoism, he wanted the soul of his beloved to be entirely a slow and painful creation of his own, freeing and purifying daily under his very eyes, the demon (as he says) hidden in the cloud. (*CW*, 217)

As the annotators point out, this seems to sum up most of the plot of Joyce's play, *Exiles*. If Robert Hand asserts several times that Richard has "created" Bertha, that she is "his own work," Richard Rowan, self-consciously playing the role of God or Pygmalion tries to free his common-law wife from too strict an adherence to a Galathean mirror image by allowing her to betray him.

Perversion, or in a religious vocabulary, sin, provides the only limit to egoism: sin brings along a sense of sundering, as Stephen says about Shakespeare, that should ultimately become productive by restarting a new life cycle. Joyce's editors point out that "Joyce's alliance to Nora Barnacle bears a vague resemblance to that which he attributes to Blake and Catherine Boucher" (*CW*, 217n). The qualification provided by the adjective "vague" is necessary, since what would strike all witnesses of daily life in the Joyce family was Nora's utter impermeability to her husband's influence. As Joyce said, his wife's personality was "absolutely proof against any influence of (him)" (*JJII*, 434), would it be going to an extreme to suggest that Lucia could only find in psychosis the shelter from a father who was all too present in her thoughts? Lucia might indeed be described as the "egoist's daughter" – and her fate was determined by her repeating this unusual legacy.

Joyce's early version of egoism consisted in a rejection of conventional values that culminated in an esthetic view of life modeled on Ibsen and Nietzsche. This is why Ibsen is praised in a letter as an "egoarch" (*LII*, 205) as we will see in the next chapter, while much later *Finnegans Wake* still makes a virtue of "eggoarchicism" (525.10). Even if this remains as a dominant and subterranean ground, Joyce experienced a turning point roughly at the time his daughter was born. Until the failed attempt to find a career in Rome, and during that stay in the eternal city, Joyce retained the illusion that he could reunite the esthetic ideal of egoism with the political movement known as anarchism. He remarks that Stanislaus objects to his "socialist tendencies" in August 1906 (*LII*, 148). In January 1907, he uses the term "anarchist" to call up his destitute life in an amusing vignette describing his shabby room, his family shivering with cold and his thwarted literary aspirations: "Title of above: *The Anarchist*" (*LII*, 206). Then in March 1907, after a moral crisis whose echoes are still felt in *Exiles*, Joyce announces that his life needs to take an entirely new direction, incriminating his state of "indifference" that puts at stake his whole career and renders the moral justification of his "artistic inclination" almost spurious: "It is months since I have written a line and even reading tires me. The interest I took in socialism and the rest has left me . . . These ideas or instincts or intuitions or impulses may be purely personal. I have no wish to codify myself as anarchist or socialist or reactionary" (*LII*, 217). This was written at the time Joyce discovered that Nora was pregnant again – and signals the decision to achieve an inner retreat and to adopt an attitude that can be equated with a purely literary egoism – a term that has to be differentiated from "egotism" as we will soon see. Joyce's attitude remained consistent during the war, and the choice of neutral Switzerland was the natural consequence of the rootlessness of an exile. And thus, among other friends in Paris, Eugène Jolas noted with some astonishment the almost fanatic avoidance of any mention of politics by Joyce in the late twenties. This attitude became more and more impossible to uphold, and shows common traits with his disavowal of Lucia's real psychic condition.

Such a close "collaborator" and acute observer of the Joyce circle in the late twenties as Stuart Gilbert points out (in a diary that appears as motivated by spite, envy and rancor as by friendship) the structural similarities between Joyce's own symptoms and Lucia's. He remarks during the various "Lucia crises" that marked the beginning of the thirties that the Joyces seem to lead "empty" lives and that all the members of the family have started emulating Joyce's motto of "silence, exile and cunning":

The truth is that all their lives (even his) are empty. They do not attach themselves to anything except ephemeral things, and tire of these so soon they are always at a loss. Thus they never, or rarely, make friends. Too self-centered . . . To fill his [James Joyce's] life he pictures himself as a victim pursued by enemies, and will not understand that most people are indifferent . . . Other people's troubles leave him cold; he is never interested in the "human" side of a book or tale or event. Hardly even the literary. It's just a fact to him. Unless it concerns his family (father for instance) or, in a less degree, his country. Nationalities interest him a little. He has still the naive enthusiasm – a little of it – for self-proclaimed rebels and the naive belief that people who have morals are hypocrites.[36]

If we read this with less spite and venom, we may observe the perseverance of the same "egoist anarchism" (indeed, having mellowed and matured) that characterized Joyce's youthful years in Pola, Trieste, and Rome. His nemesis was, at least according to Gilbert, that Lucia had mimicked this attitude with a vengeance:

The interest has centered for the last 20 days round Lucia. The typical girl left to herself and developing in all her selfishness. It is absurd to say that she never had a chance; she had every chance. Only her conceit and idleness prevented her from trying for either of the things she wanted – becoming another Pavlova or making a good match. She cultivates her father's imperious airs and spells of silence.[37]

Painful as these entries are to read, they nevertheless hit on a raw nerve. Although cynical and superior, Gilbert denies the psychiatric side of Lucia's condition as much as her father did, and like Joyce and also Nora, he blames Lucia's psychic deterioration on a systematic imitation of her father's mannerisms, infatuations, and indulgence.

In order to pull together all the strands linking the curious and ultimately lethal "egoism" of the Joyce family and the genesis of an ideology insisting on family, race, and nationality as the new site of a war waged against the rest of the world, I will now try to bring several themes together: Joyce's alleged "indifference" to human issues (all viewed, it seems, if not *sub specie aeternitatis*, at least as some manifestation of recurrent universal patterns), his determination to let his world shrink to that of an extended family, and his stubborn denial of psychoanalysis in spite of an intellectual proximity with Freud. Whereas Lacan and most Lacanians tend to collapse Joyce's "knots" and those of his psychotic daughter – as Jacques-Alain Miller writes in his introduction to *Joyce avec Lacan* ("To evoke psychosis was not just an example of applied psychoanalysis, but rather a way of questioning the discourse of the analyst *with* the symptom thought to be unanalyzable" [*JAL*, 12]), I would like to offer the counter-thesis that Joyce's later writings should not be qualified unambiguously as "psychotic" or "schizophrenic." On the contrary, if they indeed tend to approach the condition of psychosis, it is so as to provide an analysis, and perhaps a cure, of it. Joyce's deepest and most cherished delusion was that the new language he was elaborating in the thirties would be capable not just of imitating Lucia's quasi-psychotic idiom, but of actually curing it. One might indeed see in this wish the return of a repressed incestuous desire: Joyce believes that he can succeed where Jung and all other doctors have failed thanks to a "mystical" bond uniting his daughter and himself. Again, Joyce anticipates the insights of a Lacan (exactly at the same time as the French psychiatrist was elaborating a theory of "paranoiac psychosis" that the Surrealists would endorse enthusiastically[38]): both stake everything on language as a possible cure for psychosis – an idea that Freud would limit to neurotics.

Alain Manier has shown in a brilliant work[39] that what marks off psychosis from other types of neurological disorders is the way language becomes petrified and reified. Psychotic language tends on the one hand to deny the arbitrary link between signifiers and signified, and on the other hand to negate the social link that (re)motivates language for whoever speaks. Psychotic discourse, even when it looks creative in its distortion of ordinary usage, employs a language that is literalized, acquires a fixity or rigidity that often substitutes itself for bodily catatonia. One can therefore say that *Finnegans Wake* attacks directly the linguistic root of psychosis by enhancing the poetological functions of the polyglottic and punning Word, and by reconstituting the social or historical logic underlying the archeology of myths that underpins the creation of such a new language.

In other words, Lucia should not appear merely as Joyce's "anima inspiratrix," as Jung would have it, but rather as the main addressee of the *Wake*: Joyce's hope is that if he manages to reach through her multiple levels of allusions, to inhabit the darkness of a monstrous language long enough and then can still return to light in the morning, he will gain some therapeutic leverage on his daughter's condition. The utopian agency of the new "babel" both radicalizes the disjointed syntax and word condensations that are typical of feminized "little languages" (from Swift to Lewis Carroll) and points to the way out of the tunnel of hebephrenia. In fact, Lucia became the ideal reader of *Finnegans Wake* – whose pathos increased as it became obvious that she could not read the text and ended up reproducing her mother's "indifference" to *Ulysses*, but for quite opposite reasons.

If in the *Wake* the circle of history is recaptured endlessly, the cumulative effect of these melancholy recapitulations should be less a reiterative slumber than a fun-producing "wake up call" from the depth of psychosis. The element of "fun" aims thus at understanding where Lucia's *jouissance* has gone. This strategy also manages to criticize historical neuroses such as various varieties of nationalism (Irish or other) and the proliferation of psychotic messianism. Indeed, the idea of bringing "Universal History" to bear on his daughter's troubled psychic state remains caught up in the same egoistic circle I have described earlier, while escaping from the dead end of psychosis. When Joyce appeals to the endless litany of cyclical avatars of the Same and presents a Nietzschean return of the disappointingly identical – for instance, he typically presents courtship and marriage as: "for soon again 'twill be, win me, woo me, wed me, ah weary me!" (*FW*, 556. 20–21) – he means to convince Lucia that the worst catastrophe has already happened (as Winnicott would say), that her troubles are over, and that she can now share with her father the vision of a sunnier future.

Having sketched how Joyce became the Lacanian Symptom of literature, I will have to make a detour through his esthetic theories in order to follow the route linking "negative esthetics" to the philosophy of egoism that will be explored in a subsequent chapter. The loaded confrontation between endogamy and exogamy will lead us to a revision of the themes of hospitality and sodomy in the context of Joyce's desire to write a universal history of mankind. Other chapters will be devolved to the function of the reader, just sketched with Lucia here. I will subsequently have to distinguish between the plain readers, ideal readers, and revolutionary readers. Caught up in her father's revolution of language, acting as the first symptom of its disturbing effects, Lucia's tragedy was to identify with the position of the ideal reader of the *Wake* while being deprived of her no doubt brilliant future.[40] Joyce's book was made all the more dramatic as it was not only supposed to be a funny book – as indicated by the delicately paradoxical coining of "funferall" (*FW* 13.15, 11.15, and see also 458.22, 120.10)), one of the most powerful leitmotifs of *Finnegans Wake* – but it became a prophetic book with a vengeance. Joyce's messianic dreams sublimated his egoism (the wish to have a direct impact on a cherished daughter) into the decision to replace a "dream monologue" (474.4) by a "drama parapolylogic" (474.5) including all his readers, in the hope that their, our cacophonous voices would just blend into a collective "music of the future." Nevertheless, he added a prudent question mark: "The mujic of the footure on the barbarihams of the bashed?" (518. 28).

CHAPTER TWO

The ego, the nation, and degeneration

My title, "Joyce and the politics of egoism," aims at demonstrating the centrality of a moment in the history of Modernism – the transformation of a feminist bi-weekly called *The New Freewoman* into an almost identical journal called *The Egoist*, a magazine that would not only publish Joyce's major novels, but also provide Pound and his friends with a platform for the dissemination of new ideas in England. To say that Joyce should be called an "egoist" is not just flippant provocation or personal accusation but an effort to link his literary and political position to a much older debate hinged around the claims of the "individual" fighting against repressive systems, claims that were often refused as being either "egoistic" or "anarchistic." The change of name in the journals, whether it originated from its editor Dora Marsden or from her male friends, such as Ezra Pound, insists upon the importance of Max Stirner's revolutionary essay, *Der Einzige und sein Eigentum* (1844) for Dora Marsden and her collaborators. This rather obscure but scandalous tract quickly attracted Karl Marx's ire and became a cult book, sowing the seeds of philosophical anarchism among the left-Hegelians. It almost vanished from sight until it was translated into English in 1907 as *The Ego and His Own*.[1] One should include George Meredith (with his famous novel *The Egoist*) within the circle of the writers directly or indirectly influenced by Stirner's conception of radical egoism, as we will see in the next chapter. A whole genealogy of egoism could be sketched, going back to the roots of modern philosophy with Descartes's assertion of a central ego as the grammatical subject necessary for the pursuit of irrefutable truths, and on to Nietzsche's praise of egoism via Pascal's critique of "self-love" and Stendhal's idea of egotism. Stirner was the most consistent advocate of revolutionary individualism, and the curious mixture of feminists, avant-garde artists and radical thinkers in the post-Suffragism years gave to pre-war British Modernism its distinctive tone.

Stirner's advocacy of "criminality" as a last resort refusal of any authority or "cause" had found a particularly receptive audience.

Radicalizing the affirmation of Fichtean subjectivity and anticipating Nietzsche's dramatization of the artist as creator of values, Max Stirner's *Ego and His Own* still appears today as the main textbook for literary anarchism and also as Marxism's most subtle enemy, as the long section devoted to "Saint Max" in Marx and Engels's *German Ideology* proves. Michael Levenson devotes a very useful section of his *Genealogy of Modernism* to "egoism," in which he studies its links with "Imagism."[2] Although Stirner is misconstrued as a radical Hobbesian advocating a war of each against all (whereas he always insisted on the need to think a utopian and paradoxical "community of egoists"), some of his most blatant contradictions, often simply repeated by Dora Marsden and Steven Tracy Byington, the first translator into English, who was also a regular contributor to *The New Freewoman*, have been well captured by Levenson. More recently, David Weir has analyzed the importance of the general context of anarchism for Modernism, highlighting the convoluted links between Stirnerian or Tuckerian anarchism and the young Joyce's post-Ibsenian Modernism.[3] David Weir's thesis is compelling: for him, it is the whole of Modernism as a vast movement of thought bridging the gap between *fin-de-siècle* decadentism and early twentieth-century avant-gardism that owes its genesis to anarchism – not because of anarchism's strength but because anarchism was bound to fail as a political movement. In a chapter entitled "Aesthetics – From Politics to Culture," Weir writes: "In some ways, the failure of anarchism assured the success of modernism; that is, the politics of anarchism was transformed into the culture of modernism by a number of artists who gave aesthetic expression to political principles."[4]

I wish I could agree with this stimulating insight, but cannot help noticing the curious resilience of anarchism throughout the century: to say nothing of John Cage and Jackson Mac Low, whose careers unite randomness and subversion so as to provide music and language with a politically subversive function, one could see in the May 1968 Parisian "events" one, but not the only one, of the surprisingly vibrant revivals of a not yet totally defunct "urban" anarchism, with its heady mixture of Situationist dialectics and Surrealist diction. Besides, political anarchism as an active and organized force was in fact destroyed both by Franco's armies and by Stalinist repression during the Spanish Civil War; its demise dates from around 1937–38, which does not agree with the usual dates given to be the emergence of "high Modernism" at least – roughly between 1912 and 1929, to give but an average estimate.

Weir's systematic allusion to Matthew Arnold's classic *Culture and Anarchy* could be reread in view of what Terry Eagleton wrote when denouncing the disengaged liberalism of some Irish critics who refuse to engage with issues of nationalism and politics: "This bankrupt Irish Arnoldianism is particularly ironic when one considers that the title of Arnold's own major book, *Culture and Anarchy*, might well have been rewritten as *Britain and Ireland*."[5] And indeed Vincent Cheng's excellent book *Joyce, Race and Empire*[6] has documented how John Tenniel's cartoons for *Punch* could represent the Irish rebel as a wild primate with ape-like features allegorizing "anarchy" in front of a stern Britannia protecting a poor and defenseless female Hibernia.[7]

If Ireland has long stood for "anarchy" as such in the eyes of the British public, it is then quite fitting that Joyce's work should echo and denounce some of these tensions. However, *Ulysses* is often read as a cunning move by one of the most gifted Irish writers to put Dublin back on the international map and safely ensconce it in "high" and "eternal" culture. Moreover, *Finnegans Wake*, although in some sense much closer (mimetically at least) to issues of civil war, colonial conquest, clan betrayal, land spoliation, religious intolerance, and race miscegenation, in short the whole tangled and confusing colonial and post-colonial history of a still divided Ireland, works by confusing identities and stereotyping them. As Eagleton points out, there is the risk of another type of anarchy:

Something of the same ambiguity haunts *Finnegans Wake*, a work that, as its radical apologists have pointed out, confounds and commingles all distinct identities in a manner scandalous to the rigorous hierarchies of orthodox bourgeois culture. Yet . . . what you lose on the semiotic swings you make up on the Viconian roundabouts . . . The *Wake*'s anarchic differencing is possible only on the basis of a secret homogenizing of reality, a prior equalizing of all items that then enables them to enter into the most shocking idiosyncratic permutations. There comes a point, as Hegel was well aware, at which "pure" difference merely collapses back into "pure" identity, united as they are in their utter indeterminacy.[8]

Even if I am in sympathy with the idea that Joyce is fundamentally a Hegelian writer, I would not want to see in *Finnegans Wake* "the night in which . . . all cows are black"[9] to quote Hegel's jest at the expense of Schelling and all the Romantic idealists who assume that the Absolute can be "shot out of a pistol" just like that. The mistake of Romantic philosophers was to avoid a careful retracing of all the steps through which consciousness can ultimately reach back to the Absolute – which is, in brief, the main object of the *Phenomenology of Spirit*.

Finnegans Wake achieves this by plunging us *in medias res* or rather in the middle of *verba*, in a language that partly reproduces itself "anarchically" and partly needs the reader's own feedback to "work" as language. Thanks to this new "linguistic turn," Joyce's linguistic anarchism – and this is one of the contentions of this book – will not avoid facing the issue of language, a new and "revolutionary" language that aims at changing the reader, without a consideration of which one would quickly fall back on mere ideology critique. It is worth remembering that anarchism was relatively well known to Joyce, who, always very careful in presenting an image of himself, insisted in a note for his biographer, Herbert Gorman, that he was well read in the anarchist tradition, quoting among the writers he read "Most, Malatesta, Stirner, Bakunin, Kropotkin, Elisée Reclus, Spencer, and Benjamin Tucker, whose *Instead of a Book* proclaimed the liberty of the non-invasive individual." He also saw this movement of thought as quite different from classic Marxism, adding that he "never read anything by Karl Marx except the first sentence of *Das Kapital* and he found it so absurd that he immediately returned the book to the lender" (quoted in *JJII*, 142, n.). My main contention is that Joyce found in anarchism a discourse that gave sense to a subjective position that can be called "egoistic."

My focus in this book will be both more limited than Weir's Modernist contextualization of culture and anarchy, since I focus on Joyce and use the concept of anarchistic "egoism" as a hidden backbone underpinning his personal and literary trajectory, and broader, since I explore a number of critical concepts revolving around issues of egoism and its opposite notions, generosity or hospitality. Egoism, to be true, a rather fuzzy but strategic term, can be historicized (as we will see in a number of chapters dealing either with avant-garde politics or notions such as "Victorianism" or "Edwardianism"), and works at the juncture between art and politics, philosophy and literature, ethics and esthetics, artistic production and artistic consumption. Before discussing the theoretical stakes that are implied by this strategy, I will go back to Max Nordau, the first critic who perceived the centrality of the concept of egoism for an understanding of Modernism. He is of course one of Modernism's most violent detractors, but his wholesale attack on the ideology of "egomania" in

Degeneration connects usefully the "disease" of egoism with the works of Ibsen, Nietzsche, Baudelaire, Wagner, Zola, in fact anyone who had shown artistic or literary talent by the end of the nineteenth century.

FROM DEGENERATION TO THE EGOIST

Max Nordau's best-seller, *Entartung* (1892) soon translated into English as *Degeneration* (1895)[10] delivers a sweeping denunciation of the "modern" under all its shapes, which leads him to present a surprisingly clear view – *al contrario*, as it were – of the conceptual origins of Modernism. *Degeneration* was a spectacular critical success in the last years of the nineteenth century until a few critics like Wells and Shaw pointed out its howling misreadings, hasty reductions and philosophical inadequacies. In his excellent *Degeneration, Culture and the Novel*,[11] William Greenslade has sketched the entire ideological context that gave to the diagnosis of "degeneration" such a hold on the imagination of the late Victorian public.

In Nordau's book, Ibsen, Baudelaire, Nietzsche, the pre-Raphaelites, Tolstoy, Wagner, Zola are in turn taken to task and shown as so many freaks in a relentless parade of *fin-de-siècle* symptoms. Symptoms of what? Of a Darwinian regression, of the degeneracy of the human race. After enervated "mysticism," the main sign of the disorder is "ego-mania," a term Nordau distinguishes from simple "egoism": the "mystics" are relayed by the *Ichsüchtigen* in the ladder leading to madness and criminality.

It is not from affectation that I use this word instead of the terms "egoism" [*Selbstsucht*] and "egoist," so generally employed. Egoism is a lack of amiability, a defect in education, perhaps a fault of character, a proof of insufficiently developed morality, but it is not a disease . . . The ego-maniac, on the contrary, is an invalid who does not see things as they are, does not understand the world . . . (*D*, 243)

Very soon, however, Nordau bypasses his own distinction, moving freely between "megalomania" associated with "genius" and "ego-mania" connected with mental imbalance: "That egoism is a salient feature in the character of the degenerates has been unanimously confirmed by all observers" (*D*, 244). He then attempts to describe the genesis of the "ego" and uses terms that although vague and blurred should be kept in mind: "In ultimate analysis, the consciousness of the 'Ego' and notably the opposition of the 'Ego' and the 'non-Ego' is an illusion of the senses and a fallacy of thought. Every organism is related to a species, and, over and above that, to the universe" (*D*, 250). Nordau relies extensively on experimental psychology and scientific positivism (he often quotes Lombroso, Taine, Ribot, Binet, and Krafft-Ebing about "abnormal" psychology) in order to disqualify and criminalize what is not "normal" in his eyes, that is, what lacks a "healthy" relation to the world and to the others. Everything that falls short of this norm is rejected in the most brutal terms. His aim is to describe the "geniuses" as criminals and madmen. Among the Decadents and Aesthetes he debunks, he reviews Baudelaire, Wilde, Huysmans, and Barrès, to whose "*culte du moi*" he devotes relatively lucid but pointedly critical pages.

In the course of this exhaustive survey, one briefly meets Max Stirner, "a crazy Hegelian, who . . . exaggerated and involuntarily turned into ridicule the critical idealism of his master to the extent of monstrously inflating the importance – even the grossly empirical importance – of the 'I'" (*D*, 442), someone who might be the originator of the intellectual disease associated with individualism and Nietzsche's main source of inspiration. The longest section of this very loose and garrulous book is devoted to "Ibsenism" (338–415). Although Nordau notes that most of Ibsen's characters actively criticize "egoism" as in *The Pillars of Society* and *Hedda Gabler*, he does not hesitate one moment to conclude that Ibsen qualifies as an "ego-maniac": "His ego-mania assumes the form of anarchism. He is in a constant state of revolt against all that exists" (*D*, 396). Nordau quotes the famous poem in which Ibsen wishes to be more "radical," not merely "flood the terrestrial garden" but "place a torpedo under the Ark" – a poem that will resurface again and again in *Finnegans Wake* – to judge severely: "Unfortunately the Paris Communists bungled the beautiful and fertile idea by clumsy execution" (*D*, 397). With similar vehemence, he rails at Brandes's efforts to link Ibsen with the spirit of the "modern": "But this modern, this realist . . . is in reality a mystic and an ego-maniacal anarchist" (*D*, 357). Joyce will later echo these almost self-parodic strictures in adequately self-parodic terms: Shem the Penman's "Ibscenest nansence" (*FW*, 535. 19) is repeatedly denounced by Shaun who calls him: "anarch, egoarch, hiresiarch" (*FW*, 188.16)

In *Degeneration*, Ibsen's obvious companion is Nietzsche, to whom Nordau grants a measure of talent when he "rants" but who is "obviously insane from birth, and his books bear on every page the imprint of insanity" (*D*, 453). It would be a waste of time and energy to recapitulate at length the very myopic reading of Nietzsche provided by Nordau – everything he reads pushes him further to evocations of "perversion" and "anthropophobia" tinged with sadism, if not downright criminality! Nordau could not be more deluded as to Nietzsche's political position when he concludes his own "rant" by the idea that Nieztsche is a supporter of Bismarck (when he, in fact, abhorred the Prussian leader): "Nietzsche's fundamental idea of utter disregard and brutal contempt for all the rights of others standing in the way of an egoistical desire, must please the generation reared under the Bismarckian system" (*D*, 470). Nordau completed his essay too early to be able to witness in Barrès's career the conscious decision to opt for nationalism of the most rabid kind so as to escape from the wobbly estheticism and individualism he had embraced in his youth.

Nordau's hymn to positivistic common sense and his stubborn refusal of "modernity" could be entirely inscribed within the compass of Flaubert's dictionary of "received ideas" while showing negatively how pervasive and dangerous radical individualism could be felt to be at the turn of the century. Joyce's early letters show that this same tradition had colored his style and way of thinking. When, for instance, he is writing to his brother about sexual symptoms, and at a time when he ironically describes himself in Rome as "The Anarchist" (*LII*, 206) he mixes ideas of "egoism" with stereotypes about gender and sexuality:

I presume there are very few mortals in Europe who are not in danger of waking some morning and finding themselves syphilitic. The Irish consider England a sink: but if cleanliness be important in this matter, what is Ireland? Perhaps my view of life is too cynical but it seems to me that a lot of this talk about love is nonsense. A woman's love is always maternal and egoistic. A man, on the contrary, side by side with his extraordinary cerebral sexualism and bodily fervour (from which women are normally free) possesses a fund of genuine affection for the "beloved" or "once beloved" object. (*LII*, 192)

The reemergence of the concept of egoism in a less guarded context suggests that the young Joyce would have been shocked by the fervent advocacy of the term by Dora Marsden and her feminist friends. But it is tempting to consider that when Stephen Dedalus meditates on a mother's love as "the only true thing in life," he may well have "egoism" in mind.

If we have a look at the other end of the spectrum, that is to Dora Marsden's leading articles in *The Egoist*, we can see that she is at times curiously close to Nordau's definitions and diagnosis. Taken together, her editorial pieces constitute a complete philosophy of egoism as synonymous with Modernism. We will return to Marsden's analyses more fully in chapter 7, I will just briefly quote from her editorial essay of

September 1916 entitled "The 'I' and the 'Ego': A Differentiation" in order to point to hidden continuities with the critical analysis of Nordau.[12] Starting from Berkeley's definition of "being" as "being perceived," she dissociates the "I" that accompanies all perceptions from an "Ego" that will end up containing the entire world: "Let then the 'I' of ordinary speech express the normal connotation of a 'WORLD-EXCLUSIVE I' and the term 'EGO' the philosophic and 'WORLD-INCLUSIVE I'" (p. 130). This ego is allowed to expand so fully that it comprehends the "universe." As we can see, this tenet is not very far from Nordau's basic idea that the ego is one with the universe (by which he means society and nature). But whereas Nordau reaches for complete agreement and subjugation, for Marsden the main question is to ascertain when "I" and "Ego" coincide and when they diverge. Her conceptual language is informed by Berkeley and Hume, and she reprinted a philosophical paper by Professor Morgan on "Berkeley's Doctrine of Esse" in *The Egoist* of October 1916. Her drift would in fact lead her toward the post-Fichtean discussions one finds in the early texts of Hegel, or to a neo-Hegelian position similar to that of Francis Bradley – thus putting her in close proximity to T. S. Eliot, whose "Tradition and the Individual Talent" was published for the first time in the pages of *The Egoist*. Both Eliot and Marsden believe that since the ego includes the universe, death is not a fact to be feared, but a return of the individual mind to the continuous tradition that precedes it and will survive it. As Barrès had already surmised, the pure "cult of the ego" inevitably reaches its limits too soon without the support of a more global system, be it culture, tradition, or the nation.

"WHAT IS A NATION?" "– I AM A NATION."

In the summer of 1924, while he was mentally building a complex narratological architecture and delineating the main "characters" of his *Work in Progress*, Joyce visited Brittany and went especially to see Tréguier, the birthplace of Renan (*JJII*, 567). This late and unusual homage to the French writer testifies to the lasting influence of a fellow "Celt" whose considerable scientific achievements and varied linguistic knowledge had led, among other things, to the rediscovery of Phoenicians – thus, more or less directly, to Victor Bérard's interest in these early explorers of the Mediterranean world. Renan appears today as the best equivalent France can offer to Vico, much more than Michelet or Quinet, whom Joyce took as guides. Renan's personal skepticism would underlie a systematic anthropological reinterpretation of comparative mythology and his linguistic expertise in Hebrew and other Semitic languages helped him approach religious phenomena with considerable authority. It is for his skepticism concerning the life of Jesus that he is quoted three times in *Stephen Hero*, including the famous paradox: "Renan says a man is a martyr only for things of which he is not quite sure" (*SH*, 180) This "not being quite sure" will apply all the more poignantly to Renan's definition of a nation.

Joyce had read Renan with considerable interest in 1905, especially his *Recollections of My Youth* and his *Life of Jesus* and was able to improvise a funny parody of his "Prayer on Acropolis" in a letter to Stanislaus (*LII*, 109). Perhaps Joyce was aware that it was in 1882 (March 11, to be precise), the year he was born – let us not forget that *natio* originally means "something that is born"[13] – that Renan had read his famous essay "What is a Nation?" to a rapt audience in the Sorbonne. "What is a Nation?" was written in the context of the Prussian occupation of the German-speaking portion of France known as Alsace-Lorraine after their victory in 1870. As most historians agree, the debate about the essence of a nation redoubled at that time.[14] For Renan, who examines the various claims made by nationalists of both camps, a nation in the modern sense of the term cannot be founded on any concept of race, blood, religion, or geography (all these claims are criticized successively) but only on the collective will of the people. "A nation, therefore, is the result of a great sense of solidarity, constituted by the sacrifices people have made and are willing to make. Although it assumes a past, it defines itself in the present by a tangible fact: the agreement, the desire clearly expressed, to continue life together. The existence of a nation involves a daily plebiscite."[15]

As Renan writes, the constitution of a nation implies a long history although it is not merely the collective memory of a group honoring founding fathers and their high deeds but a "forgetful memory." Lots of real historical events must be forgotten in order to allow for the vital interaction or melting pot that generates the subjective sense of belonging to a nation. Renan gives the example of the unification of France in the thirteenth century that entailed savage religious crusades on the part of the north against the south: it is normal, even inevitable that these past horrors should be forgotten. Or again he adds that in order to be a Frenchman, one "should" have forgotten the St. Bartholomew massacre. The individual feeling of belonging to one nation entails a curious balance between memory and forgetting. One might simply ask what happens to a collective memory when it cannot forget the feuds and betrayals of the past? This is in part how Joyce saw the "nightmare of history" reflected through Irish eyes, and why *Finnegans Wake* advocates forgetting as much as remembering – hence the double and contradictory injunction: "Forget, remember!" (*FW*, 614. 23).[16]

Memory coupled with forgetting should provide a powerful engine for the production of an irrational "national sentiment," an affect that works as a performative and constitutes the impression of belonging to an "imagined community," as Benedict Anderson has shown.[17] Both Renan and Joyce are attentive to the risks implied in this notion, above all the risk of a sentimentalism seen as the exaggeration or perversion of this legitimate sentiment. How can one distinguish between a genuine national sentiment and its perversion? This is a question to which we will return in chapter 7, when discussing what Meredith calls "sentimentalism" or the denial of the links between the subject's position and the acknowledgment of a collective debt (since most nations constitute themselves by managing a real or symbolical debt). Sentimentalism can be deadly, as the recent history of "national" minorities has shown, and it operates in ways that have been sketched by Stirner's critique, by endowing a city, a date, a hero, or martyr with a sacred aura. The sacralization of the "cause" for which one is ready to sacrifice one's life implies a mystifying mechanism that will cancel out irony, skepticism, and a commonsense reluctance to let collective ideals encroach upon one's life.

Leopold Bloom attempts to negotiate between conflicting definitions of nationality when he tries, not always successfully it is true, to provide his own definition. His wish to steer a course between strong antinomies, or to avoid the forceful equation of a citizen with a collective identity lands him in terminological difficulties. Let us return to this often quoted passage:

– But do you know what a nation means? says John Wyse.
– Yes, says Bloom.
– What is it? says John Wyse.
– A nation? says Bloom. A nation is the same people living in the same place.
– By God, then says Ned, laughing, if that's so I'm a nation for I'm living in the same place for the past five years. (*U*, 12: 1419–25)

Ned Lambert's rude irony may exhibit the inadequacy of Bloom's definition, but also points out to insufficiencies in a "nationalist" discourse that will have otherwise to stress race and blood as main factors. When Bloom is finally asked pointedly whether he "belongs" to the Irish nation, his reply is positive:

– What is your nation if I may ask, says the citizen.
– Ireland, says Bloom. I was born here. Ireland. (*U*, 12: 1430–31)

Bloom's invocation of nationality by birthright implies indeed that he should have partly "forgotten" (in Renan's sense) his Austro-Hungarian lineage, a point of view that is not shared by his fellow Dubliners. However Joyce's irony soon cuts against them, for when they "remember" his Jewishness and exotic origins, the text both indicates that Bloom is a Sinn Fein sympathizer, and moreover that the nationalist customers of the Citizen's pub are much closer to the pro-British administration than they would want to acknowledge:

– Isn't that a fact, says John Wyse, what I was telling the Citizen about Bloom and the Sinn Fein?
– That's so, says Martin. Or so they allege . . .
– He's a perverted Jew, says Martin, from a place in Hungary and it was he drew up all the plans according to the Hungarian system. We know that in the castle. (*U*, 12: 1621–1636)

The allusion is quite topical: Arthur Griffith had just finished publishing the installments of his main political essay, *The Resurrection of Hungary* in the *United Irishman* in June 1904 and he was under close watch from the center of British administration and police situated in the "castle." Indeed, he was arrested soon after the 1916 Easter Rising although he had taken no part in the planning of the failed insurrection. As Joyce's friend Padraic Colum, who was quite close to Griffith at that time, writes in a later memoir, the 1904 publication of *The Resurrection of Hungary* was "an event in Irish history": "To the post-Parnell generation it dramatized an alternative to Parliamentarianism with its performance that had become routine; to the generation moulded by the Gaelic League it offered a politic that befitted an integral nationalism."[18] It is not known whether Arthur Griffith, whose anti-Semitism was notable and peaked in 1904,[19] got the idea to look up the Hungarian events of 1849 from one of his Jewish friends (like Michael Nyok). However, he had discovered a model in the way a "nation" like Hungary refused to see its sovereign status annulled by a "State" (the Austro-Hungarian Empire). After a few years of turmoil, Francis Joseph became King of Hungary in exchange for the right of Hungarians to legislate for themselves as a free and associated nation. As Renan insists in "What is a Nation?" the double monarchy of the Habsburgs was not a nation but a State administrating at least two (if not more) nations. Hence the resurgence of the problem of "nationalities" throughout the twentieth century, from the Balkans to the former Soviet Empire. However, the main political goal pursued by Griffith in 1904 – and to which Bloom lends his sympathy – was the restoration of the Irish parliament that had been granted in 1782 and abolished in 1800 by the Act of Union. This program came through during the general election of December 1918, when Sinn Fein candidates won by a crushing majority. In January 1919, they implemented Griffith's politics by refusing to take up their seats in Westminster and instead proclaimed themselves "Dail Eireann" – the first parliament of the Irish Republic.

Much earlier, when Arthur Griffith was looking for a name for a fledgling nationalist movement just before his departure for South Africa in 1897, he either invented it himself or took it from a poem in Gaelic written by Douglas Hyde, then President of the Gaelic League: "Waiting for help from France, waiting for help from Spain; the people who waited long ago for that, they got shame only . . . // It is time for every fool to have knowledge that there is no watchcry worth any heed but one – *Sinn Féin amhain* – Ourselves alone!"[20] The cunning of history can be shown by the fact that the very terms that mark the birth of modern Irish nationalism, the Sinn Fein movement that looms so large in *Ulysses* and *Finnegans Wake*, convey a strong suggestion of isolationism in its refusal of alien imperialism. Whereas Stephen's anti-nationalist position in *Stephen Hero* is consistently described as "egoistic" (Stephen has to "acknowledge to himself in honest egoism that he could not take to heart the distress of a nation the soul of which was antipathetic to his own, so bitterly as the indignity of a bad line of verse" [*SH*, 151]), the pluralization introduced into "egoism" by "Ourselves alone!" entails a significant shift from Stephen's esthetic anarchism to a Leopold Bloom who fully assumes his Irish nationality while refusing the xenophobic excesses of sentimentalist nationalism. The aim of this book is to explore the evolution of Joyce's political and esthetic response to the various ethical dilemmas posed by the nationalist ideology he had fled but could not help acknowledge and the internationalist Modernism he belonged to – or rather "came into his own" as a successful writer living in exile. For at the time he was writing *Ulysses* in a neutral Switzerland while war raged in Europe, Joyce was engaged in a critical revision of his juvenile *alter ego*'s anarchistic attitude: as we will see, the issue of hospitality and "charity" clearly embodied by a "Jewish" Leopold Bloom acquires the crucial ethical dimension that appears to be lacking both in youthful estheticism and in shrill proclamations of xenophobic nationalism.

If we turn to the canonical expressions of Stephen's anarchist credo of "non serviam," the issue becomes more complex when we superpose two famous triads of ideological "bad objects" whose negativity has often been taken for granted. The first triad of Irish idols links forcefully the features associated with Irish nationalism which stress Catholicism against the oppressor's official Protestantism and Gaelic as a recently discovered weapon against *beurla* or English. Stephen exclaims: "You talk to me of nationality, language, religion. I shall try to fly by those nets" (*P*, 220). However, in a later discussion, we see a different triad of "bogeys" Stephen wishes to reject:

I will not serve that I which I no longer believe whether it call itself my home, my fatherland or my church: and I will try to express myself in some mode of life or art as freely as I can and as wholly as I can, using for my defence the only arms I allow myself to use – silence, exile and cunning. (*P*, 268–69)

If we apply the motto of: "silence, exile and cunning" reciprocally to family ("home"), nationalism ("fatherland"), and religion ("church"), we review successively the three "collective fictions" whose mystification the young artist wanted to avoid being tricked by. But why does he not mention language? Is it because he has settled the issue with "silence"? Anyway, how can one "fly by" the net of language? Will it be by using one language (English) to the detriment of another? Stephen's hopelessly mixed metaphors denounce him as a "sentimentalist" who refuses to acknowledge a debt: "My ancestors threw off their language and took another, Stephen said. They allowed a handful of foreigners to subject them. Do you fancy I am going to pay in my own life and person debts they made?" (*P*, 220). In *Ulysses*, we know that Stephen does acknowledge his own debt at least in a very revealing IOU dedicated to the writer AE – even if he still will not pay. But in the *Portrait of the Artist as a Young Man*, Davin's enraged question: "Are you Irish at all?" (*P*, 219) could rhyme with the Citizen's question facing Bloom's doubtful status.

Finally, one of the lessons taught by Ned Lambert's quip is that if "I" can be a "nation," it is because a nation, to succeed in its claims for autonomy, needs to create an "imagined" identity or the fiction of an "ego." As a matter of fact, "Ireland, Island of Saints and Sages" (1907) begins by forcefully equating individual and national characteristics: "Nations have their ego, just like individuals" (*CW*, 154). It looks as if Joyce resorted in this Triestine essay written in Italian to a kind of "wild psychoanalysis" of the Irish taken as a coherent group. This lecture owes a few insights to Renan's *Recollections* since Renan insists from the beginning upon the idea that Celtic culture has been shaped by saints and mystics who would often come from Ireland. Joyce's concept of a collective "ego" finds its roots in the Middle Ages whose "mystical" demarcations attest to an ancient heritage: "even a superficial consideration will show that the Irish nation's insistence on developing its own culture by itself is not so much the demand of a young nation that wants to make good in the European concert as the demand of a very old nation to renew under new forms the glories of a past civilization" (*CW*, 157). This lecture provides a blueprint for Joyce's later texts: the idea that Gaelic is a Phoenician idiom will later be grafted to Victor Bérard's inquiry into Odysseus' travels across a Mediterranean sea already mapped by its first voyagers; and the idea that Ireland has systematically assimilated invaders such as the Vikings or the English conquistadors seems to be at the root of the *Wake*'s exploration of hostility and hospitality.

As Joyce states: "the Danes, the Firbolgs, the Milesians from Spain, the Norman invaders, and the Anglo-Saxon settlers have united to form a new entity" (*CW*, 166). In this ancient and "mystical" nation, language, race, and nationality have been hybridized and intermingled in a tapestry woven by history:

Our civilization is a vast fabric, in which the most diverse elements are mingled, in which nordic aggressiveness and Roman law, the new bourgeois conventions and the remnants of a Syriac religion are reconciled. In such a fabric, it is useless to look for a thread that may have remained pure and virgin without having undergone the influence of a neighbouring thread. What race, or what language . . . can boast of being pure today? And no race has less right to utter such a boast than the race now living in Ireland. Nationality (if it really is not a convenient fiction like so many others to which the scalpels of present-day scientists have given the coup de grâce) must find its reason for being rooted in something that surpasses and transcends and informs changing things like blood and the human word. (*CW*, 166)

Clearly, Joyce debunks the myth of racial or ethnic purity upon which nationalist sentimentalism starts building its reconstruction of history.

THE "EGO'S OWN" OR "CHANGING THE SUBJECT"

Joyce's useful caveat alerts us to the need to be clear as to what defines these ruling "fictions" that keep such a hold on our lives. While arguing for a revised concept of "egoism" in connection with Modernism, I am aware that I will have to be extremely cautious, especially if I wish to avoid the danger of a merely fashionable "political reading." As Seamus

Deane wrote in an essay on "Joyce and Nationalism," a prevalent critical assumption used to be that Joyce was resolutely apolitical and limited
his genius to formal and stylistic innovation:

It is well known that Joyce, like Stephen Dedalus, considered himself to be the
slave of two masters, one British and one Roman. It is equally well known that
he repudiated the Irish revival . . . Repudiating British and Roman imperialism
and rejecting Irish nationalism and Irish literature which seemed to be in the
service of that cause, he turned away from his early commitment to socialism
and devoted himself instead to a highly apolitical and wonderfully arcane practice of writing. Such, in brief, is the received wisdom about Joyce and his relationship to the major political issues of his times.[21]

Deane notes however that the critical tide had turned around 1985,
when "some revision of this estimate" began. One could push back the
watershed in time, send readers back to Dominic Manganiello's *Joyce and
Politics* (1980) or even to Colin MacCabe's seminal *James Joyce and the
Revolution of the World* (1978). More recently, Trevor Williams has identified the 1975 Paris Joyce Symposium as the moment when the "apolitical" view of Joyce was shattered, an analysis with which I
wholeheartedly agree.[22] The Paris symposium highlighted a clash
between two cultures: I can still conjure up the dismay and the shocked
disbelief of American scholars when Philippe Sollers asserted that
English was a "dead language" after the publication of *Finnegans Wake*
not to speak of the bafflement that met Lacan's talk described in chapter
1. This book wishes to pay homage to such moments of inspiration and
confrontation, to re-read productive misunderstandings that verged
more often on comedy than on tragedy by reopening some of the moot
issues.

   Besides the fact that a different critical language inspired by Marxism,
psychoanalysis, feminism, linguistics, post-structuralism, and deconstruction – although the last two terms had not been "invented" then –
was brought to bear on Joyce for the first time, a major communication
problem centered around a more delicate conundrum: how could one
see the political element in Joyce given the biographical "fact" of his
rather aloof position in Irish matters and his quasi-autobiographical
projection into a fictional double presenting a young esthete whose main
wish it was to leave behind him Ireland's burden of tangled responsibil-
ities, and who remains cagey of any involvement in the nationalist cause
from the early texts until at least *Ulysses*? In brief, it turned out that the
political French were stressing the issue of a revolutionary language (a
language that was enough to place Joyce among a radical avant-garde,

on a pedestal that included at the time President Mao and Antonin Artaud), whereas the more conservative American specialists were always returning to either issues of esthetics or biography. Whereas the French could say, like Mallarmé, that "the Book is the bomb!" (pointing to the adequately red hardback cover of the jacketless Faber edition of *Finnegans Wake*), the "Joyceans" could only see in the "artist's" politics non-involvement, detachment, critical aloofness, and they had no difficulty in pointing out the real-life Joyce's lack of very visible political commitment.

What has changed then since 1985 cannot be attributed to a gradual and always fragile acceptance by American academics of "French" or "continental" approaches to literary theory. The spate of books written on Joyce from the perspective of post-colonial theory, like Enda Duffy's *The Subaltern Ulysses* (1994), Vincent Cheng's already quoted *Joyce, Race and Empire* (1995) or Declan Kiberd's very influential *Inventing Ireland* (1996), seems to show that there is by now a consensus. The political readings of Joyce have won the day, but they now tend to address a slightly different critical predicament. What is still the object of heated controversy is the role one is willing to grant to Joyce's alleged critique of nationalism. While Vincent Cheng remains quite prudent and balanced, some recent Irish scholars, like Emer Nolan[23] have tried to reassess more positively the nationalist discourses in *Ulysses*, seeing in a character like the Citizen just a counterpart to Bloom's idealism, while criticizing what may appear as liberal complacency in other critics' internationalist position. Seamus Deane, Terry Eagleton, and David Lloyd would belong to a camp more prone to striking a balance between Bloom's measured tolerance and the political struggle that was going on in Ireland at the time. Colin MacCabe, a Marxist critic deemed too close to Barthes and Lacan, is suddenly transmogrified into a "liberal," almost accused of betraying the cause of the "subaltern"'s resistance or of being blind to the way Joyce's "minor" literature functions as a vehicle for revolutionary aspirations.

A relatively similar evolution has marked recent trends in Modernist studies. In the last two decades, whether critics have tended to redefine boundaries, from Tyrus Miller's useful notion of "late Modernism"[24] or Peter Bürger's distinction between a purely esthetic modernism and a political avant-garde, or again attempted to put on the map female writers who have been excluded from prior canonization (the excellent anthology *The Gender of Modernism*[25] is a good case in point), there seems to be a general agreement that "high Modernism" is essentially apolitical, at best internationalist because not really committed to any other cause than high culture, or at worst tainted with fascism and anti-Semitism: Eliot, Lewis, Pound, and Yeats present a formidable rightist front, barely counterbalanced by Woolf's liberal sympathies and Joyce's disdain of authoritarian ideologies. At times "pink," never really "red," high Modernism floats too "high" above the cultural landscape precisely because it systematically refused to separate the issue of politics from the issue of language. In that context, it seemed to me crucial to revisit in a historicized manner the fate of Eugène Jolas's concept of the avant-garde in the *transition* years while understanding what the waning of avant-garde ideology in the thirties could mean for Joyce (as will be the object of chapter 2).

I would like to suggest that Joyce originally found his own political and ethical impetus in postures associated with egoism. Egoism defines more than an early phase in Joyce's career, as was the case with his anarcho-syndicalism or his brief infatuation for socialism, which ended with his return from Rome to Trieste: it sketches the ways in which a writer can learn to "become his own" or to "own himself" . . . until he becomes a "saint" or "martyr" of literature. Exactly as Sartre could describe Jean Genet as "Saint Genet, actor and martyr,"[26] Joyce has been described as a saint (and an actor) by a number of writers, from Adrienne Monnier and Gide to Lacan. The saintly posture looks more Schopenhauerian than Stirnerian indeed, but as Stirner suggested, radical individualism defined by a refusal to "serve" any other cause than that of the subject's own entails a rethinking of "ownership" and a desire of owning . . . the entire world of discourse at least. Such a radical ambition cannot but modify our usual apprehension of the structure of the subject.

This is what Stephen has in mind when he shocks Bloom by declaring grandiosely that "Ireland must be important because it belongs to me" (*U*, 16: 1164–65). When Bloom fails to understand what might belong to whom, Stephen adds impatiently: "We can't change the country. Let us change the subject" (*U*, 16: 1172–74). The hilarious pseudo-grammatical commentary provided by a visibly baffled Bloom is worth quoting in full: "At this pertinent suggestion, Mr. Bloom, to change the subject, looked down, but in a quandary, as he couldn't tell exactly what construction to put on belongs to which sounds rather a far cry" (*U*, 16: 1172–74). Even if "Eumaeus" flaunts its tired syntax, grammatical *non sequiturs*, and exhausted language, Bloom is quite right in assuming that the only cause worth some effort – for Stephen at least – is that of language, in so far as it can "change the subject," that is, replace the old monolithic entity that underpins metaphysical or ideological discourse with a fractured, unstable but also at times monstrously hypertrophied ego.

By pointing out unexpected links and echoes between Stirnerian egoism and Lacan's late transformation of his standard term of "subject" (by which he usually means "the divided subject of desire") into a new and symptomatic ego that he needed in order to read Joyce, I will try to show how the ego generates more than a theme that might be equated with the "self" or "individual": it provides a structure that concerns as much language as "Life" (which is why I will need to study the way nature, or more precisely, these particular animals that appear to be born of our bodies, lice). When life is perceived as an autotelic and self-reproductive system, as we will see in chapter 5, it is not necessary to romanticize or "transfigure" it as Yeats was always tempted to do. Life understood in this sense is "always already" ready for writing, as it were, it abounds in verbal felicities and ready-made constructs that only need an accurate recorder, provided the subjective relation between the writer and his audience has changed. Thus issues of textual and ethical hospitality become a dominant vector in *Ulysses*, in a textual process where the encounter with sodomy will force us to examine the reverse of egoism. For modernist egoism is refused as soon as it generates an "incestuous" endogamy. The door should be left open for another reader closer to what I call a "genetic reader."

It will be necessary to hold fast to both sides of the critical discussion, the political-linguistic side and the side concerned with esthetic theory and biographical issues. In Lacan's view, as we have seen, Joyce's unique status among Modernist writers derives from his transformation of his ego as saintly symptom of literature. Lacan's approach owes not a little to Heidegger's philosophy of language, a philosophy that needs and questions the concept of "origin" in a discourse that flirts with ontological "anarchism."[27] To save time and space, I will refer to the formulas of "The Way to Language" that stress both the transitivity (through the act of pointing or designating) and the intransivity (since language refers above all to itself) of poetic language. Heidegger envisages a foundational task that consists in "bringing language as language to language" without forgetting a need to "own" something, at least through poetry: "*What bestirs in the showing of saying is owning.*"[28] His punning discourse plays with notions of propriety and appropriation understood as "event" (*Ereignis* and *das Eigene*) that might call up shades of Stirner. Just as Stirner's "vanishing" ego leaves a new world and new language after his demise ("In the *unique one* the owner himself returns into his creative nothing, of which he was born . . . I have founded my cause upon Nothing"[29]) while Heidegger's language traverses reflexivity in order to abolish itself as a pure "pointing" (*Zeige*) or "showing" of the world.

Heidegger develops the implications of his two formulas with the qualification that one should avoid solipsistic or "egoistic" implications that might be created by purely autotelic self-mirroring. Language understood as poetic language (*die Sage*) allows us to "own" something which is not yet "its own" but a future event that will "come into its own." To stick to a Joycean context, we might think of the epiphany as a mode of pure showing. The epiphany is a showing which nevertheless cannot bypass the issue of its own language if it only wishes to "record" something that will remain, or if we want either author or "new reader" to actually "own" anything at all.

This is how Heidegger sums up the complex issue:

> Thus freed to its own space, language can concern itself solely with itself alone. That sounds like the common discourse we hear about egoistic solipsism. Yet language does not insist on itself, is not a self-mirroring that forgets everything else because it is enamored of itself [*nur eigensüchtigen*]. As legendary saying [*die Sage*], the essence of language is an appropriating showing that in fact disregards itself in order to release what is shown into its own, into its appearance [*in das Eigene seines Erscheinens zu befreien*].[30]

What matters is to let the world appear in a new "phanein" that somehow also invokes language. This could provide a philosophical commentary of what Eliot expressed in the poetic language of "Marina": for him, the writer's role is to "make" – and thus make us "own" – through a *poiesis* blending memory and forgetfulness, conscious knowledge and unconscious knowledge. The speaker blends the trauma of past disaster (Hercules' slaughter of his children) and the discovery of a mysterious new birth:

> I made this, I have forgotten
> And remember . . .
> Made this unknowing, half conscious, unknown, my own.[31]

CHAPTER THREE

Joyce the egoist

I began the last chapter with the historical "coincidence" that saw a convergence between Joyce's youthful egoistic anarchism and the creation of the review called *The Egoist*. Another coincidence was replayed more recently when a French magazine that had been similarly baptized *Egoïste* was requested to sell its name to Chanel – so as to launch a new line of after-shaves and perfumes for men called "*Egoïste*." While the magazine known as *The New Freewoman* was renamed *The Egoist* in 1914 – Dora Marsden's decision to rechristen her own magazine was announced in December 1913 – the name *Egoïste* was bought from Nicole Wisniak, who had started it as a fancy fashion magazine in 1977. In 1990 Wisniak sold the name to Karl Lagerfeld for Chanel (the sum of the transaction was not disclosed); he then launched the very successful after-shave brand. This has not prevented *Egoïste* from continuing its publication.[1] It is rather bewildering to witness how the same pattern has been repeated. In each case, a bright young woman starts a magazine and then sells the name or even the contents as well to what can be described as a male multinational (even if Chanel was founded by a woman).

I still remember the first advertising campaign when Chanel launched *Egoïste* in 1990. It is a publicity film, in which one discovers an Italian palazzo with a stately park seen from a distance, and as the camera comes closer, suddenly a pair of wooden shutters bursts open, and a beautiful woman shouts: "Egoïste!" Another window opens, and then another, until the entire façade is full of shouting women all crying "Egoïste!" at the top of their voices. The advertising campaign for the "Platinum" version of "Egoïste" is more recent: it is a photograph showing a man barely clad in a towel who boxes with his own shadow on the wall, and is seen in the act of delivering a direct blow to the stomach of this huge figure who has just dropped a bottle of the precious liquid, spilling in the air . . . The change in the campaign is undoubtedly symptomatic: from a series of beautiful women accusing some invisible man – is he their joint lover in what looks like some modern harem? – of being "selfish" (perhaps by dedicating himself to another woman, or to all the other women?), we have shifted to a single muscular man who appears to be fighting with himself so as to finally retrieve his after-shave from his own shadow. This tends to prove at least that the brand name is not felt to be an insult any more: male egoism seems to have been condoned by publicity at least.

This change in ideological fashions could suggest a new "performative" agency of certain key signifiers, and publicity is one of the best sites to observe important mutations (however, in this context, one will be tempted to replace *Egoïste* with the new men's perfume by Caron, *L'Anarchiste*, with its ominous caption: "*C'est dans le noir que se reconnaît l'Anarchiste.*"[2]) I am of course not only punning on "perfume" but also calling up Derrida's playful analysis of Molly Bloom's many yeses in *Ulysses Gramophone.*

Can one sign with a perfume? Just as we cannot replace *yes* by a thing which it would be supposed to describe . . . so it would be impossible to replace the *yes* by the names of the concepts supposedly describing this act or operation, if indeed this is an act or operation . . . Think back to Bloom in the chemist's. Among other things, he speaks to himself about perfumes. And remember, too, that the *yeses* of Molly (moly), the herb, also belong to the element of perfume. I could . . . have turned this paper into a treatise on perfumes – that is, on the *pharmakon* – and I could have called it *On the perfumative in Ulysses.*[3]

Molly, however, likes the mixing of opoponax and violet (*U*, 18: 463), while her perfume, called *Peau d'Espagne*, has a composition that is never fully disclosed: "Sweet almond oil and tincture of benzoin" – and then Bloom stops (*U*, 5: 490). Its orangeflower-water scent would no doubt be quite different from the pungent and racy smell of Chanel. Joyce owned a copy of Augustin Galopin's *Le Parfum de la femme* (Paris, 1889)[4] and he would have been thrilled or delighted by *Egoïste*. Would he have preferred the straight *Egoïste* or its more recent, more metallic, less fruity version called *Egoïste Platinum*?

We know from one passage of *Finnegans Wake* that if Joyce had kept all his affection for the magazine that launched his literary career ("I'm so keen on that New Free Woman with novel inside" [145. 29]) he was quite dismissive of the feminine element that had dominated it up to a point. The context, when quoted in full, dramatically qualifies the tone of the speaking voice:

Of I be leib in the immoralities? O, you mean the strangle for love and the sow-iveall of the prettiest? Yep, we open hap coseries in the home. And once upon the week I improve on myself I'm so keen on that New Free Woman with novel inside. I'm always as tickled as can be over Man in a Surplus by the Lady who Pays the Rates. (145. 25–31)

Joyce debunks the neo-Darwinism that was rampant among the editors and contributors of the magazine and depicts it as a fashion magazine devoted to self-improvement.

Another reference, in *Ulysses* this time, confirms the idea that Joyce remained skeptical about the change of name, even if he was grateful for the publication of his novel – but let us note, in *The Egoist*, and not in *The New Freewoman*: "I believe, O Lord, help my unbelief. That is, help me to believe or help me to unbelieve? Who helps to believe? *Egomen*. Who to unbelieve? Other chap" (*U*, 9:1078–80). Joyce plays on the Greek *ego*, followed by the intensive particle *men* (meaning "really") which, in a dialogue, would mean "yes, truly." Gifford and Seidman, among others, see this as an allusion to *The Egoist*, a magazine that indeed encouraged Joyce at a time when he had the greatest difficulties in getting published. The "other chap" could accordingly be George Roberts, who hesitated to publish *Dubliners* and finally destroyed the sheets in 1912. In fact, Joyce goes even further than merely alluding to the magazine: the passage directly quotes from the leading article by Dora Marsden in the August 1, 1914 edition of *The Egoist* (which was still serializing *A Portrait of the Artist as a Young Man*). Dora Marsden meditates on the concept of "Authority" and skillfully links "to believe" with "to leave doubt":

The voices of authority echo one to another all the world round with the cry of "Believe, believe." They mean, "Leave decision, leave it, leave it to us," in effect asserting that knowledge is a spurious form, a degraded type of the ideal which is lack-of-knowledge . . . The sacred is indeed the first weapon of defence against the prying questions of intelligence . . . Very naturally, therefore, all that one believes is by acquiescence of belief made sacred. "My beliefs are sacred," they would be no doubt, were the decision left with the believers, but the believer, as the history of belief shows, is encompassed about with enemies: both from within and from without . . . Spontaneously bursts from him the cry: "I believe, help thou my unbelief. I have abandoned the quest: do thou (namely, sluggishness, comfort, whatnot) smother this itch I have to return to pry and poke."[5]

Both Joyce and Mardsen quote Mark 9: 24, who tells the story of the father of a possessed child who answers Jesus's injunction: "If thou canst believe, all things are possible to him that believeth." Both include the famous phrase in a context that makes it inevitable to stress the value of doubt and the need to resist any authoritative injunction to believe.

In other articles, Marsden develops her analysis of the "word-games" by which authority imposes itself on individual consciences; this genealogy of the belief in morality and sin looks extremely modern, with echoes of Nietzsche and adumbrations of Wittgenstein's later strategies. She exposes in critical light the "grammar of assent" that was so dear to Cardinal Newman. Marsden's deconstructive and anarchist semantics announces her later development of a "science of signs." It is in this context that one may reinscribe Stephen's dialogic meditations on belief. If such an intertextual network looks promising, I shall nevertheless try to show that one cannot equate *The Egoist* people with a bunch of *Ego-Men*. A different gendering of egoism will thus be the subject of the next section.

FROM *THE NEW FREEWOMAN* TO *THE EGOIST*

Let us recapitulate: in January 1914, an obscure London journal known as *The New Freewoman* changed its name to *The Egoist*. In recent years, the change has become a subject of intense debate among scholars of literary Modernism, who have urged that it signals a key transformation within literary Modernism itself, a turn away from Modernism's earlier affiliations with militant feminism and a move toward a more agonistic and decidedly male Modernism. The work of Joyce, who published *A Portrait of the Artist as a Young Man* and much of *Ulysses* in the journal during the next years, has also become a crucial site for the unfolding of this debate, in part because his affiliations with the journal were critical to his early career and left lasting traces throughout his work, and in part because he has long been viewed as the paradigmatic master of Modernist prose.

How were the relations between Modernism and feminism played out in the change of the journal's name? What were the gender affiliations of egoism, and how did they overlap with the increasingly troubled status of the self and notions of modern heroism, and in what ways were they linked with the kind of relentless linguistic experimentalism so typically associated with Joyce? These have recently become pressing questions, and I propose to reconsider them by teasing out Joyce's complicated associations with egoism, viewed here as a set of philosophical commitments that intersect in complex ways with contemporary debates about gender, politics, and language. It is crucial to reopen a rather complex issue which has been explored by the excellent book Bruce Clarke has devoted to *Dora Marsden and Early Modernism.*[6] Clarke has deeply modified the way critics had so far viewed the famous take-over of a feminist magazine by phallocratic Modernism. Let us recall a few facts first.

Dora Marsden had been a classmate of Christabel Pankhurst since 1900 at the Manchester Victoria University and remained associated with Suffragism since then. She was a militant in the Women's Social and Political Union (WSPU), and spoke for instance at the huge rally that took place in June 1908 in Manchester, a meeting that drew 150,000 persons. By 1908 she was a salaried organizer of the movement, drew attention by her spectacular harassment of Winston Churchill at the Southport Empire Theatre in December 1909, when she shouted prop-aganda from a skylight in the dome, and almost fell to her death when the police caught her! She was repeatedly jailed, force-fed through the nose like many militant suffragettes. After what was termed "Black Friday" in November 1910, when two women died by police brutality, she was felt to be too radical in her positions, and condemned by the Pankhursts. In 1911, she resigned from the WSPU, and founded *The Freewoman: A Weekly Feminist Review*, which lasted from November 1911 till October 1912.

The Freewoman was a unique magazine, an open forum for suffragists, feminists, anarchists, socialists, Uranians (the gay liberation movement of the period) but also spiritualists, money-reformers, poets, and esthetes. The magazine went bankrupt, but was resuscitated under the name of *The New Freewoman: An Individualist Review* in June 1913, opening its columns to writers such as Rebecca West, Ezra Pound and Richard Aldington. Then the name was changed in January 1914 to become *The Egoist*. The last issue of *The New Freewoman* contained a note saying: "It is proposed that with our issue of January 1st, 1914, the title of THE NEW FREEWOMAN be changed to THE EGOIST" (15 December 1913), and reproduced a letter signed by five men, Upward, Pound, Carter, Kauffmann, and Aldington:

We, the undersigned men of letters who are grateful to you for establishing an organ in which men and women of intelligence can express themselves without regard to the public, venture to suggest to you that the present title of the paper causes it to be confounded with organs devoted solely to the advocacy of an unimportant reform in an obsolete political institution.

We therefore ask with great respect that you should consider the advisability of adopting another title which will mark the character of your paper as an organ of individualists of both sexes, and of the individualist principle in every department of life.[7]

This could be read as the sign of a takeover by men who wish to erase all traces of feminism – a takeover that would have been prepared by the famous "Imagiste" issue of August 1913, in which Rebecca West paves the way for Pound and his friends. Then in October 1913, Pound published "The Serious Artist" and "Religio" in an issue that features Aldington, Byington, Upward, and Rémy de Gourmont. When Harriet Weaver became the main editor of *The Egoist* it seemed that a male-centered Modernism had ousted and replaced an earlier and more radical feminism. Such has been for instance the accusation launched by Rachel Blau Du Plessis, who, in her *Pink Guitar*, is extremely critical of Marsden's betrayal of feminism.[8] Moreover, Bruce Clarke conclusively demonstrated that Dora Marsden herself engineered the change of name, to the point of soliciting the letter from these already reputed "men of letters."

Indeed, if one reads closely the front page of the first issue of *The New Freewoman*, one cannot miss the dominantly Stirnerian tone. Here is what Dora Marsden writes in her leading article:

This is the epoch of the gadding mind. The mind "not at home" but given to something else, occupied with alien "causes" is the normal order and as such must be held accountable for that contemning [sic] of the lonely occupant of the home – the Self – which is the characteristic of the common mind . . . Hence the popularity of the "Cause" which provides the Idol to which the desired self-sacrifice can be offered. The greater the sacrifice the Idol can accept the greater is it as a "Cause," whether it be liberty, equality, fraternity or what not.[9]

This rhetoric of the "Cause" is directly influenced by the opening statement of Max Stirner's *The Ego and His Own*, which had been translated into English in 1907 by Benjamin Tucker (who was also a regular contributor to *The New Freewoman*).

Stirner quotes the first line of a famous drinking poem by Goethe, "Vanitas! Vanitatum Vanitas!" "*Ich hab' mein Sach' auf Nichts gestellt*" – which can be translated as "I have set my cause on nothing," and develops the idea:

What is not supposed to be my cause [*Sache*]! First and foremost, the Good Cause, then God's cause, the cause of mankind, of truth, of freedom, of humanity, of justice; further, the cause of my people, my prince, my fatherland; finally even the cause of Mind, and a thousand other causes. Only *my* cause is never to be my concern. Shame on the egoist who thinks only of himself![10]

Stirner then describes the "egoism" of those who require us to work for them, such as the Prince or God, and decides to "take a lesson from them" and instead of serving them, to serve himself first: "God and mankind have concerned themselves for nothing but themselves. Let me then likewise concern myself for *myself*, who am equally with God the nothing of all others, who am my all, who am the only one [*der Einzige*] . . . Nothing is more to me than myself!" (pp. 4–5).

It is thanks to Stirner relayed via Tucker and Byington that Dora Marsden criticizes the way the two Pankhursts define Suffragism as a "Cause": "'The Cause to which I have given my life.' This is a message, the last but one of Mrs. Pankhurst," and she comments on Mrs. Pankhurst's rhetoric, noting that six years earlier, she would have only have said: "I want the vote given to me." She has fallen into the trap of absolute dedication to a cause. "She began to 'lead a cause' and imperceptibly the Cause became Leader – leading where all causes tend – to self-annihilation. Mrs. Pankhurst may die and great is the Cause. What Cause? The Cause of the empty concept – the fount of all insincerity: the Cause of the Symbol – the Nothing worked upon by the Dithyramb."[11]

Or again:

Accurately speaking, there is no "Woman movement" . . . If primarily women are to regard themselves as Woman or as the Mother, their satisfactions as individuals would be subordinated to an external authority: the requirements of the development of Woman or Mother *as such* – Empty concepts again . . . The few individual women before mentioned maintain that their only fitting description is that of Individual: Ends-in-themselves. They are Egoists. They are autocrats and government in their autocracy is vested in the Self which holds the reins in the kingdom of varying wants and desires, and which defines the resultant of these different forces as the Satisfaction of Itself. The intensive satisfaction of Self is for the individualist the one goal in life.[12]

This flamboyant statement was published in the first issue of *The New Freewoman*, which proves that anarchism was the dominant inspiration and not feminism. No wonder that one finds an advertisement for Stirner's book, *The Ego and His Own* (with the caption: "The most powerful work that has ever emerged from a single human mind") in a list of titles including *Anarchism* by Eltzbacher and *State Socialism and Anarchism* by Tucker. Dora Marsden had indeed moved from post-suffragist feminism to post-feminist anarchism, and was already building up her revolutionary deconstruction of political discourse and everyday language, in what she later called her "Egoist semantics." Let us now take a closer look at her model, Max Stirner.

"ANARCH" AND "EGOARCH" (188.16):
STIRNER'S GHOSTLY EGOISM

One could stress the difference between the American translation (with the subtitle "The Case of the Individual Against Authority") and the original version – *Der Einzige und sein Eigentum*, which clearly situates it among the *Junghegelianer* and the Berlin "Free spirits." Stirner radically criticizes and simplifies the system of Hegel's *Phenomenology of Spirit* by distinguishing between two great periods, that of the "Ancients," or the world of ancient wisdom, and that of the "Moderns," which he identifies with Christianity. Christian theology, because it is based upon a mystique of transcendent love, remains a resolute adversary of egoism, which refuses to sacrifice personal interest to a cause that is a generous but mystifying abstract idea.

Theology for Stirner is nothing but a systematic belief in ghosts. Stirner more than energetically mimics that which is whispered in contemporary ears by the "Romantic" discourse of the so-called Moderns:

> Yes, the whole world is haunted! Only is haunted? Nay, it itself "walks," it is uncanny through and through, it is the wandering seeming-body of a spirit, it is a spook . . . Everything that appears to you is only the phantasm of an indwelling spirit, is a ghostly "apparition" . . . to you the whole world is spiritualized, and has become an enigmatic ghost; therefore do not wonder if you likewise find in yourself nothing but a spook.[13]

Everything has become spectral in a fundamentally haunted modernity. Stirner's response lies in a reduction of investment to the Ego – that is, to a transcendental egoism which will resist the constraints of abstract ideas. Unicity combats generality somewhat like the drive-struggles against the powerful fictions of the Freudian super-ego. Accordingly, Stirner refuses to admit that love can be exercised in the name of an external value:

> If I cherish you because I hold you dear, because in you my heart finds nourishment, my need satisfaction, then it is not done for the sake of a higher essence whose hallowed body you are, not on account of my beholding in you a ghost; i.e. an appearing spirit, but from egoistic pleasure; you yourself with *your* essence are valuable to me, for your essence is not a higher one, is not higher and more general than you, is unique like you yourself, because it is you. (*EO*, 54)

This idea could be profitably paralleled with Joyce's notes for *Exiles*.

Stirner would probably have been forgotten as a mere oddity, a minor Hegelian, had he not become the butt of Marx and Engels's ferocious humor in *The German Ideology*, a work that curiously monumentalizes him by making him the main "enemy" of Marxian dialectics. *The Ego and His Own* is accused of embodying ideology; the central "ego" as "unique" is reduced to the function of a ghost, thereby demonstrating the culmination of an ideology that is essentially ghostly. Stirner becomes the whipping boy and the scapegoat of historical materialism, and like Finn in the *Wake*, he quickly turns into a "hegoak" (*FW*, 5.7). In order to criticize him, Marx and Engels feign a tactical incomprehension of the parodic tone so crucial in *The Ego and His Own*. They deliberately remain deaf to the ironies that are rife in Stirner's evocation of a "phantasmagoria" and write:

Without realizing it, Saint Max has so far done no more than give instruction in the art of spirit-seeing, by regarding the ancient and modern world as the "pseudo-body of a spirit," as a spectral phenomenon, and seeing in it only struggles of spirits. Now, however, he consciously and *ex professo* gives instruction in the art of ghost-seeing.[14]

To be sure, Stirner does not explain the history of Christianity through the "empirical conditions" and "industrial relations and relations of exchange" connected to a given form of society. For Marx and Engels, Stirner remains a prisoner of the spirit he denounces: by dint of crying "ghost," he has effectively transformed himself and his conceptual world into a spectral phantasmagoria.

Certainly, there is little need to reenact the Marxist trial of idealism and ideology (who would escape whipping?). It suffices to note how the philosophical debunking performed by Marx and Engels hinges around purely literary strategies; it is as if Stirner's book was referred back to a fictional world of shadows from which it should never have detached itself. There also remains the enigma of the curious relentlessness of Marx and Engels whose 350 pages of mocking remarks devoted to Stirner surpass by close to twenty pages the entire volume of *The Ego and His Own*; this is a rare feat of polemical overkill. Like Bouvard and Pécuchet, who in their desperate quest for knowledge fling at each other the epithets of "materialist" and "idealist," Marx and Engels manage to quote almost *all* of Stirner's essay! As Derrida suggests in his *Specters of Marx*,[15] Marx and Engels appear to have been miffed by the fact that Stirner spoke better and before them of ghosts and spectrality! At stake in this struggle for the reduction of ghosts is the staunch Marxist refusal to conceive of an a-relational relation, an "I" which only positions itself as "Ego" or the "Unique" in order to refute any positioning and hence disappear.

Marx and Engels reduce to a "magi:al incantation" the rhapsody on the term of the "Unique" which concludes Stirner's treatise. They remark on the unstable function of this term, a non-conceptual concept, when they write that the "Unique" becomes a word which is "simultaneously more and less than a word" (*GI*, 449) and conclude with hints of a surreptitious return of a Christian repressed: "'Sancho'-Stirner has found as the object of his Quixotic quest a pure and empty word which plays the role of Christ the Redeemer – and redeems itself from any link with reality" (*GI*, 449–50). However, the dialectic of an anti-dialectic enunciation that has been invented by Stirner could be seen as heralding later insights such as the main intuition of Nietzsche's critique of the self (there is at least one unmistakable allusion to Stirner's "Unique" in *Thus Spake Zarathustra*), of Adorno's "negative dialectics," or, with more exactitude, of Blanchot's *Neuter*, a neutrality more passive than passivity. The "I" only calls itself "Ego" to transcend itself and vanish once again in its own enunciative process.

This yields a paradoxical foundation, the enunciation of an "Ego" by which All is inverted into Nothing and vice versa. The famous final paragraph of *The Ego and His Own* confirms this idea:

I am owner of my might, and I am so when I know myself as *unique*. In the *Unique one* the owner himself returns into his creative nothing, of which he is born. Every higher essence above me, be it God, be it man, weakens the feeling of my uniqueness, and pales only before the sun of this consciousness. If I found my cause on myself [*Stell' Ich auf Mich meine Sache*], the unique one, then my concern rests on its transitory, mortal creator, who consumes himself, and I may say: // I have founded my cause on nothing. [*Ich hab' Mein' Sach' auf Nichts gestellt*].[16]

Is this merely, as *The German Ideology* maintains, a play on words, the absurd exploitation of a tautology which detaches itself from language in mysterious and transcendent fashion? One may understand, however, how the derisive epithets of "Saint Max" and "Sancho" need an enunciative montage without which the philosophical critique could not work. Stirner is slowly cornered at the intersection of two texts – the Bible and *Don Quixote* – which play a driving polemical role in the Marxist critique of ideology, allegedly presented in the name of historical materialism. Indeed, the last word of the caustic review of Sancho's thought is left to Cervantes.

If Marx saw in Stirner proof by incompetence and self-parody of the bankruptcy of the speculative system of German idealism, one might counter by saying that Stirner not only "invented" modern anarchism, but also radicalized the question that would be taken up by Lacan more than a century later about the paradoxes of subjective enunciation – as one can observe in the last sentences of *The Ego and His Own*: The conceptual question,

"What is man?" has then changed into the personal question [an alternative translation would be: it is up to You to answer], "Who is man?" With "what" the concept was sought for, in order to realize it; with "who" it is no longer any question at all, but the answer is personally there present at once in the asker: the question answers itself. (*EO*, p. 366, modified)

Stirner is a writer who produces a work in order to extol the pleasure of life perceived as the Ego's auto-delectation and self-erasure: everything is Ghost for the unique mill of the Ego. The Ego is All and Nothing at once, and the non-totalizable source of negativity introduced into the world. This would recall Fichte rather than Hegel; here, the combination of their theses provides an unassailable position – except if you manage to convince the Ego that he is just another ghost. Which is what Marx and Engels have attempted to do, with a modest measure of success.

THE POLITICS OF EGOISM

It is not a mere coincidence that Joyce's work should have found its way into the pages of Mardsen's magazine. If we are to pay attention to what Stanislaus Joyce has to say, his elder brother distinguished himself early by a Stirnerian attitude. At the beginning of his diary, in 1903, when James was putting together material for a tentative autobiography, Stanislaus notes:

Jim is a genius of character . . . He has, above all, a proud, wilful, vicious self-ishness, out of which by times now he writes a poem or an epiphany, now commits the meanness of whim and appetite, which was at first protestant egoism, and had, perhaps, some desperateness in it, but which is now well-rooted – or developed? – in his nature, a very Yggdrasill.[17]

In these pages where Stanislaus confesses that he has modeled his life on that of Jim, he accordingly expresses fears that he might have followed his brother's egoism and is relieved to hear from his aunt that this was not the case. He also values the fact that Poppie, his sister who was one year older, had none of the detested selfishness:

Poppie is the most unselfish person I know ... She seems to wish, if anyone is
to suffer, that she should be the victim. What an extraordinary sense of duty
women have! ... Aunt Josephine tells me I underrate myself and that I am not
an egoist. The fact that I think constantly about myself should prove her that I
am. Yet I take myself at Jim's valuation of me, because it is my own, perhaps.
(*DD*, 58–59)

As for his elder brother, Stanislaus can point out inconsistencies in his
system:

His [James's] nature is naturally antagonistic to morality. Morality bores and
irritates him. He tries to live on a principle of impulse. The justification of his
conduct is the genuineness of impulse. The principle is itself an impulse, not a
conviction. He is a polytheist. What pleases him for the moment is his god for
the moment. He demands an absolute freedom to do as he pleases ... This kind
of life is naturally highly unsatisfactory and his conduct bristles with contradictions. (*DD*, 52)

What Stanislaus exposes here is the combination of lax socialism and
easy Nietzscheism that was so dominant a pose among young esthetes at
the turn of the century. This element is nevertheless a major component
of "early Modernism" – as James himself seemed to be aware. Here is
again the Diary:

Jim boasts – for he often boast now – of being modern. He calls himself a socialist but attaches to no school of socialism. He marks the uprooting of feudal principles. Beside this, and that subtle egoism which he calls the modern mind, he
proclaims all kinds of anti-Christian ideals – selfishness, licentiousness, pitiless-
ness. What he calls the domestic virtues are words of contempt in his mouth.
He does not recognize such a thing as gratitude. He says it reminds him of a
fellow lending you an overcoat on a wet night and asking for a receipt.
(Gratitude is, after all, such an uncomfortable sentiment – thanks with a grudge
at the back of it.) As he lives on borrowing and favours, and as people never fail
to treat him in their manners as a genius while he treats them as fools, he has
availed himself of plenty of opportunity of showing ingratitude. (*DD*, 54–55)

One should not blame Stanislaus for what could appear as a jaundiced
assessment. His brother's earlier works, what remains of *Stephen Hero* and
the 1904 "Portrait of the Artist," all stress the need of systematic egoism.
At the opening of chapter 17 of *Stephen Hero* we can read that Maurice
has been "corrupted" by his brother's idle habits, while Stephen resents
the family pressure that is put upon him. He is reluctant to "satisfy the
family" by choosing a remunerative career. "He thanked their intention:
it had first fulfilled him with egoism; and he rejoiced that his life had
been so self-centered" (*SH*, 53). His rejection of Irish society is based

above all upon a loathing for Irish Catholicism – but he also refuses the role of a political activist or "demagogue." If his work can change this society, so much the better! This cannot become a program:

The attitude which was constitutional with him was a silent self-occupied, contemptuous manner and his intelligence, moreover, persuaded him that the tomahawk, as an effective instrument of warfare, had become obsolete. He acknowledged to himself in honest egoism that he could not take to heart the distress of a nation, the soul of which was antipathetic to his own, so bitterly as the indignity of a bad line of verse . . . (*SH*, 151)

In Joyce's autobiography, the denunciation of egoism is left to others, such as Lynch, who seems at one point upset by "Stephen's unapologetic egoism, his remorseless lack of sentiment for himself no less than for others" (*SH*, 156).

This is the same picture that we find in the early "Portrait of the Artist" (1904): the third page of the manuscript describes the "enigma of a manner" that is supposed to protect Stephen: "It was part of that ineradicable egoism which he was afterwards to call redeemer that he imagined converging to him all the deeds and thoughts of the microcosm." This thought cannot simply be ascribed to youthful enthusiasm, since we find it in Stephen's mouth at the close of *Ulysses*, in "Eumaeus," when Stephen declares to a baffled Bloom "that Ireland must be important because it belongs to [him]" (*U*, 16: 1164–65). One could observe traces of this grandiloquent and slightly paranoid egoism in Lucia's attitude in the 1930s, since she seemed to have taken too literally the idea that Ireland actually belonged to her father.

By a typically Fichtean reversal, the early "Portrait of the Artist" transforms egoism into negoism: "His Nego, therefore, written amid a chorus of peddling Jews' gibberish and Gentile clamour, was drawn up valiantly while true believers prophesied fried atheism and was hurled against the obscene hells of our Holy Mother." (*APA*, 14). The position of what the *Wake* calls a "Negoist Cabler" (*FW*, 488. 21) is here described as a mere "outburst," for the artist seems ready to join a communal movement:

already the generous idea had emerged from a thirty years' war in Germany and was directing the councils of the Latins. To those multitudes, not as yet in the wombs of humanity but surely engenderable there, he would give the word: Man and Woman, out of you comes the nation that is to come, the lightening of your masses in travail; the competitive order is employed against itself, the aristocracies are supplanted; and amid the general paralysis of an insane society, the confederate will issues in action. (*APA*, 13–14)

As Manganiello has shown in his groundbreaking *Joyce's Politics*,[18] Joyce's position was closest to the specifically southern anarcho-syndicalism of the times. The reference to a new thirty years' war probably alludes to the evolution of German socialism after 1875, that is, after the Gotha Congress that tried to bridge the gap between anarchists and communists. But the shift advocated from Germany to Italy does not point toward a Marxist solution to the conflict: Joyce clearly inclines toward anarchism as an ideology that can accept and even foster egoism.

Two couples of concepts need to be linked here: egoism and heroism go together on the one hand – as we shall see in chapter 4, this sketches both an esthetic and an ethical position via a "heroic" *Ego Nego* – whereas socialist internationalism has to be seen in its complex interaction with Irish nationalism. When Griffith decided to rename his *United Irishman* (it had been sued for libel in May 1906) *Sinn Fein*, his choice of the Irish phrase corresponding to "Ourselves alone" was a decisive move toward practical and economic solutions for Ireland rather than an hitherto sterile parliamentary agitation. Ireland would start being its own and stop following other causes: it would boycott British products and develop its own industries and banking system. All the letters Joyce wrote in 1906 show him endorsing most of Griffith's program, with an extraordinary clear-sighted analysis of his strengths and weaknesses: "In my opinion Griffith's speech at the meeting of the National Council justifies the existence of his paper [*Sinn Fein*] . . . so far as my knowledge of Irish affairs goes, he was the first person in Ireland to revive the separatist idea on modern lines nine years ago" (*LIV*, 110).

From Rome, Joyce voices two important reservations about language and race: "What I object to most of all in his paper is that it is educating the people of Ireland on the old pap of racial hatred whereas anyone can see that if the Irish question exists, it exists for the Irish proletariat chiefly" (*LIV*, 111). And about a month later:

You ask what I would substitute for parliamentary agitation in Ireland. I think the *Sinn Fein* policy would be more effective. Of course I see that its success would be to substitute Irish for English capital but no-one, I suppose, denies that capitalism is a stage of progress. The Irish proletariat has yet to be created. A feudal peasantry exists, scraping the soil but this would with a national revival or with a definite preponderance of England surely disappear . . . For either *Sinn Fein* or Imperialism will conquer the present Ireland. If the Irish programme did not insist on the Irish language I suppose I could call myself a nationalist. As it is, I am content to recognize myself an exile: and, prophetically, a repudiated one. (*LIV*, 124–25)

This "prophetic" repudiation allows Joyce to look even further into the future than the contemporary nationalist movement, whose ultimate success he seems to envisage here, while admitting that he will probably never return.

To contextualize Joyce's balanced assessment, it is worth recalling that Marx and Engels themselves had advocated nationalism as an acceptable solution for Ireland in spite of their well-known internationalist leanings. In a letter Marx wrote to Kugelmann in April 1868, he begins by asserting that: "The Irish question predominates here just now."[19] In the same letter, he announces the overthrow of the Church the English established in Ireland as a bulwark to landlordism. In December 1869, writing to Engels, who was then preparing a monumental *History of Ireland* that he would never complete, Marx announces that it is vital that the International Council of the Workers should discuss the Irish question:

For a long time I believed that it would be possible to overthrow the Irish regime by English working-class ascendancy . . . Deeper study has now convinced me of the opposite. The English working class will *never accomplish anything* before it has got rid of Ireland. The lever must be applied in Ireland. That is why the Irish question is so important for the social movement in general. (*IIQ*, 382)

Just one year before Marx died (1883) – but also less than one week after James Joyce's birth, Engels wrote to Kautsky (February 7, 1882): "I . . . hold the view that *two* nations in Europe have not only the right but even the duty to be nationalistic before they become internationalistic: the Irish and the Poles. They are most internationalistic when they are genuinely nationalistic." (*IIQ*, 432)

Although Engels remained unaware that a future literary genius had just then been born who would apply this precept with a vengeance, he had no patience with what he considered an anarchist deviation of armed nationalism – namely direct action as advocated by the Fenians. He strongly condemned terrorist coups such as the Phoenix Park assassination of 1882: "Thus the 'heroic deed' in Phoenix Park appears if not as pure stupidity, then at least as pure Bakuninist, bragging, purposeless *'propagande par le fait'*" (*IIQ*, 436). The same letter urges Eduard Bernstein "never (to) praise a single Irishman – a politician – unreservedly, and never identify yourself with him before he is dead" since "Celtic blood and the customary exploitation of the peasant make Irish politicians very responsible to corruption" (*IIQ*, 436). Engels then quotes O'Connell's famous bribes and the famous rejoinder of one of the Land

League leaders who was responding to the reproach that he had sold his country: "Yes, and I was damned glad to have a country to sell."

Joyce's political egoism evolved from his deep identification with Parnell, but also from a meditation on the causes of his failure. He never wavered in his condemnation of the Catholic Church who had abandoned the nationalist leader for moral reasons, but also never doubted that Irish politicians had betrayed the only leader who could have brought about a peaceful transition to national independence. After this parliamentary failure, separatism appears as the only way out. This also applies in the domains of art and culture: the motto "I am my own" offers the only valid course. And this realization goes beyond Joyce's private mythology to encompass a major component of Modernism.

I have already alluded to Levenson's *Genealogy of Modernism* and the idea that, among turn of the century intellectuals, "liberalism decomposed into egoism."[20] I would like to complicate the issue still further by alluding to a book that attempts to demonstrate that Joyce was neither an Egoist nor a Modernist. In his provocative *The Antimodernism of Joyce's Portrait of the Artist as a Young Man*,[21] Weldon Thornton mounts a systematic attack on Modernism, a Modernism seen as a philosophical notion that goes back to Galileo and Locke. Locke's pioneering distinction between primary and secondary qualities was to generate the entire movement of skepticism in regard to the power of human consciousness. What Thornton subsequently brands as "the Modernist Syndrome" is the separation between subject and object that Cartesian philosophy achieved and that culminates as egoism.

Modernism is defined by the conjunction of two movements: individual skepticism in the realm of society and culture, and in epistemology, a split between subject and object, mind and matter. Modernism is thus the combined creation of Galileo, Bacon, Descartes, Hobbes, Newton, Hume, and the Enlightenment philosophers. When this ideology identified itself with modernity especially after the French Revolution it led to the dissolution of a unified social psyche: Wilde's paradoxes and witty inversions of the commonsensical beliefs still held dear by the previous *doxa* are based on a strict hiatus between the world of empirical object and the mind, free to reconstruct a world out of nothing (*TAJ*, 29–31). Egoism would thus appear as the outcome and main symptom of early Modernism.

Thornton could be said to belong to the camp of the "Stephen-haters." He presents young Stephen as a would-be artist, and never as the spokesman of the author. It is such a de-authorization of the central character that allows Joyce to combine techniques derived from two antagonistic traditions, symbolism and naturalism. Their combined energies help create an original type of *Bildungsroman* whose aim is to "expose the paltriness of the modernist view of the self" (*TAJ*, 57). Modernism having been identified with atomic individualism, according to Thornton, Joyce aims at reconstructing the self as a full, social, and organic entity, therefore at fighting against egoism under all its shapes. The isolated or egoistic "self" is heard, felt, or seen through its "individuating rhythm," with a careful alternation of social and individual modes of investment moving from outer to inner, then again outer and inner approaches, while running the gauntlet of social, sensuous, religious, and finally esthetic temptations.

When Thornton writes that Stephen's language cuts across the artificial distinctions between self and world that have been generated by Modernism, he is not only undermining his own categories – social vs. individual, inner vs. outer – that were instrumental in his structural description of the novel's progression, he is also enacting a program which belongs to the same category as, say, Lawrences's early novels, *The Waste Land*, and Pound's *Cantos*. *A Portrait of the Artist as a Young Man* has often been commended for its insistence on the creative value of language. Thornton has first to deny that Joyce reduces thought to language – an idea that is nevertheless crucial in Marsden's egoist semantics. Thornton then states his opposition to those who wish to see language as Joyce's sole theme (*TAJ*, 117) and quotes Joyce's letters and essays in an effort to prove that Joyce himself would never collapse language and thought. His discussion then focuses on the fifth chapter, a chapter which appears all the more deceptive as the entries in Stephen's diary betray his inadequacies as much as they convey his hopes and plans. Is this a sign of Joyce's refusal to identify his character with his language, a sign that what he is attacking is a superficial version of Modernism debunked through a parodic exposition of Stephen's immaturity?

Joyce's presentation of the progressive liberation of a "young man" who chooses the arduous path of artistic rebellion against all the traps and trappings of family values, religious models, and national politics is no doubt partly ironic and parodic. In Thornton's words, "we see that while Stephen aspires to the Enlightenment program of complete self-knowledge, Joyce wishes us to realize how specious that aim is, and how simple and superficial a view of the psyche it involves" (*TAJ*, 152). For instance, Stephen remains very Irish in spite of himself, which proves that Joyce works often against his "hero"'s declared values; however, this is not sufficient to convince us that the main goal of the novel is to bridge the gap between self and world, inner and outer values that Galileo and Descartes had opened under our feet.

Most critics who belong to Thornton's "reconstructive" camp would then follow Stephen through *Ulysses* and show how badly he needs Bloom's full humanity and *caritas* to compensate for his failings and shallowness. But what of Molly's monologue? And what to do with *Finnegans Wake*? Thornton notes correctly that it is "a book devoted to radically a-personal elements, generic elements, perhaps even pre-human elements, in human experience" (*TAJ*, 61). Relying more systematically on Jung's view of the psyche, and still refusing to believe that this text evades traditional models of meaning, Thornton has to confess to a certain bafflement: "In light of Joyce's concern in his earlier works with "individualism," one of the most striking things about *Finnegans Wake* is the absence in it of anything like individual characters" (*TAJ*, 61). His critical honesty forces him to acknowledge that the *Wake* cannot be brought in line with the alleged "message" of *Ulysses* ("*Ulysses* is in some degree paradigmatic of how Joyce feels we should respond to our own life-crises – namely, by tempering our sense of ego and of our separateness from one another, but not by abandoning the conscious self and the values that it brings into being. Not so in *Finnegans Wake*" [*TAJ*, 62]). This says a lot about Joyce's intractability (and probably justifies the whole "experiment" of his later work): he has managed to write a text that can be seen to resist all humanistic recuperations – but by expanding his earlier egoism. Or perhaps by preferring a novelistic model of egoism to a philosophical concept.

In the fiction that escapes from the autobiographical sphere, Joyce often provides interesting critiques of egoism, especially when it appears not as the expression of the self's liberation but as nihilistic impotence. The "case" of Mr. Duffy would provide a good example of this critique. "A Painful Case" shows how a man can condemn a woman to degradation and finally to an ignominious death through his rejection of love: "He thought that in her eyes he would ascend to an angelical stature; and as he attached the fervent nature of his companion more and more closely to him, he heard the strange impersonal voice which he recognised as his own, insisting on the soul's incurable loneliness. We cannot give ourselves, it said: we are our own."[22] Is Mr. Duffy the negative version of the egoist? Perhaps, especially when we remember that this story is based upon an incident that happened to Stanislaus Joyce. Let us take this as an opportunity to return to his diary, and to what it has to say about literary egoism, or more precisely about Meredith's famous novel, *The Egoist*.

THE BOOK OF EGOISM: "CRIBBED OUT OF MEREDITH" (*U*, 14: 1486)

A long and self-conscious passage in the Dublin *Diary* is devoted to a systematic comparison between Henry James and George Meredith. Stanislaus values James over Meredith and finds many faults with two main novels, *Richard Feverel* and *The Egoist*. "*The Egoist* is later and more mature work, but its construction is far worse. It drags intolerably until within about 100 pages of the end, and then ends like a farce by Pinero" (*DD*, 120). He then sums up the plot, stressing its artificiality and obscurity ("Vernon Whitford and Colonel de Craye evidently know as much about the affair as Meredith himself") and concludes: "Perhaps what is called a 'plot' has little attraction for me, but it seems to me that *The Egoist* has to be written again and that the man who will write it must be able to write without a 'plot,' directly from his characters" (*DD*, 121). One could surmise that this is precisely the kind of advice that Joyce paid attention to when he rewrote *Stephen Hero* as *A Portrait of the Artist as a Young Man*. I am not merely suggesting that the novel is a variation on the theme of *The Egoist*, but also that *Ulysses* attempts to overcome aporias of anarchist egoism by fusing the main themes of two novels: *Richard Feverel* – for the "father and son" intrigue linking Bloom and Stephen, as some explicit allusions make clear – and *The Egoist*. This last point needs more explanations.

Let us review briefly the basic ingredients of this novel. The hero is Sir Willoughby Patterne, a rich and handsome country squire who has reached the age of marrying. He hesitates between the "dashing" and wealthy Constantia Durham and a shy and romantic neighbor, Laetitia Dale, who happens to be a poet as well. He first chooses Constantia as more of a match appropriate to his standing, when she suddenly marries someone else. Wounded personally and socially, he turns back to Laetitia, to whom he promises that they will eventually marry, but to cover the social embarrassment caused by Constantia, he spends three years traveling in America with his cousin. When he returns, his mother looks down upon Laetitia, and he meets his ideal partner, Clara

Middleton. She unites all the qualities of the others, is well off, independent, her father is a renowned scholar, she is only eighteen but assuredly beautiful and clever. She lets him court her, but when she has grudgingly accepted to be engaged to him and is presented as the official "betrothed," she slowly realizes that he is an intolerable egoist who wants to keep her in his world, and will never allow her the autonomy she requires. He behaves like a feudal lord who expects absolute devotion from his subjects: "I confess to exacting that kind of dependency. Feudalism is not an objectionable thing if you can be sure of the lord. You know, Clara . . . I do not claim servitude, I stipulate for affection. I claim to be surrounded by persons loving me . . . To be the possessor of the whole of you! Your thoughts, hopes, all."[23]

The painful slowness of the novel that had been denounced by Stanislaus Joyce corresponds to the long internal struggle within Clara, who is at first in love with Willoughby, or at least flattered by his "devotion," and who slowly comes to the conclusion that she must reject him if she is to remain "her own." At one point she thinks: "My mind is my own, married or not" and the narrator adds: "It was the point in dispute" (*E*, 64). Love implies possessiveness and she cannot accept the limitation of her freedom that it entails. She pretends to be jealous of Laetitia (still in love with Willoughby, despite his two rejections), a ploy which works up to when the two young women become friends. In a friendly and intense discussion, Clara admits to having become an "egoist" herself ("I have latterly become an Egoist thinking of no one but myself, scheming to make use of every soul I meet" [*E*, 132]), adding in self-defense that women need different weapons: "But then women are in the position of inferiors. They are hardly out of the nursery when a lasso is round their necks" and she finally systematizes the main opposition between male and female egoism: "Here is the difference I see; I see it; I am certain of it: women who are called coquettes make their conquests not of the best of men; but men who are Egoists have *good* women for their victims; women on whose devoted constancy they feed; they drink it like blood" (*E*, 133). Laetitia, who first thinks that she is hearing "discursive observations upon the inequality in the relations of the sexes" then understands that this discourse concerns Clara and her – her role has been outlined by her new "friend."

Clara finds help and support when a friend who is also a rival of Willoughby, Colonel de Craye, who is half-Irish and a born seducer, comes upon the scene. Clara more or less openly allows him to flirt with her, and almost runs away, followed nevertheless by Vernon,

Willoughby's cousin who is secretly in love with her. She will eventually leave with him (this has been asked of her by Willoughby, who had rather see her go with his cousin than with his rival). She loses her social respectability by doing so, but seems in the end to have found her freedom. Willoughby marries Laetitia, who by now has lost all her illusions, and just accepts the deal because she needs the money and power. She too has become an egoist as she explains in the penultimate chapter.

Meredith bases his system on "science," that is the theory of evolution. Why has Clara yielded to Willoughby's entreaties? "He looked the fittest; he justified the dictum of science. The survival of the Patternes was assured" (*E*, 35). Egoism is a vestige of an archaic past, and sends us back to primitive man: "The Egoist, who is our original male in giant form" (*E*, 191). The splendid mansion of the Patternes was built out of such primitive accumulation of wealth and egoism: "Aforetime a grand old egoism built the House. It would appear that ever finer essences of it are demanded to sustain the structure: but especially would it appear that a reversion to the gross original, beneath a mask and in a vein of fineness, is an earthquake at the foundations of the House" (*E*, 6–7). Willoughby's naive egoism is thus an "anachronic spectre" coming from the past of his family and mankind. He is therefore ridiculous – comedy is the only medicine one can apply to his case. The novel opens with the parallel presentation of the "Book of the earth" which can be called "the Book of egoism" (*E*, 3) and of the imps of the comic spirit who can try to correct egoism. However, the Egoist also inspires pity (and we know that as Meredith said, he was portraying himself under the disguise of Sir Willoughby Patterne): "The Egoist surely inspires pity. He who would desire to clothe himself at everybody's expense, and is of that desire condemned to strip himself stark naked, he, if pathos ever had a form, might be taken for the actual person" (*E*, 6). The uneasy mixture of comedy and pathos makes for narrative slowness, while conversely dramatic ironies abound. For instance, it is Willoughby who warns Clara never to marry an egoist: "Beware of marrying an Egoist, my dear!," he blurts out, forgetting that Clara will be tempted to apply the term to him (and she does, grasping it avidly), as Meredith explains: "None of them saw the man in the word, none noticed the word; yet this word was her medical herb, her illuminating lamp, the key of him . . . Egoist! She beheld him – unfortunate, self-designed man that he was!" (*E*, 82). Meredith has come by a different route to Stirner's circularity linking mental concept and active realization, utterance, and performativity. In the novel, the simple mental evocation of the word "Egoist" by any character propels the action, leads to new realizations and to a series of imitative and disruptive tactics.

This generalized performativity is philosophically very impressive while it brings one supplementary problem to the novel's economy: it fails in bringing out the "comedy" that would work as a real antidote to egoism. Despite its links with the famous lecture delivered in 1877 on "Comedy and the Uses of the Comic spirit" (*E*, 431–50), *The Egoist* can never become funny enough to propel itself beyond mere psychological delineation, despite its advertised ambition. The satire never really takes off (perhaps because the theme was too painfully close to Meredith's own life) – whereas *Ulysses* manages to be consistently comic, in the very spirit advocated by Meredith, without ever flaunting comedy as a key to or a consequence of the idea of the book. This is where Joyce has clearly gone beyond Meredith – but he may have been helped by Stanislaus's gruff remarks.

Thus, the central issue in the interpretation of Meredith's novel is to decide whether Clara becomes an egoist, and if she does, what this can mean. We have seen that Laetitia has at the end and that she cynically admits her disillusionment with Willoughby and romantic feelings. For Jenni Calder, Clara has learned from Willoughby the uses of egoism, which forces her to think of herself and to refuse the lure of self-sacrifice that is expected of women.[24] One finds a few passages in which Meredith clearly approves of feminine retaliation facing male egoism: "Let women tell us of their side of the battle. We are not so much the test of the Egoist in them as they to us. Moments of similarity shown in crowned and undiademed ladies of intrepid independence suggest their occasional capacity to be like men when it is given to them to hunt" (*E*, 191). Clara is also betrayed by her own father in her struggle, since he cannot understand her desire to be "her own," and would prefer her to make a socially rewarding marriage.

Like Richard Feverel, Clara will have to discover herself as Unique and her own through an "ordeal." It is likely that Meredith had heard of Stirner's book, although it was not available in English at the time. Egoism smacks also of capitalism as the next stage after feudal society: the Egoist wishes to buy a wife who will be treated as a beautiful ornament, and merely add to his riches. And what is fundamentally condemned by Meredith is the lack of reciprocity that egoism entails: "In the hundred and fourth chapter of the thirteenth volume of the BOOK of EGOISM, it is written: *Possession without obligation to the object possessed approaches felicity.* // It is the rarest condition of ownership" (*E*, 110).

Meredith explains how possession generally entails some vestigial obligation to the object owned. Not in one case only: "Our possession of an adoring female's worship is this instance" (*E*, 111).

This analysis is very close to what Meredith attacks under the name of sentimentalism in *The Ordeal of Richard Feverel* – a sentence that is quoted, as we remember, by Stephen Dedalus when he sends his Parthian shot, the telegram to Buck Mulligan: "'Sentimentalists,' says *The Pilgrim's Scrip*, 'are they who seek to enjoy without incurring the Immense Debtorship for a thing done.'"[25] Sentimentalism, as an attempt to negate a sense of debt, is a weaker form of egoism: at least an egoist behaves more or less consciously like a despot. This is why avid readers of Meredith such as Harriet Weaver and Dora Marsden could embrace egoism but never accept sentimentalism. When Harriet Weaver congratulated Marsden on the change of name from *The New Freewoman* to *The Egoist*, she wrote that it would be a "good challenge to sentimentalism"; in a similar way, when Marsden expresses doubts about Allen Upward as an editor, she writes: "I am terrified he will turn out a sentimentalist."[26] Bruce Clarke explains how the spirit of anarchism penetrated the stronghold of Suffragism through a reference to *The Egoist* – as early as December 1911 – in a leading article by Selwyn Weston, who showed that the seemingly self-effacing protagonist, Vernon Whitford, was "no less an egoist than Willoughby."[27] The logical development for the two female editors was then to replace Meredith by Stirner, in a development which was the exact inverse of Joyce's own progression through various modes of egoism.

One passage in Meredith's *Egoist* seems to be even more relevant to the situation of Stephen than the famous subtitle of *The Ordeal of Richard Feverel – A History of Father and Son*; it is the analysis of dissociation brought about by the pain of jealousy to the Egoist, who realizes that he is about to lose his prize. When Willoughby manages to control himself, above all by thinking that Clara has been touched by scandal, he reunites with himself, but in what alarmingly looks like a parody of Christian theology, Meredith explains how he becomes his own Father *and* his own Son:

Consider him indulgently: the Egoist is the Son of Himself. He is likewise the Father. And the son loves the father, the father the son; they reciprocate affection through the closest ties . . . The Egoist is our fountain-head, primeval man: the primitive is born again, the elemental reconstituted. Born again, into new conditions, the primitive may be highly polished of men, and forfeit nothing save the roughness of his original nature. He is not only his own father, he is ours; and he is also our son. We have produced him, he us. (*E*, 324–25)

While noting how this page debunks in advance Ayn Rand's egoist philosophy, I would like to suggest too that Meredith can allow us to understand not only the critique of Stephen's juvenile egoism, the illusion he entertains of a "mystical" self-begetting, but also how a female ego's realization both overcomes egoism and signifies its culmination. In this sense, Molly Bloom, as a "happy" adulteress, derives in direct descent from Clara Middleton, for she universalizes egoism in her "pre-human" and "post-human" functions when she becomes identified with the earth as Gea-Tellus. The "father-and-son" intrigue vanishes from the "plot" in order to allow for the apotheosis of a female being who can assert independence beyond immanence and transcendence. "Penelope" and Clara Middleton finally gain their freedom by contradicting themselves a lot and by losing a little in reputation. Thus can they be free and also accept life in all its manifestations. And when Gea-Tellus becomes one with a principle of paradoxical narratology, based upon orality so as to never really tell us the tale we expect, but to let language deploy itself in all its masks and obfuscations, we have reached the *terra non firma* of *Finnegans Wake*.

In the *Wake*, it is Shem, constantly described as "self exiled in upon his ego" (*FW*, 184.7), who provides another version of "eggoarchicism" (525.10), that is of anarchist egoism, as another development of Stephen Dedalus's position. However, there can be no stable "Egoname" (485.5) in the *Wake*, only functions relying on the interchangeability of names. The male egos are clearly caught up in a constant struggle for domination, whereas with phrases such as the "itch in his egondoom" (343.26), Joyce winks at the Freudian struggle between the id and the ego, parodically reduced to an itching condom that announces that the kingdom of a male ego is doomed.

Schizophrenia appears as the feminine counterpart of male "Negoism" (488. 21), but the affirmation of life as flux entails a division of the self (Issy) in a Romantic or Wagnerian death achieving a reunion with "Allself," as we can surmise from a passage in II, 4, in which we see the Four with Tristan and Isolde: "eysolt of binnoculises memostinmust egotum sabcunsciously senses upers the deprofundity of multimathematical immaterialities wherebejubers in the pancosmic urge the allimanence of that which Itself is Itself Alone . . . intuitions of reunited selfdom . . . in the higherdimissional selfless Allself" (394.30–395.2). However, this neo-Hegelian conflation of ego and Allself cannot be taken as a final solution to the problem of egology. We will have to explore a few more consequences of this knot in the following chapters.

I would like to conclude this chapter on the larger consequences of egoism. First, in a typically Modernist fashion, it seems that the only way for Joycean egoism to go beyond its narcissistic shortcomings is to blend with language. If Joyce's strong ego could be opposed to Pound's volatile and esemplastic personality, they share a fundamental attitude, well captured by Olson who was writing about Pound: "Ez's epic solves problem by his ego . . . thus creates the methodology of the Cantos, viz, a space-field where, by inversion, though the material is all time material, he has driven through it so sharply by the beak of his ego that he has turned time into what we must now have, space & its live air."[28] Joyce's last epic also solved all problems through an ego – however, this ego passes different hurdles. We can recognize them in the famous "eagles" that will come to "pull out the eyes" of the frightened baby tuckoo at the beginning of *A Portrait of the Artist as a Young Man*. These eagles embody the threatening super-egos of a Law that is administered by women as well as by men. Throughout his career, the strategy adopted by Joyce will remain the same: by hiding under the tables of the Law, he multiplies his "I's" in order to avoid the frightening beaks. For him, paradoxically, moral courage is founded on the lability of the "I"; this derives from the main property of a Stirnerian Unique who is also *causa sui*, or as Ayn Rand would write, a "Prime Mover." Thus egoism can never be equated with an essentialism of the self. Joyce shared with Pound the motto of "Never explain, Never apologize." The concept of "apologizing" deployed as a haunting theme in the first pages of *A Portrait of the Artist as a Young Man* (we are never told whether young Stephen did apologize in front of Dante, but we know that he keeps suffering from his eyes) is an original moral law that has to be subverted, for an apology is synonymous with excuse, and an "ex-cuse" is a way of ex-causing oneself, of refusing the single "cause" one has to become, namely oneself. Like Stirner, Joyce chose to become his own cause and consistently refused to apologize.

With Joyce, egoism has to be distinguished from egotism (a distinction which, as we have seen, does not really make sense for Ayn Rand). Joyce never wrote his *Recollections* as Renan did, or kept private Memoirs as Stendhal did, which included his *Souvenirs d'Egotisme*, a diary he kept between 1821 and 1830.[29] The main dissociation would follow this division: if egotism implies the heroic cultivation of the self, as we find in Romantic and post-Romantic literature, from Goethe to Barrès, via Stendhal, Baudelaire, and Gide, egoism implies a radical anarchism refusing any authority. Egotism remains a literary posture that has been highly developed in French literature, possibly because of the centrality of Montaigne, and the important debate between Pascal and Montaigne that dominated most of the discussions about moralism and anti-moralism in France during the seventeenth and eighteenth centuries. Egoism never severs its ties with politics, and appears closer to German, Danish, or English frame of minds. Joyce always appeared impatient of literary egotism. For instance, in a conversation with Arthur Power to which I shall return, Joyce insisted that *Ulysses* critiqued egotism.[30] A few years later, *Finnegans Wake* also stressed the limitation of egotism with its meta-narrative logics based on a-personal sigla and statements such as: "Cockran, eggotisters, limitated." (*FW*, 137. 8). Joyce's initial Stirnerian position nevertheless forced him to see the ghosts surrounding the anti-Romantic "facts" he claimed he had never left aside. The egotist, like the ego, owns himself or herself only after having been reconciled with the various ghosts of an unconscious past.

"The Ego and His Ghosts" would bring us by a circuitous way from Ibsen, the main "egoarch," to Wakean idioms like "me altar's ego in miniature" (*FW*, 463. 7). It is an endless recirculation of a-personal subjects that can then "guide them through the labyrinth of their samilikes and the alteregoases of their pseudoselves" (576.32–33). The task devoted to feminine characters is less to eradicate than to sublimate egoism by creating a new and vital affirmation. This explains why the feminist "egoism" Joyce found in Dora Marsden, Harriet Weaver, and later Sylvia Beach was so instrumental in his career and sustained him so well throughout his life. The *Egomen* who helped himself believe in him were above all women! They were devoted, dedicated, and loved him, not sexually, not as a person, but as a cause, a cause he defended less than he embodied it. The paradox of Joyce's cunning is that these several *Egomen* needed to defend *him* in order to uphold the cause of literature.

As Lacan suggests in the Joyce Seminar I examined in the first chapter, the Irish writer becomes the *sinthome* who enacts our entire culture, a modern avatar of Aquinas. Joyce's only cause is the cause of writing, understood less as literature than as a psychic apparatus. Egoism never reclaims the subjective self as the source of values, but points to an "other" cause that contains the keys of the structure of a subjectivity constituted by language. In this movement, Joyce betrays a fundamental alliance with a post-feminist position such as Dora Marsden's, who remained a feminist in spite of her repudiation of her former suffragist ideology. Whatever our personal affects may be, egoism does not foster rejection or hate, for it aims at producing a paradoxical love for the symptom.[31]

Can we, readers, continue loving Joyce when we know that he was such an egoist? I have shown that this was not Lacan's case, but hope to have proved that we should, that we have some "cause" to love him, at least for his moral courage and his integrity, in a word for a literary saintliness well captured by Adrienne Monnier.[32] Since I started this chapter by referring to the French fashion magazine, *Egoïste*, I will end by quoting the epigraph of the June 1996 double issue in the hope that it may have some bearing on the "work of the symptom" generated by Joyce's writing, above all because it manages to provide the simplest definition of egoism I know: "An Egoist is just somebody who doesn't think of me."[33] Or, to try another image, one might paraphrase Duchamp's portmanteau-word linking "ghost" and "guest" ("A guest + a Host = a Ghost").[34] The arch egoist of language embodied by Joyce has to be written with an "h": as an "eghoist," he is the ghost who unites his guests and his hosts.

CHAPTER FOUR

The esthetic paradoxes of egoism: from negoism to the theoretic

The relation between Joyce's esthetics and his works of fiction has always been a vexed one. The gradual incorporation of the fragments of juvenile esthetics considered as an independent discourse into the very stuff of fiction entails a conspicuous disappearance of "theory" as such.[1] It is less, as we will see, a disaffection of the author with his own theories as a refusal to let theories stand on their own, without a strong link to their enunciator. We have witnessed a similar tension at work in Lacan's theory of the literary symptom accompanied by a no less symptomatic "return of the ego."

Joyce's perception of his own canon in the making, as evinced by the proud assertion made to his mother from his first Parisian "exile," announced among other his projects an esthetic theory. In a blustering manner, he outlines a work-schedule filling up the two next decades: "Synge says I have a mind like Spinoza! . . . I am at present up to the neck in Aristotle's Metaphysics . . . My book of songs will be published in the Spring of 1907. My first comedy about five years later. My 'Esthetic' about five years later again. (This *must* interest you!)." (*LIV*, 19). Surprisingly, Joyce was quite right about the first date: *Chamber Music* was actually published in 1907, while *Exiles* (if it can be called a "comedy") was only started in 1914. But no "Esthetic" was ever published or written – unless we count the few reviews and essays collected under the title of *Critical Writings* and add to them a few theoretical passages in *Ulysses* (1922), mostly culled from Stephen Dedalus's ruminations on art, paternity, creation, and rhythm.

Behind the striking disappearance of this esthetic theory, it looks as if Joyce always returned to a principle of esthetic apprehension that could bridge the gap between the fiction and the never to be completed esthetic treatise. On the one hand, there is the concept that Joyce proffers so obtrusively yet obliquely at the beginning of *Dubliners*, when he tantalizingly suggests that our reading will be patterned by a "gnomon," an incomplete figure in which meaning is made manifest through lack and darkness. On the other hand, one meets early enough the crucial and much debated term of "epiphany" – understood as a principle of revelation by which the hidden sense is perceived as groping toward a presentation in full light. Both principles interact so as to bypass, exceed, and finally undermine any explicit "theory" of their meaning, production, and functioning. This complex movement also helps redefine the very notion of esthetics understood as just an "esthetic theory." However, one of the preliminary questions we have to pose is whether Joyce gave a specific meaning to the term of "theory," since "theory" appears as a site or knot connecting a number of cruxes or paradoxes. I would like to suggest that we need to posit four distinctions, or paradoxes,[2] in order to understand more fully Joyce's strategic revisions of "theory."

THE FOUR PARADOXES OF JOYCEAN ESTHETICS

A first distinction derives from the age-old bifurcation of "esthetics" caught up between the meaning of "sense perception" (as one finds in Kant's first *Critique* when he talks of "transcendental esthetics" as a first step into the discovery of pure reason) and the meaning of "discourse bearing upon beautiful objects" (as would be the object of Kant's third critique of judgment). The point has been made by numerous critics that Joyce's Aristotelian point of departure led him to stress the concept of "natural process" as a way of unifying these two levels. Thus, the famous commentary on Aristotle's *e tekhne mimeitai ten physin* one finds in the 1903 Paris notebook ("This phrase is falsely rendered as 'Art is an imitation of Nature.' Aristotle does not here define art; he says only, 'Art imitates Nature' and means that the artistic process is like the natural process"[3]) leads to the genetic theory of artistic development that will constitute the backbone of *A Portrait of the Artist as a Young Man*.[4] I will explore one important consequence of this "theory" for the parallel genesis of nature and art in the following chapter. As the example of "lice" will show, the making of a work of art implies indeed "artistic conception, artistic gestation, and artistic reproduction" (*APA*, 209), which entails "a new personal experience" as it puts the production of artifacts on a par with that of living beings. A further paradox is that the male artist will have to imitate or steal even the feminine role in gestation and reproduction. The theory will vanish only insofar as it teaches him how to "give birth" to art. Much as the theory cannot be abstracted from a personal experience of revelation, its ternary structure should also become identical with an ideal genesis that transcends sexual division. Here lie the seeds of what I will later describe as the "genetic reader" called upon by Joyce.

As Stephen explains to a bemused Lynch, "Aristotle's entire system of philosophy rests upon his book of psychology" (*APA*, 208), which justifies his effort aiming at paralleling formal structures of the work of art with the stages of the mind's apprehension of it. Psychology and esthetics are both underwritten by a more fundamental "genetic reason." Esthetics cannot become a "science of the concrete" or a "science of the particular" (and if it fails to do so, it remains a dead letter, pure abstraction devoid of real content) without accounting for its genesis. This is the entire crux of *The Portrait of the Artist as a Young Man*, in which the description of esthetic experience not only explains how any subject is bound to follow in Stephen's steps and apprehend the three stages of the individuating beauty in an object, but is also entirely integrated into a quasi-biographical narrative. Such a narrative then has to document the key-position of "the subject of enunciation" while remaining fixed on the desired vision of an "essence" of beauty.

The second paradox follows from the first in that it addresses a difficulty arising from the usual definition of esthetics understood conventionally as a discourse elaborating the modalities by which we apprehend or contemplate the beautiful. "Theory" is indeed a loaded term, hesitating between the vague idea of "abstract discourse" while retaining something of its old connection with "contemplation." It might be useful to distinguish between the Marxist (in its Althusserian version, especially) sense of "theory" as dialectically joined with "praxis" and the more etymological sense of "contemplative," in the mystical or solely artistic use of the term. Any danger of confusion could be avoided by an opposition between a "theoretical" approach and a "theoretic" position. Such a distinction is not a mere linguistic quibble since it was offered as quite necessary by a philosopher of Esthetics that Joyce had read and used with great profit during his Dublin years, Bernard Bosanquet. Bosanquet's final explication of these terms is to be found in a late book consisting of a collection of lectures published in 1923, the year of his death, *Three Lectures on Aesthetics*.[5] Here is what Bosanquet has to say about the idea of "contemplation," in a passage in which he is trying to qualify an earlier definition of the "aesthetic attitude" as that "in which we imaginatively contemplate an object, being able in that way to live in it as an embodiment of our feeling" (*TLA*, 29–30):

Now, I am uneasy about this word "contemplate." No doubt it makes a very good distinction against the practical and the theoretical frames of mind; which in contrast with it are very much like each other. For, I think, we must distinguish the theoretical, at least in modern usage, from the "theoretic." "Theoretic" is pretty much "contemplative," while "theoretical" indicates a very busy activity aimed at putting together hypotheses and testing them by facts. It is in this sense that it is so sharply opposed to "theoretic" or contemplative. (*TLA*, 30)

Bosanquet's dichotomy starts off a series of binary oppositions: theoretic is opposed to theoretical as passive is opposed to active and as the fragment is opposed to totality. The theoretical intellect associates facts and ideas, it starts from experiences considered as "praxis" and moves toward the conceptual. It aims at a general dialectization of sense experience and general deductive ideas. The theoretic intellect, closer to pure "vision," remains passive and contemplative. It seizes forcibly, in a direct glance, what the mystics were trying to express in their "negative way" or apophatic revelation. Aristotle would represent the theoretical mind, while Plotinus would be on the side of the theoretic.

Following Lacan's hint, I would like to suggest here another verbal echo, probably not intended by Bosanquet, but one that Joyce could not help hearing in the term itself, the inevitable overtones of "heresy" in "theoretic." Very early, the youthful Stephen Dedalus is presented as a "hero" when he manages to link the production of an esthetic theory with an attitude of refusal or subversion of dominant values. Stephen should properly be called a "hero" only insofar as he appears as a theory-hero who is also a "theo(h)er(h)etic." It is therefore quite logical that the earliest manifestations of Stephen's theories should be accompanied by acts of negation.

In *Stephen Hero*, one can discern a fetishization of the word "theory" – the term being a short cut for "aesthetic theory" but brandished in a repeated gesture of distancing and negation. If, as we have seen, "theory" thus understood is never too far from its sense of "contemplation," the subsequent question concerns the movement that brings the subject from pure perception (determined, for instance, by the categories of space and time) to a heightened sense of revelation – as when Stephen is described exultant, under the shock of the vision of a young girl wading in the sea at the end of chapter IV in *A Portrait of the Artist as a Young Man*. All in all, Stephen could almost appear as a disciple of Ruskin, when the latter opposes "aesthesis" and "theory" in *Modern*

Painters: "The mere animal consciousness of the pleasantness (in the perception of Beauty) I call Aesthesis, but the exulting, reverent and grateful perception of it I call Theoria."[6] Theoria would thus provide another name for the artistic task consisting in the "recording" of these "most delicate and evanescent moments," to quote Stephen's definitions in *Stephen Hero*. A third paradox of esthetic theory will therefore be generated by the forceful link one must establish between the individual subject and the discourse of the collective body to which he or she willy-nilly belongs.

As Wlad Godzich has stressed in his useful introduction to De Man's essay, "theoria" cannot be divorced from its political function, especially if we remember that "theoria" is originally a plural that meant in Athens the succession of official witnesses who could testify that such or such an event had really, actually taken place. The individual "aesthesis" had to be relayed by the official "theoria," a theoria grounded in a deixis of the "here and now" but underwritten, countersigned by the polis. Theoria announces that any particular event is capable of being narrated.

This points to another gap in Stephen's youthful formulations, since the rewriting of *Stephen Hero* as *A Portrait of the Artist as a Young Man* tends to leave out most social reference from his system. Yet Stephen seems to be in search of recognition, at least by his peers, if not from his "masters." Hence the dialectical turn of his meditations: Stephen needs a number of "witnesses" before he can authorize himself. The main issue, however, is less the accusation of "bourgeois individualism" that is leveled against him by his fellow students at the university than the consideration of the mechanisms by which any statement will be authorized. Stephen, like Joyce, will then often appear in the uncomfortable position of pretending to subvert all types of "authority"[7] while caught up in a tremendous effort of "self-authorization."

Finally, a last paradox would have to point to the quandary in which post-Kantian esthetics found itself: is esthetics merely the conventional discourse about judgments of taste and beauty understood as that which "pleases" a social majority, or can it be capable of a more radical approach to negativity? Kant's analysis of the Sublime paves the way for Hegel's critique and reappropriation of an infinity that is perceived when the subject faces certain natural spectacles (a wild tempest tossing ships, distant armies charging across lands, the ineffable symphonies of clouds at sunset) and then understands how these sights exceed the powers of conception of the human imagination. If, as Zizek has shown, we have here in a nutshell the entire invention of Hegelian dialectics,[8] do we have to follow Kant's return toward the interiority of the moral law? In this well-known analysis, the subject, comprehending that he cannot comprehend, will transform his utter abasement facing an excess of infinity as perceived into a purely ethical infinity that he can still contain within his own categories. In Joyce's case, what remains to be assessed is whether his esthetic categories can be translated into the bifurcation of beauty and the sublime. As Ginette Verstraete's book on the "feminine sublime" shows, this entails changing the field of reference and abandoning the confrontation between Kant and Hegel in order to use the different model provided by Schlegel's esthetics.[9] A new "feminine sublime" would then be born, a sublime that might also encompass ugliness and ridicule. Even if Joyce was probably not aware of Schlegel's theses, he shares his basic insight into the duplicity, irony and reversibility of any gendered version of the sublime. I will now turn to study a number of key passages in the early works so as to suggest how Joyce could have slowly worked toward a resolution of these esthetic antinomies. Egoism can be shown to function not merely as a moral or political term, but as the keystone of this system of "disappearing" esthetics.

HEROISM AS ESTHETIC NEGATION: "EGO NEGO"

In the first "Portrait of the Artist" (1904), the radicalization of esthetic egoism leads to a position of absolute negation: Stephen's consistent "Ego Nego" defines him, in the words of *Finnegans Wake*, as a "Negoist" (*FW*, 488.21). One sentence from the 1904 text finds its way literally into *Stephen Hero*: "It was part of that ineradicable egoism which he was afterwards to call redeemer that he imagined converging to him the deeds and thoughts of the microcosm" (*APA*, 259, and *SH*, 34). This anticipates with little modification Stephen's proud assertion in "Eumaeus"("But I suspect . . . that Ireland must be important because it belongs to me" [*U*, 16: 1174]), which we have already analyzed in chapter 2. Such Stirnerian posturing borders on delusions of grandeur in its shrill assertion of the ego's utter centrality. What "redeems" this egoism, however, is the idea that Stephen will not "keep" what is "given" to him since he is a "spendthrift saint" (*APA*, 258). Sanctity is therefore the salvation of the egoist. As an egoist, Stephen will have to play the part of the "saint" who desires "an arduous good" (*APA*, 260) and of the "spendthrift" since, like his father, he cannot resist giving again what has been offered to him, at least under the form of words.

We have seen in chapter 1 how Lacan's concept of the *sinthome*

included all the characteristics of sainthood. The saint, as Lacan has
shown in *Television*[10] manages to own, condense and redeem the essential value of the world by excluding himself from it. Like the Hegelian
"Beautiful Soul," but with more efficiency, the saint and the egoist
negate everything in their banal surroundings that annoys them in the
name of the power of beauty. Stephen has chosen as his muse "the
image of beauty" (*APA*, 260), and it is thanks to this unwavering resolution that he keeps ideological authority and religious conformity at a
distance.

A similar model for this youthful confession documenting a personal
struggle with an ambitious esthetic program can be found in Rimbaud's
moving recapitulation of esthetic failure in *A Season in Hell*. Rimbaud's
original expectations ("I shall now unveil all the mysteries: mysterious
religious or natural, death, birth, future, past, cosmogony, void. I am a
master of phantasmagoria"[11]) have to be shattered after he realizes that
he cannot "fix" vertigos or stabilize his hallucinations: "My health was
threatened. Terror came upon me . . . I was forced to travel, to distract
the enchantments crowding in my brain."[12] Rimbaud's well-known
ambivalence toward religion and art is similar to the tone of: "A thousand eternities were to be reaffirmed, divine knowledge was to be reestablished. Alas for Fatuity! as easily might he have summoned a
regiment of the winds" (*APA*, 261). We would find an identical confession bearing less on "negative esthetics" than on the discovery of the
impossibility of constituting full-fledged esthetics. What pushes Stephen
out of the despair and impossibility that mark Rimbaud's esthetics is an
innate belief in his worth coupled with a Fichtean negative assertion.
"His Nego, therefore, written amid a chorus of peddling Jews' gibberish
and Gentile clamour, was drawn up valiantly while true believers prophesied fried atheism and was hurled against the obscene hells of our Holy
Mother: but that outburst over, it was urbanity in warfare" (*APA*, 265).
Egoism rewritten as Negoism eventually saves him from Rimbaud's
apocalyptic silence.

The "Portrait" ends on a socialist plea for revolution that sounds
rather at odds with the previous profession of esthetic isolationism.
Nevertheless, this revolutionary position is the only way of bridging the
gap between the individualist rebellion and the collective dimension it
has to acquire, or between an early "egoistic mysticism" and Stephen's
admission that he, after all, is also Irish, even if he chooses exile. I have
already commented upon the apparently trite statement that opens the
1907 essay entitled "Ireland, Island of Saints and Sages" ("Nations have

their ego, just like individuals" [*CW*, 154]). If the Irish nation can reach its "ego" when it sees the core of its identity summed up by the phrase "Island of Saints and Sages" (a phrase that has to be unpacked and entirely explicated in the lecture itself), Joyce is also aware that his historical survey of Ireland leads to a critical (or suspensive) analysis of nationalism. When he sums up the British conquest of the island or the Act of Union of 1800, he stresses the two combined factors of Irish corruption and Irish betrayal, adding: "From my point of view, these two facts must be thoroughly explained before the country in which they occurred has the most rudimentary right to persuade one of her sons to change his position from that of an unprejudiced observer to that of a convinced nationalist" (*CW*, 162–63). This illuminating text written in Italian appears not only as a synthesis of the individual and the collective that was still lacking in *Stephen Hero* but also as a blueprint for the whole bulk of *Finnegans Wake*. It is only in the *Wake* that Joyce manages to overcome the paradox of the collective versus the singular "theoretician" and he does so partly by getting rid of any conventional "character" and replacing them with "sigla" or mere narratological functions.[13] By that time, the term of "theory" is not really useful any longer, since the new writing in a new language can successfully negotiate between the beautiful and the sublime on the one hand, and the sublime and the ridiculous on the other hand. We do find some "theories" about the excremental nature of writing as a bodily production of Shem's, but they are couched in such a language and caught in such complex narratological determinations that it would be impossible to extract them from their context and ascribe them to Joyce, as so many of the earlier theories have been.

What remains more difficult to understand perhaps is the link between Joyce's early egoistic estheticism and the revolutionary consequences he ascribes to it – all of which revolves around the recurrent and loaded use of the word "theory." One of the major differences between the first "Portrait of the Artist"– a text that announces the final *Portrait* in its bold cinematographic montage of different scenes and in its non-chronological, synthetic approach – and *Stephen Hero* is the shift in the meaning of the word "theory." In the first "Portrait of the Artist" of 1904, "theory" has still a negative value; we see this when Stephen opts for "the lower orders" in which a "confessor did not seem anxious to reveal himself, in theory at least, a man of the world" (*APA*, 258). In *Stephen Hero* on the contrary, the term of "theory" is flaunted with a curious and almost mechanical insistence.

Stephen's heroism consists in the ardor and candor with which he strives to reach his goal of artistic self-generation through the egoistic production of a theory. His "ordeal," to use a term Meredith often employed, consists in serial negotiations with figures of authority who can validate his "theories" and also recognize their marginal – or subversive – status. However, Stephen's esthetic theory (understood as a theory of the apprehension of the beautiful) has constantly to be detached from the process of sublimation that produces it. This is why it is crucial for Stephen to refuse the President of the University's move, when the latter attempts to push the discussion of beauty into a discussion of the sublime (or, for that matter, of saintliness). Both are discussing Aquinas's famous *pulchra sunt quae visa placent*, when the President adds:

– But he means the sublime – that which leads man upwards.
– His remark would apply to a Dutch painter's representation of a plate of onions.
– No, no; that which pleases the soul in a state of sanctification, the soul seeking its spiritual good.
– Aquinas's definition of the good is an unsafe basis of operations; it is very wide. He seems to me almost ironical in his treatment of the "appetites." (*SH*, 95)

After all, one doesn't see why a Dutch still life representing onions on a plate could not be called "sublime." Or why a plate of onions could not help the soul turn upward in the hope of sanctification. However, Stephen's deft rhetorical move forces the President to leave the field of esthetics and to move into ethics, which proves to be his mistake: he will then add lamely – in an ironical foreshadowing of one of Pound's most recurrent mottoes: "The cult of beauty is difficult" (*SH*, 96) – probably hoping to force Stephen to confess an impenitent estheticism. It would be tempting to stress the "difficulty," not so distant from the "arduous good" the young esthete was searching after, as a weakened form of sublime.

At that juncture, however, Stephen is eager to avoid any subjective reduction of his theory to its position of enunciation: "My conviction has led me nowhere: my theory states itself" (*SH*, 96). This is already the attitude one sees him taking at the end of his Shakespeare discussion in "Scylla and Charybdis" in *Ulysses* when he confesses that he does not believe in his own theory. The really "sublime" moment occurs when the author of the theory can renounce the paternity of the discourse, cutting as it were the umbilical cord linking the words to their enunciator, thus letting the theory follow its own course.

Later in the book, when Stephen argues with a more amenable interlocutor, Father Artifoni, "about the beautiful and the good" (*SH*, 170), he
has managed to bridge the gap between art and nature on the one hand,
and between the good and the beautiful on the other hand, by a systematic reference to "process." This process could be called a process of
"sublimation": "To talk about the perfection of one's art was not for him
to talk about something agreed upon as sublime but in reality no more
than a sublime convention but rather to talk about a veritably sublime
process of one's nature which had a right to examination and open discussion" (*SH*, 171). The next paragraph states the stakes implied by this
qualification: "It was exactly this vivid interest which kept him away
from such places of uncomely dalliance as the debating society and the
warmly cushioned sodality" (*SH*, 171). If we agree to see in Stephen's fascination for the theory of Beauty the consequence of a "sublime
process," it is clear that he is constantly going to be precipitated from the
sublime to the ridiculous (as *Finnegans Wake* will confirm in a revealing
parenthesis at 445.27).

What prevents the constant movement back and fro between
moments of sublimation and moments of debunking – a strategy that is
fully developed in *A Portrait of the Artist as a Young Man* – is that *Stephen Hero*
is open in its middle, and holds precisely by the hole of the Real that
gapes in its middle. It is not a coincidence that a long manuscript beginning and ending with unfinished sentences – at least in the current
edition, with the additional pages concluded by "but when he was a few
paces" (*SH*, 253) while it jump-starts with "anyone spoke to him mingled
a too polite disbelief with its expectancy" (*SH*, 23) at the beginning of
chapter 15 – should be punctured roughly in its middle by the recycling
of one of the most painful and cruel epiphanies: the question of an help-
less mother asking Stephen whether he can give any advice about the
suspicious liquid oozing away from Isabel's (Georgie's in real life)
stomach. In spite of the minimal reworking of what was epiphany 19
(Joyce adds in *Stephen Hero* "a voice of a terrified human being" and "like
the voice of a messenger in a play") the sheer horror betrayed by the
question limns a limit of language and leads the reader to an unnamable zone.

Thus "The hole . . . the hole we all have . . . here" (*SH*, 163) refers to
– what? This first riddle, after all, seems to resist better than "the word
known to all men": if most readers believe it points to the navel – as I do
– there are some who insist upon seeing it as the anus, in which case "the
hole in Isabel's . . . stomach" would be a distortion attributable to a desire

to be polite. "Do you know anything about the body?" remains as an insistent and disturbing question – and no doubt echoes in *Ulysses* with Buck Mulligan's medical knowledge of how a "dogsbody" can die and rot, and with Leopold Bloom's curiosity about everything that concerns body orifices. Lacan's concept of the Real could define this locus as the crucial point where gnomonic negativity and epiphanic elision meet. This convergence forges a *deixis* that cannot show, that does not "present" but merely points to the unpresentable or the unspeakable.

This crux is not merely the locus of death and putrefaction, it also leads by another way to the ineffable *jouissance* that letters and literature attempt to circumscribe. Both Lacanian metapsychology and Joycean "theoretic" drift thus merge when they meet a limit, a border – this encounter with the limit of language could call up, as Wittgenstein often said, the realm of ethics, or the pure function of silence in theory – in a movement that is not too far from what classical esthetics used to call the discourse of sublimity.

Joyce's concept of the sublime in *Finnegans Wake* appears very close to what Burke calls a "natural sublime" marked by "difficulty." As Burke noted in his *Philosophical Enquiry into the Origin of our Ideas of the Sublime and the Beautiful*,

Another source of greatness is *Difficulty*. When any work seems to have required immense force and labour to erect it, the idea is grand. Stonehenge, neither for disposition nor ornament, has any thing admirable; but those huge rude masses of stone, set on end, and piled each on other, turn the mind on the immense force necessary for such a work. Nay the rudeness of the work increases this cause of grandeur, as it excludes the idea of art, and contrivance . . .[14]

Can one say that Joyce attempts to "exclude the idea of art and contrivance" in his new idiom? I would like to suggest that the obvious difficulty of his work was if not produced, at least enhanced, by an attempt to solve the four esthetic paradoxes I have sketched.

THEORETIC SUBLIMATION AND THE SUBLIMINAL LANGUAGE OF NIGHT

Colleen Jaurretsche's book[15] on Joyce's mysticism gives us a good idea of how Joyce's language is haunted by its own margins and limits. She implies with her title, "The Sensual Philosophy," that Joyce's negative theology or apophatic mysticism should not be understood as an individual variation or aberration on traditional religion, but as a discourse that addresses the senses, eroticism, love, and desire, apprehended as the logical consequence of a general esthetic system. Out of the tradition of mystical theology Joyce was tapping in his Dublin years, out of his interest in occultism and theosophy, his fascination for Blake's visionary powers, his study of Dionysius the pseudo-Aeropagite, we gather a unique and original philosophy of "limit stages" and an esthetic of negativity. However, this wide and vague tradition is seen by him as typically "Irish." Thus, Dionysius, who is quoted in "Ireland, Island of Saints and Sages," is only one among the relatively uncanonical influences who can make sense of a tradition of Irish mysticism and link a "sensual philosophy" with the paradoxical discourse of absence and unknowing.

Joyce read the anonymous *Cloud of Unknowing* and above all St. John of the Cross's *Dark Night of the Soul* to see in "darkness" the most apt image able to materialize the almost ineffable process of "forgetting" that leads to a mystical fusion with God. Such a union is not devoid of sexual overtones, as any reader of St. John of the Cross can notice. *The Dark Night* is an erotic poem, and all the mystical writers put forward the "pleasure of nothing," the sensual dissolution of the self when it meets with an ineffable divine lover. Joyce's critical writings are also bathed in the light of mystical theology, described, as we have seen, as a specifically Irish trait. With the *Wake*, Joyce's decision to confront and explore the Night as such, shows how negative theology turns into sensuality if not lewdness (with Shawn as John facing an enamored and enraptured Issy).

Moreover, I would like to stress the importance of the cultural context provided by Jolas and the *transition* group of writers who, starting in 1927 but with increasing force in the thirties, stressed the affinities between Joyce's *Work in Progress* and what they called "the language of night." Jolas had started reading St. John of the Cross early and quite independently of Joyce, and this reading nourished his fascination for all sorts of mystical and paradoxical discourses. In *transition* no. 23 (1935), an issue partly devoted to "James Joyce and his new work," Jolas sketches "a Little Mantic Almageste" in which he lists Blake, Boehme, Madame Guyon, and St. John of the Cross among many other mystics as the forerunners of the new language of myth and the unconscious developed by the group of experimental writers and artists he keeps promoting – Joyce representing of course the culmination of such a process in his eyes. The language of night confronts the inexpressible: it attempts to posit esthetic discourse in the place once occupied by negative theology. While Rimbaud's "impossible" marks an unpassable frontier that lyricism could not breach, here language justifies its activity when facing the task of extending and subverting the usual communicational model.

While pursuing the negative way, Joyce's last book attempts to provide a solution to the four paradoxes of esthetics I have distinguished earlier. The first level consisted of the distinction between *aesthesis* as sensual perception and esthetics as a discourse regulating the conditions requested for the production or perception of the beautiful and sublime. This gap is bridged as soon as the reader's perception of any word, sentence, paragraph in the book is suspended between contradictory or undecidable levels of sense. Something is indeed perceived, if only vaguely, but the hesitation that adheres to what would normally be restricted by univocal linguistic functions pushes the reading to the level of the meta-discourse of esthetics as well. Thus any word, sentence, paragraph of *Finnegans Wake* will not only carry several meanings but will also refer to the book's structure and therefore to its various insights into beauty, the sublime, and the ridiculous. Such self-reference is not necessarily foregrounded, does not inevitably provide the more important level, but will always remain as a reflexive potentiality.

Among the paradoxes already posited, theory as social authentication was seen to interact with individual acts of contemplation. As we have seen, Joyce's esthetic individualism led him to assume more and more radically the role of the Saint, that is, someone who dares to confront the unspeakable Other and become a cultural or collective "sinthome" – at least when he was writing his last work. Finally, Joyce wishes to embody the spirit of a collective ego, to be one with or to "atone," as Stephen would say, with its ethical substance (Hegel's *Sittlichkeit*). This "ethical substance" is not, in Joyce's case, limited to Ireland and to its divided community, but includes the whole of Europe, and reaches forward into the linguistic domains of Africa, Asia, Australia and America. As he hoped, individual artistic toil might redeem and perhaps heal the diseases of the collective spirit such as xenophobic nationalism, fascism, and religious bigotry. The new language should in the end create a new and different reading practice strong enough to subvert those ideologically reactionary values that are still latent in the old *Sittlichkeit*. Such a movement, with its ethical and political drift, cannot just be comprehended by the purely esthetic categories of the sublime and the beautiful. As Eagleton and Verstraete have shown in totally opposite ways,[16] the *Wake* systematically debunks these ancient categories by constantly sublimating and desublimating itself.

The last opposition between the sublime and the beautiful is overcome by the "subliminal" as the locus of infra-discursive linguistic production and by sublimation as a process of transformation from the individual to the collective. The subliminal defines the domain of the language of the night proper while sublimation stresses its social disseminations in a Babelic idiom. In III, 3, an episode I will analyze more systematically in a later chapter, a typical reply of sleeping Yawn to the Four analysts begins with a "Yes" and ends with a "No." Between the two assertions, the voice shifts from one speaker to another and attributes the negation to the "small other" represented by the brother:

– Oyessoyess! I never dramped of prebeing a postman but I mean in ostralian someplace, mults deeply belubdead; my allaboy brother, Negoist Cabler, of this city, whom 'tis better ne'er to name, my said brother, the skipgod, expulled for looking at churches from behind, who is sender of the Hullo Eve Cenograph in prose and worse every Allso's night. High Brazil Brandan's Deferred, midden Erse clare language, Noughtnoughtnought nein. Assass. (*FW*, 488.19–26)

The dialectization of the contraries is still subsumed by the oppositional logic that stylizes Shem and Shaun as the fighting brothers. Both have recognizable features and voices, but whereas Shaun is characterized by a constant oscillation between the sublime and the ridiculous, Shem's writerly capacities are attributable to what we have already examined, that is a process of sublimation: "this Esuan Menschavik and the first till last alshemist wrote over every square inch of the only foolscap available, his own body, till by its corrosive sublimation one continuous present tense integument slowly unfolded all the marryvoising moodmoulded cyclewheeling history" (185. 34–186.2) This goes beyond a simple admission of the autobiographical nature of the book, for Shem, even when he allegorizes the process of creation by the means of writing also refers to Gertrude Stein's theory of the "continuous present."[17]

The fourth paradox revolved around the issue of the theoretic versus theoretical. In his last years, Joyce, probably heartbroken by his daughter's private tragedy, seems to testify to a deep familiarity with the spirit of utter nothingness. This is why he expressed this despair when writing to his son Giorgio, at the age of fifty-three: "My eyes are tired. For over half a century, they have gazed into nullity where they have found a lovely nothing."[18] One might be tempted to stress the irony of the adjective "lovely" – with innuendoes of the "beautiful" and of the "meaningless." The tone of this passage is very close to that of Mallarmé's last letters, especially when the French poet stresses the proximity of beauty and nothingness.[19] The "Nothing" Joyce admits of having gazed at for too long could also be called "God," or the Hegelian "absolute master," Death. While it points to the hollowing of Presence that can be ascribed to negativity, there is in this Nothing an irreducible and undialectizable element, a tragic factor that underpins any "writing of the disaster" (to quote Blanchot). But it pertains to the theoretic vigilance of the "theo-heretic" – a godlike heretic, as it were – to dare contemplate this nega-tivity without flinching: only then can the theo-heretic receive praise meet for Saint or Sage.

Yet is no body present here which was not there before. Only is order othered. Nought is nulled. *Fuifiat!*
   Lo, the laud of laurens now orielising benedictively when saint and sage have said their say. (*FW*, 613. 14–16)

CHAPTER FIVE

Theory's slice of life

We have seen how the problematization of theory implies for Joyce a detour through particulars before witnessing theory's own disappearance. I shall now focus on one of those particulars, the image of lice in Joyce's works, so as to point out the links between the reversibility of the sublime and the ridiculous and the applicability of this theme to Joyce's overall esthetic project. Since *The Songs of Maldoror* were published in the pages of *The Egoist* at the same time as the editors of the magazine started their collaboration with Joyce, it is quite possible that he came across Lautréamont's famous hymn to lice: "If the earth was covered with lice, as the seashore with sandgrains, the human race would be annihilated, dying in horrible pain. What a spectacle! And I, with angel's wings, motionless, contemplating it."[1] The remarkable translations of *The Songs of Maldoror* by Aldington were serialized in *The Egoist* from October 1914 to January 1915, and then they stop abruptly on a misleading "To be continued."[2] For Ducasse, lice provide an image of aggression and debasement, introducing a gothic esthetic of excess in universal destruction. Aldington started his serialized version of *The Songs of Maldoror* by translating a general introduction to Lautréamont by Remy de Gourmont which described the poet as talented but "diseased" and half-crazy, a "mad genius," whose irony nevertheless redeems a baroque and violent imagery. To show the presence of irony, de Gourmont quotes the following passage: "You, young man, must not despair, for you have a friend in the vampire, in spite of your contrary opinion. If you count the parasite which causes the itch you will have two friends."[3] In this short survey of Lautréamont's *œuvre*, the stress is laid upon despicable animals such as toads, lice, bats, and vermin. Here is another passage quoted as typical:

The bloodsucker's brother [Maldoror] walked slowly in the forest . . . At last he cried: "Man, when you meet a dead dog turned up against a lock-gate which prevents the stream carrying away, do not, like others, pick up the worms from its swollen belly and consider them with amazement, do not bring out your knife to cut them up . . ."[4]

I will not heed Maldoror's warning when investigating the peculiar function played by lice in Joyce's works. For Joyce as for Ducasse, lice embody the stubborn resistance of nature or the body to ideas: they exemplify both "negoistic" trends preventing a theoretical movement toward the universal, when they do not appeal to universal history.

When I chose Blake's wonderful *Ghost of a Flea* for the cover of a book,[5] I had not foreseen that ghosts of fleas or lice would come back to haunt me. As I happened to visit the remarkable Georges de La Tour exhibition organized by the National Gallery of Art in Washington in October 1996, I saw once more a painting that had fascinated me previously. Often called *La femme à la puce* (*The Flea Catcher*), one takes its subject for granted although the title was not given by the author. The catalogue introduction by Conisbee stresses the indeterminacy of its topic:

There have been many attempts to identify the subject of *The Flea Catcher* . . . The seriousness and the air of contemplation with which La Tour invests this apparently banal subject give it all the feeling of a religious work. Rosenberg has hinted that it may represent a scene from the Bible, yet to be identified. Others have interpreted the woman as Hagar, the Magdalen, the Virgin sequestered by Joseph when he heard of her expectant state, and as a pregnant girl given shelter by a charitable foundation such as the Order of Notre-Dame du Refuge in Nancy. Is she really crushing a flea? Would it not rather be a louse? And is another one visible on her stomach?[6]

My thesis is that the questions whether this enigmatic young woman is seen cracking a flea, a louse, or rosary beads, and also whether she is pregnant or not, both have a direct and special relevance to the esthetics developed by Joyce in his early novels.

Joyce would no doubt answer the query of the exhibition curators with his own questions. We see how in *A Portrait of the Artist as a Young Man* Stephen, following young Joyce's own habit, writes down strange questions and develops his theories by looking for adequate answers ("In finding the answers to them I found the theory of esthetic which I am trying to explain" [*P*, 214]). Thus the issue of lice is addressed by this kind of internal dialogism: "*Can excrement or a child or a louse be a work of art? If not, why not?*" (*P*, 214). The sequence of these three terms is surprising, which is no doubt why Lynch laughs and replies: "Why not, indeed?"

However, one needs to consult the Paris Notebook to find an adequate context: "Question: Why are not excrements, children and lice works of art? Answer: Excrements, children and lice are human products – human dispositions of sensible matter. The process by which they are produced is natural and non-artistic . . ."[7] What appears as slightly shocking here is not just that children should be so readily equated with lice and excrement – which is a sure way to dismiss them from the sphere of artistic productions – but that lice should be considered as purely *human* products, "*human* dispositions of sensible matter." Joyce's jottings on Aristotle had no doubt convinced him that lice were properly not animals, but bodily creations, innate productions that could be linked with the famous "fingernails" the godlike artist is always paring (*P*, 215). Lice and nails are linked in a meditation that takes the intimate parallelism of art and nature as its source (one has not forgotten how, in the same Paris Notebook, Joyce comments on Aristotle's *e tekhne mimeitai ten physin* to stress the idea that it only means that "the artistic process is like the natural process" [*CW*, 145]).

The circuitous route going from Joyce back to Aristotle can be rewarding if it leads us to unresolved problems dealing with physical life. In the work known as *Problems* (which is probably not from Aristotle but from his students) we find many interesting questions about the topic of sweat:

Why does sweat occur neither when men are straining nor when holding their breath, but rather when they let it go? . . . Why do the upper parts sweat more than the lower? . . . Why does sweat from the head either have no smell or less than sweat from the body? . . . Why do men sweat more when they have not sweated for a long time? . . . Why do we sweat more in the back than in the front? . . . Why does sweat flow from the head and the feet most of all when people grow hot? . . . Why do men who are nervous sweat in the feet and not in the face? . . . Why do men sweat more asleep than awake? Is it because sweat originates from within, and the parts within are warmer, so that the internal heat melts and expels the internal moisture? Or is it because it is probable that something is always flowing off from the body, but it is unnoticed because there is nothing by falling on to which it will be collected? There is evidence for this: the hollow parts of the body always sweat.[8]

Aristotle describes very convincingly human beings as sweating beings, especially when asleep, for, as Joyce was well aware, we are all "sweaty-funnyadams" (*FW*, 65.5). Similarly, *Finnegans Wake* appears as a book written with much sweat (so much so that sweat turned into ink: "In the ink of his sweat he will find it yet" [563. 19–20]). The result of the book is not so much a nightmare as an endless damp (if not entirely wet) dream, sad and funny at times, from which we can only wake up drenched in sweat: "When he woke up in a sweat besidus it was to pardon him, goldylocks, me having an airth, but he daydreamed we had a lovelyt face for a pulltomine" (615. 22–24). The pantomime may be a "legpull" but it is one which will have had us toil and sweat over it, as all readers should know. Why is it important to know as much as possible about sweat, especially when one claims to be an "aristotaller" (417.16)? Because sweat produces more than salty water – strange animals are also generated from it:

Why does a change of water cause lice to increase on those who have them? Is it because there is a failure to digest the moisture owing to the disturbance produced, which is due to the variation with those who change their water frequently? This produces moisture, especially in the region most liable to it. Now the brain is moist; consequently the head is always moist. This is obvious from the fact that most hair grows there. The dampness of this region is most liable to produce lice. This is clear in the case of children, for they are often moist-headed and most liable to discharge from the nose and flow of blood, and it is at this age that lice are commonest.[9]

Aristotle believes that lice are self-generated and equates the production of lice with the activity of the brain. Stephen is therefore a good Aristotelian when he exclaims that his mind directly produces vermin (I shall return to this crucial passage in *A Portrait of the Artist as a Young Man*). Like Aristotle, Stephen believes that lice are self-begotten. "Lice are produced out of flesh. When lice are going to be produced, as it were small eruptions form, but without any purulent matter in them; and if these are pricked, lice emerge. Some people get this disease when there is a great deal of moisture in the body; some indeed have been killed by it . . ."[10] This popular medieval belief is echoed by Bloom in *Ulysses* when he remembers the strange illness Sir Guinness's brother was rumored to have suffered from: "Still the other brother lord Ardilaun has to change his shirt four times a day, they say. Skin breeds lice or vermin" (*U*, 5: 306–307).

Strangely enough, one of the first victims of lice was an egregious casualty: he was no less than Homer himself! According to an old anecdote, passed on to us by various authors including Heraclitus, here is the sad story of how Homer died. He was watching children who asked him to solve a riddle. They said: "What we have seen and caught, we left behind. What we have neither seen nor caught, we bring with us" (Fr. B 56 DK). According to Heraclitus, Homer's death was caused by his failure to explain the riddle.[11] Although he was the "wisest of all men," he was nevertheless deceived by a simple and childish riddle! A fatal puzzle proved his inability to reach the wisdom of children, who appear closer to the essence of time as cosmic play and pure becoming. Heraclitus' fragment puns on the etymology of *Homeros* suggesting "blindness" and of *phtheir* (louse) calling up *phtheiro* (I destroy, I corrupt). It is as though the destructiveness often etymologically ascribed to Helen – as in the famous passage of *Agamemnon* by Aeschylus, where Helen is accused of destroying "men, cities and rule" by a pun that finds its way into Pound's seventh Canto[12] – had been transferred to the most minute and despicable creature on earth. Here is the full fragment: "Men are deluded as to their knowledge of visible things, a little like Homer, who was nevertheless wiser than all the Greeks taken together, for children who were killing lice deceived him when they said: What we have seen and caught, we left behind; what we have neither seen nor caught, we bring with us."[13] Poetic wisdom betrays its impotence since it cannot sublimate either bodily refuse or teeming vermin, in which one recognizes an allegory of the invisible nature of the flow of time. The authors of an interesting book on *Greek Insects* believe that these boys had caught some fish they had left behind, but carried lice with them. Let this red herring rot on the shores of Greece! Curiously, Davies and Kathirithamby have been as deceived as Homer once was, for it is much more plausible and philosophically telling to assume that Homer's mischievous children had referred to lice in both cases. Heraclitus' exalted obscurity manages to make lice the topic of philosophic discourse, even though it remains impenetrably obscure: it succeeds where epic poetry fails, and finds in lice an image of an invisible but pervasive life-force, life dimly glimpsed as an endless stream of becoming that cannot be arrested, just momentarily caught in the prism of a mocking riddle. In this riddle, a riddle that I would be tempted to allegorize and generalize, the lice seem to function in a curious way: they are invisible, alien bodies, yet produced by my body's secretions. If I see them, I can catch them and kill them. But if I don't – which is more often the case – I have to carry them with me. Isn't this a remarkable description of the unconscious? A knowledge that is hidden somewhere on or in my (now happily balding) head, a knowledge, which like nostalgia, I carry with me when I am not aware of the knowledge *it* knows.

IDEOLOGICAL LICE

During his ill-fated stay in Rome, Joyce writes to his brother, who has stayed in Trieste: "On Saturday last I went up to the headquarters of the

black lice to find out if they had chosen their general. A carman told
(me) they had elected a German and were now at their pranzo."[14] This
is how Joyce reports the election of Francis Xavier Werns to the position
of General of the Jesuits in September 1906. This is only one example
of a recurrent trope, evincing a strong animus against Jesuits and priests
– a feeling entirely shared by James and Stanislaus. Thus, the image of
lice follows a complex evolution in Joyce's works, and I will just try to
sketch the rhetoric they generate. A first stage is clearly provided by the
metaphor of the parasite. For Joyce, the main paradigm of social para-
sitism is Catholicism. Priests share with lice their typical black color and
a tendency to swarm in huge numbers. In Joyce's systematic critique of
religion, the term of "lice" functions as a privileged trope denouncing
the "plague of Catholicism." *Stephen Hero* develops the figure resound-
ingly:

In a stupor of powerlessness he reviewed the plague of Catholicism. He seemed
to see the vermin begotten in the catacombs in an age of sickness and cruelty
issuing forth upon the plains and mountains of Europe. Like the plague of
locusts described in Callista they seemed to choke the rivers and fill the valleys
up. They obscured the sun. Contempt of human nature, weakness, nervous
trembling, fear of day and joy, distrust of man and life, hemiplegia of the will,
beset the body burdened and disaffected in its members by its black tyrannous
lice. (*SH*, 198–99)

Joyce opposes the "exultation of the body in free confederate labours"
to what has been corrupted by "the pest of this vermin." This type of
critique returns also at the close of the early "Portrait of the Artist"
(1904) and echoes the rhetoric of anti-clericalism so dominant at the end
of the nineteenth century, especially in its anarchist versions. Bakunin,
Kropotkin, or Stirner all rail against the "parasites" that are to be found
among the clergy. The most entertaining variation on this theme is to be
found in "Scylla and Charybdis" when Stephen elaborates on Johann
Most's pamphlet, *The Deistic Pestilence* (1902). Most's advocacy of the 1882
murder in Phoenix Park made him popular in Ireland, and his anarchist
paper, *Die Freiheit*, had some audience at the time.[15] Most constantly
attacked "the race of parasites" that was not limited to priests but
included capitalists and their slaves. When Stephen describes Jesus as
"nailed like bat to barndoor" and sent as "Agenbuyer" (*U*, 9: 494–95),
one cannot help equating the "agenbuyer" (Old English for redeemer)
with Stephen's remorse: it is as if the "agenbite of inwit" (*U*, 1: 481, 9:
196, and 809, 10: 875 and 879) was felt to be the relentless bite of a divine
louse! "They wash and tub and scrub. Agenbite of inwit. Conscience.

Yet here's a spot" (*U*, 1: 481). Stephen's refusal to serve is a refusal to be clean. The proud *Non serviam!* – coupled with an archaic hydrophobia – entails an ethics of uncleanness since real lice are preferable to the bite of moralistic lice. Besides, it is not easy to get rid of any parasite. As Stephen must admit: "Catholicism is in your blood" (*SH*, 211) and the ritual cleansing of the inner body implies a more complex rhetorical machinery than that of the sweaty skin.

Stephen's juvenile rhetoric often sounds close to tones one finds in Pound's "Hell Cantos," with blasting and damning passages like:

> The slough of unamiable liars
> bog of stupidities,
> malevolent stupidities, and stupidities,
> the soil living pus, full of vermin,
> dead maggots begetting live maggots,
> slum owners,
> usurers squeezing crab-lice, pandars to authority . . .[16]

The other side of the image would appear with particular force in Kafka's "Metamorphosis," when Gregor Samsa is transformed over-night into *"einem ungeheuren Ungeziefer"* (a monstrous vermin) by a parodic embodiment of a derogative term used for Jews in Germany and Austria at that time. Vladimir Nabokov the entomologist discovered that the insect Gregor has turned into was closer to a beetle than to a louse or a cockroach. According to Nabokov's formidable reading, Gregor's tragedy is that he never discovered that he had wings concealed in his back.[17]

The role of priests as parasites is double, since they are known to transform their constituencies into vermin. Being fundamentally barren (celibate) themselves, they nevertheless generate . . . lousy children! In *Stephen Hero*, Stephen's anger is fueled by the contrast between the slums and the priests inspecting "these warrens full of swarming and cringing believers, he cursed the farce of Irish catholicism" (*SH*, 150–51). In *Dubliners*, when the main character of "A Little Cloud," Little Chandler, hurries to meet Gallagher, he catches a glimpse of the grimy streets of Dublin populated by lice-like children:

The golden sunset was waning and the air had grown sharp. A horde of grimy children populated the streets. They stood or ran in the roadway or crawled up the steps before the gaping doors or squatted like mice upon the thresholds. Little Chandler gave them no thought. He picked his way deftly through all that minute vermin-like life and under the shadow of the gaunt spectral mansions in which the old nobility of Dublin had roistered. (*D*, 71)

This vision of the slums recurs in Joyce's works as late as *Finnegans Wake* where we find the passage on "respectability" (*FW.* 543–45) with its slums with "copious holes emitting mice" (*FW*, 545. 8).

What is perhaps more revealing in the opening of this story is the denunciation of Chandler's facile sentimentality about "life" in general. He contemplates the sun that "flickered upon all the moving figures – on the children who ran screaming along the gravel paths and on everyone who passed through the gardens. He watched the scene and thought of life; and (as always happened when he thought of life) he became sad" (*D*, 71). A strong association has been established in the reader's mind between life and lice on the one hand, children and lice on the other hand. We are likely to forget it during the pub scene, but at the end, when Chandler is disturbed by his baby's cries, we must realize that the baby has indeed become a louse for him. Lucky for the poor brat that the wife comes back early enough! The vision of a "narrow cell," an open tomb ready for a dead woman, is no doubt intended as the place he wishes to send his wife as soon as possible (*D*, 84). The irony of his final "tears of remorse" is that they seem to stem also from an anticipated mourning of his family's demise.

Dubliners is full of strange – floating – worms, such as the "faints and worms" mentioned by the child narrator of "The Sisters." In the original version, the words were italicized, and were clearly explained by the distillery in which Cotter worked. In the final version, they float without any mooring between the other signifiers haunting him, like gnomon and simony. These "worms" are attributed to Cotter's former stories about the distillery: they belong to its technical vocabulary (the coiled tube coming out of a still) and contribute to the realism of the story. One could pun on Cotter's name, and see in his unfinished sentences a way of holding this naturalism at a distance, as it were, of cutting or slicing the worm, thereby making it more ambiguous. Is it life, or death, that it refers to? When Mr. Duffy meditates on the death of Mrs. Sinico at the end of "A Painful Case," and sees himself "outcast from life's feast" (*D*, 117), the apparition of the train "like a worm with a fiery head winding through the darkness, obstinately and laboriously" and "reiterating the syllables of her name" (*ibid.*) is a good enactment of the "inbite principle," yet remains undecided as to its meaning: the train "means" both a solitary and absurd death for the man who has refused to love, and the continuation of life for the "prostrate creatures" who busy themselves with their "venal loves" by the wall in the park. A whole study could still be devoted to Joyce's complex links with what has been described as Naturalism by Zola and his followers. They claimed Flaubert as their master, and one of the major exponents of French Naturalism was Maupassant, with whom Joyce was competing when writing *Dubliners*.

One of the basic principles of the movement was a belief in science and social reportage that would cure the ills of society. A true case study would slowly force people to see the hidden causes of prostitution, drunkenness, child abuse, workers' exploitation, and so on. This was the age of the various "physiologies" of love and mores, founded upon a belief in the organic unity of all beings. As Balzac had already stated in the Foreword to his monumental *Human Comedy* (1842), "Just as there are zoological species, there are social species too." Consequently, one of the basic ideas associated with Naturalism was that of the "slice of life" technique. *Dubliners* is still based upon such a principle, refining it with two important modifications: a life can be seen in a moment of decision, or indecision, as with Eveline. And the "slice" has to be taken literally, there has to a cut – a cut that hesitates between life and death, darkness and light, the obscurity of a gnomon and the flash of an epiphany. Combining techniques inherited by Symbolism and from Naturalism, the "slicing of life and (as) lice" creates a strategy of displacement, hesitation, postponement.

This strategy belongs in a fundamental sense to Joyce's esthetics, or perhaps, more crucially, to Stephen's. When Stephen hallucinates lice as his body's productions, he has already crafted the Villanelle and he can now fully associate the writing of poetry with sexuality. He is talking with his friends on the steps of the Library while Emma (E. C.) passes. This vision calls up a line he misquotes ("*Darkness falls from the air*"). He needs to feel a louse crawl on his neck to realize not only his mistake but also the sordid state he has fallen into:

A louse crawled over the nape of his neck and, putting his thumb and forefinger deftly beneath his loose collar, he caught it. He rolled its body, tender yet brittle as a grain of rice, between thumb and finger for an instant before he let it fall from him and wondered would it live or die. There came to his mind a curious phrase from Cornelius a Lapide which said that the lice born of human sweat were not created by God with the other animals on the sixth day. But the tickling of the skin of his neck made his mind raw and red. The life of his body, illclad, illfed, louseaten, made him close his eyelids in a sudden spasm of despair: and in the darkness he saw the brittle bright bodies of lice falling from the air and turning often as they fell. Yes; and it was not darkness that fell from the air. It was brightness.

Brightness falls from the air.
He had not even remembered rightly Nash's line. All the images it had awak-
ened were false. His mind bred vermin. His thoughts were lice born of the sweat
of sloth.

He came back quickly along the colonnade towards the group of students.
Well then, let her go and be damned to her. She could love some clean athlete
who washed himself every morning to the waist and had black hair on his chest.
Let her. (*APA*, 233–34)

The terror induced by the discovery of a louse on Stephen's neck could
be interpreted in Bakhtinian terms as the carnivalized return of the
repressed body (let us remember that, as a consequence of this hallucination, Stephen still lacks a body in the various schemes of correspondences for *Ulysses*). The dirty body debunks Romantic idealization, and
prevents any attempt to soar above sordid everyday life in a squalid
Dublin. This episode is presented, however, as a scene of hallucination:
Stephen believes that he can directly think lice, that his thoughts have
become grotesquely embodied as lice, which blurs the boundaries
between humanity and animality, and also between the body and thinking. One could say that this scene is parallel, while inversing it, with the
discovery of the word "foetus" on a student's desk in Cork. In both cases,
the Real (in the Lacanian sense) of sexuality erupts, first as carved letters,
then as lice crawling on his flesh. It looks as if the father's foetus had
finally given birth to lice.

Lice, children, letters, and words have many common points: they are
"litters" supposed to give a body to thoughts; they are born from bodily
fluids; like the offspring of poor and pious Catholic families, they tend
to multiply uncontrollably; this proliferation increases risks for the pop-
ulation's health; the disease is easily passed on to other people, as a result
of either casual acquaintance or more intimate encounters. Such a
contagious infection has also affected literature, in this case, poetry-
writing, which remains Stephen's main artistic goal. The remarkable
exchange between Nash's song (from *Summer's Last Will and Testament*)
and Cornelius a Lapide literally transforms the line of poetry into a
louse. Stephen needs to visualize the numerous lice falling around him
in order to discover his oversight. The first version ("*Darkness falls from the
air*") may have been suggested by desire, allegedly favored by obscurity.
The very line is however quite obscure, even if the text says: "*Brightness
falls from the air.*"

It is worth noticing that William Empson takes the passage as a crucial
example of "ambiguity" in his well-known essay. For Empson, the line is

an example of "ambiguity by vagueness" and he lists the many meanings that can be attached to it. He then alludes to the theory that "air" had merely been a misprint for a more material "hair": "It is proper to mention a rather cynical theory that Nash wrote or meant 'hair'; still, though less imaginative, this is very adequate . . ."[18] It all makes more sense if one visualizes little bright bodies falling from the hair: the dirge for a dying beauty makes all the more sense.

What one finds in Cornelius a Lapide's commentary on the Bible is not very different either from Nash or from Aristotelian dogma: the lice created from human bodies are not fully "created," therefore cannot be ascribed to God's creation of animals on the sixth day. The Latin text confirms the importance of the Aristotelian opposition between actual form and potentiality: "*pulices, mures aliique vermiculi, non fuerunt hoc sexto die creata formaliter, sed potentialiter, et quasi in seminali ratione.*" The reason why this passage has stuck in Stephen's mind is probably that lice are seen here as a debased version of the *logos spermatikos* dear to Stoician philosophy. If his own sexual unrest has found an adequate metaphor, curiously, the final result is astringent and negative. Rather than embrace corruption in the mind and the body, Stephen's shame makes him reject Emma's temptation. This is why the paradoxical outcome of this passage is his decision to let Emma "go and be damned." The hallucination of a clean rival "who washed himself every morning to the waist and had black hair on his chest" provides an ironical anticlimax. Stephen lets Emma go where athletes gather so that he may keep his own lice.

The only person who seems to be entitled to have him all, body, lice, and soul, is therefore his mother. It is in *Ulysses*, that, in a very symptomatic fashion, Stephen's mother appears repeatedly in connection with lice. This is how she is described: "Her shapely fingernails reddened by the blood of squashed lice from the children's shirts" (*U*, 1: 268–69). The relatively crude sight metaphorizes her effort to keep her children healthy, to cleanse them, and also to bring them up as good Christians. The famous "word known to all men" might thus be not "love" but simply "lice"! Because of the mother's doomed efforts, she then, by a sort of metonymic displacement, becomes a bloody "ghoul," a "chewer of corpses." The drama of her metamorphosis into a horrible ghoul enacts all of Stephen's contradictions concerning religion and the family. There is nevertheless for him a "crack-up" in the mirror: lice – like ghosts – have a habit of appearing at the moment when representations fail (like the error about the line from Nash's song) and exhibit their constitutive gap: "Stephen bent forward and peered at the mirror held out to him, cleft by a crooked crack. Hair on end. As he and others see me. Who chose this face for me? This dogsbody to rid of vermin. It asks me too" (*U*, 1:135–37). What does this "it" refer to? The mirror, or the mother's body? Is the task implied that of "getting rid of vermin" or of seeing oneself as others see one?

Here, Stephen echoes Robert Burns's famous 1785 poem, "To a Louse (*On Seeing One on a Lady's Bonnet at Church*)," the second stanza of which ends with an allusion to a "poor body" not far from his mother's: "Gae somewhere else and seek your dinner / On some poor body." Here is the relevant passage from the last stanza:

> O wad some Pow'r the giftie gie us
> *To see oursels as others see us!*[19]

The other's point of view – which could adequately be called a vision *sub specie pediculi* or "the louse's viewpoint" – becomes possible once the mirror of narcissism has been cracked. A similar point of view is offered to Bloom in the second half of the "Nausicaa" episode, when, after having thought of the smell of menstrual periods and of his own smell, he says to himself: "See ourselves as others see us" (*U*, 13: 1058). However, unlike Stephen or Chandler, Bloom does not allow himself to be swayed by the evocations of lice, worms, and maggots. At the end of his visit to the cemetery, his meditation on corpses rotting among "maggoty beds" leads him to a positive affirmation: "Warms beds: warm fullblooded life" (*U*, 6: 1005). It is against this lyrical and often circular assertion of life's creativity and resilience that Stephen, like Plato's Sophist, will feel the need to divide and cut, at least between the bodily purifications and the soul's cleansing (see *The Sophist*, 274 b-c, for the example of the technique of "lice-catching").

Similarly, in Stephen's musings at the end of the *Portrait*, the curious and exotic name of Cornelius a Lapide is relayed by another Lepidus, one who is quoted by Stephen when he reflects on the problem posed by Cranly about a crocodile and a baby who has just fallen into a river; the mother can only retrieve the baby if she is able to tell the crocodile what it will do next – a very old riddle, as old as the problem of children with lice, but a poser which seems to annoy Stephen ("This mentality, Lepidus would say, is indeed bred out of your mud by the operation of your sun" [*P*, 250]). The reference is to a moment of comedy in *Antony and Cleopatra* when Antony makes fun of a drunk and sick Lepidus. Lepidus offers a curious extension of the abiogenesis or spontaneous generation theory to . . . crocodiles, when he says: "Your serpent of Egypt is bred now of your mud by the operation of your sun: so is your crocodile" (*Antony and Cleopatra*, II, vii, 26–27). Then a humorous dialogue starts in which Antony parodies Lepidus's credulity:

LEP. What manner of thing is your crocodile?
ANT. It is shap'd, sir, just like itself, and it is as broad as it hath breadth: it is
    just so high as it is, and moves with its own organs. It lives by that which
    nourishes it, and the element once out of it, it transmigrates.
LEP. What colour is it of?
ANT. Of its own colour too.
LEP. 'Tis a strange serpent. (*Antony and Cleopatra* II, vii, 40–47)

Antony reduces abiogenesis to pure tautology, but when Stephen quotes him, he seems to denounce an Irish "Nilemud" that would generate the mentality of his friends, and by extension, of all the Irish people, which includes his own family. When he meets his father by accident, the exchange is less than cordial: "Wants me to read law. Says I was cut out for that. More mud, more crocodiles" (*P*, 250). The sarcastic remark, "More mud, more crocodiles," is meant to "cut" his father's speech, and stop the cycle of internal generation. Stephen's heroic egoism will allow him to cross the muddy river safely, helped, no doubt, by his rather discourteous habit of "cutting" (when not slicing) through predictable discourses.

Cutting or editing is nevertheless often necessary when dealing with Joyce's texts and I shall now give a personal example of this. The translation of *Ulysses* into French is said to be authoritative, and the Pléiade editors were not allowed to change it. It was therefore difficult to decide what to do when I realized that the passage of "Scylla and Charybdis" in which Stephen thinks: "Forgot: any more than he forgot the whipping lousy Lucy gave him" (*U*, 9: 1134) had been mistranslated as: "pas plus qu'il n'a oublié que l'ignoble Lucie la pouilleuse lui avait donné le fouet."[20] According to our guidelines, I could only annotate, and allude to the tradition according to which Shakespeare got his revenge on a brutal Sir Lucy by writing a bawdy ballad on him ("Lousy Lucy"). Shakespeare's revenge was indeed completed when the French translators turned him into a woman. A further irony is that Lucy is the name that was arbitrarily given to the oldest woman discovered in Africa. An ancestor of humanity who also had, it seems, lice.

A similar confusion of genders can be noted when Simon Dedalus calls his son a "lazy bitch" in the *Portrait* (*P*, 234). This may also explain why Stephen insists that aesthetic theory should focus on "the phenomenon of artistic conception, artistic gestation and artistic reproduction" (*P*, 209). Esthetic theory as Stephen sees it is not to be distinguished from the "Generation of animals" – assuming that he too, is an "animal" as well as an "artist." Aristotelian theories of the generation of the animals underwrite a general concept of Life in general, a Life to which Stephen decides to devote himself through his Art, as all the first essays and "critical writings" confirm. If Life can be epitomized by vermin (which being supposedly born out of lifeless matter, manifests therefore the absolute "triumph of life") we understand how Joyce's double program, partly naturalistic, implying the "slice of life" technique, and partly symbolist, taking language as a site which negates all the rest of the world, moves toward the sublimation of self-begetting without renouncing the underlying allegory of the body implied by the transformation. A mystical abiogenesis functions as a key concept in Joyce's affirmation of Life through Art. Mystical or mythical? How far are we from real history or the real science of biology? When Bloom dreamily answers to Virag's encyclopedic lore of sexual life, he muses aloud: "The cloven sex. Why they fear vermin, creeping things. Yet Eve and the serpent contradicts. Not a historical fact" (*U*, 15. 2445). I will now investigate the connection between Joyce's historical myth and the biological knowledge it presupposes.

"THE USES AND ABUSES OF INSECTS" (*FW*, 306. 30)

If lice can function as a metaphor of religion, ideological and political simony or usury, they come closer to a metonymy of life seen in all its aspects, a life which can encompass the idea of hair (to quote Plato) as well as the idea of a triangle. It is time to stress once more Joyce's fundamental anti-Platonism, since for him, the essence of life can never be reduced to an aspiration to the abstract truth of essences. Joyce follows Aristotle in refusing the imposition of a mathematical model when defining universal truths. What matters is to understand the causes and ends of the manifold manifestations of life, life seen as a biological principle which can be subdivided, classified, but never abstracted from a degree of physicality. This broad philosophical context can help us when we move toward *Finnegans Wake* and to what could be called an allegory: lice begin to function as a complex allegory linking spontaneous generation, debasement or bodily shame, writing and being alive, cutting oneself while yet surviving.

Lice are never a "central" theme of *Finnegans Wake*, precisely because they play the role of a debased insect, the hidden reminder of a major issue, abiogenesis. As an allegory of literary self-generation, lice can be seen either in a Freudian fashion as the "refuse" of art (as Freud says about his methodology in *The Moses of Michelangelo*) or in a broader manner, as defining a new parodic streak inherent in Joyce's synthetic language. In the *Wake*, the louse appears as a multilayered shifter connecting communication in its most material sense with the sublime spirit or soul. This appears in several passages, for instance in the Franco-English pun of "pounautique" in II, 3: "Skibbereen has common inn, by pounautique, with pokeway paw, and sadder raven evermore, telled shinshanks lauwering frankish for his kicker who, through the medium of gallic" (315. 33–36), a strangely unfinished sentence, without a final period, that tells us how the Skipper has found a way of communicating through a *pneumatique* (i.e. a telegram sent through the pneumatic communication system available in Paris between the wars). This also alludes to the "nautical louse" mentioned by Aristotle, and to Greek *pneuma*, or soul. "Summer is icumen in" the famous Old English refrain leads to Poe's "Raven" in a chapter that is full of technological inventions, from radio to television. The scene also takes place in a "public plouse" (338.4)!

The main character associated with lice in the *Wake* – this is no surprise – is Shem. Like Stephen, Shem is often introduced as a dirty parasite and a snobbish Parisian: "Let him be Artalone the weeps with his parisites peeling off him" (418. 1–2). The whole Shem chapter includes, of course, many eggs and omelets and some lice: among the factors that prevent Shem from memorizing poetry, one finds "the foxtrotting fleas, the lieabed lice" (180. 18–19). The systematic use of the vocabulary of dirt and derision often cuts both ways, since the "plebs" accusing Shem, or Shaun himself, are never without any blemish: "Again there was a hope that people, looking on him with the contemp of the contemptibles, after first gaving him a roll in the dirt, might pity and forgive him, if properly deloused, but the pleb was born a Quicklow and sank alowing till he stank out of sight" (174. 36–175. 4). By an unexpected linguistic twist, the lowness and dirt that are typical of Shem turn him into an exile and also an outlaw, both an "outlex" (169. 3) and a puling *pulex* (or flea). Professor Jones says: "I am closely watching Master Pules" (166. 20) in a passage that plays on sexual reversibility and the fear that "mites" may reproduce themselves anarchically: "My solotions for the proper parturience of matres and the education of micturious mites must stand over from the moment till I tackle this tickler hussy for occupying my uttentions" (166. 28–30). This passage takes place in the middle of the story of Burrus, Caseous, and Margareena. It may be worth remembering in this context that Aristotle had already noted that cheese, especially cream cheese (I mention this with a Philadelphian fondness) had the property of generating – again by pure abiogenesis – the smallest mite or louse of all, the *akari* (a name that is still used today for the microscopic skin-lice that we all carry on our bodies):

Also an animal is produced in cream cheese which is getting ancient, as in wood, and this is considered to be the smallest of all living creatures; it is known as *akari*, and is white and small. Others are found in books . . . and generally speaking small creatures are found in almost anything, both in dry things which are turning moist and moist ones which are turning dry, anything which contains life.[21]

This biological atom will surface again in Pascal's disquisition on the two infinites, under the name of *ciron* ("mites" in Krailshamer's translation).[22]

The entire passage of *FW* 161–68 could be read in the light of the doomed search for the smallest "atom" of living matter. For Aristotle, the law of life is the interaction between humidity and some dry substance. The unwelcome generation of "Shems" in the *Wake* obeys such a disturbing pattern, which constantly disrupts the usual boundaries opposing life and death. This introduces us to one of the basic laws of the book, one which goes beyond the characterization of Shem alone, and helps define the nature of Law in the text. Here, we have again to move from Aristotle to our own post-Biblical world or reference to realize that sweat as labor is indeed the basic postlapsarian factor that explains the genesis of all life, human or animal. The reincorporation of outlawed elements is a basic feature of Joyce's plea for linguistic and biological productivity. In *Finnegans Wake*, a revised story of the Fall explains that since Genesis humanity has not only to be condemned to sweat and toil, but also to survive as all animals do, with the difference that men create language, cities, laws . . . and lice. As early as the first chapter we find: "He dug in and dug out by the skill of his tilth for himself and all belonging to him and he sweated his crew beneath his auspice for the living and he urned his dread, that dragon volant, and he made louse for us and delivered us to boll weevils amain" (24. 3–6). Laws are here linked with the cult of dead ancestors and all the funeral rites performed for them. But laws are nothing if not contingent. A meeting "of all sections and cross sections . . . of our liffeyside people" is to take place "under the shadow of the monument of the shouldhavebeen legislator" (42. 19–25). The "lousy laws" provided by the failed legislator are often thrown back to an impotent God as a constant reproach. Shem as Jerry or Devil is no doubt partly responsible for the failure of the best intentions ("but, laus sake, the devil does be in that knirps of a Jerry sometimes" [27. 8–9]), but this is because a superior law of life seems to regulate all civilizations, according to a Viconian scheme of Providence. However, Providence gets another name in the *Wake*: writing. "There'll be bluebells blowing in salty sepulchres the night she signs her final tear. Zee End. But that's a world of ways away. Till track laws time" (28. 26–30).

Writing is one of the central concerns of *Finnegans Wake*, not just because this is an extremely self-reflexive book, but also because Joyce attempts the creation of a universal history that would both encompass a history of writing, of printing, of the book, and present itself as a natural history of signs. Which is why letters come closer to nature, and for instance become insects that bite: "Huntler and Pumar's animal alphabites, the first in the world from aab to zoo" (263 F 1). The text is forever elaborating on its own "inkbottle authority" (263. 24) and describes its printed lines as rows of ants, earwigs or lice moving on the page. "But look what you have in your handself! The movibles are scrawling in motions, marching, all of them ago, in pitpat and zingzang for ever busy eerie whig's a bit of torytale to tell" (20. 20–23). It is probably enough to note that if the animals vary their forms and species (we have in the same passage: "See the snake wurrums everyside" [19.12] and also simple "owlet's eggs" [19.9]), we can never lose sight of the original midden heap or turf or garbage mound in which letters, litters, and vermin are found to proliferate suddenly as so many "wigworms" (282.13). This is a constant creation *ex nihilo* retelling the origin of language and letters: "We are once amore as babes awondering in a world made fresh where with the hen in the storyaboot we start from scratch" (336.15–17).

The central trope allegorizing all these tensions, especially the struggle between the ear and the eye, is the earwig, the emblem and main pet of the *Wake*. It is well known that the name of the insect derives from the popular belief that these insects can crawl into the ears of sleeping people, hence its name of *Forficula auricularia*. It appears very early in the *Wake*, in the Mutt and Jeff dialogue, a passage that connects ancestors' burial grounds ("And thanacestross mound have swollup them all" [18. 3–4]), the fertility of the earth ("This ourth of years is not save brickdust and being humus the same rotourns" [18. 4–5]), and the kind of insects that can be found in the mound: "The gyant Forficules with Amni the fay" [18. 11]). The insect is systematically associated with sepulture: the early times of Dublin saw, as a Shaunian narrator explains, ladies who used "to carry, as earwigs do their dead, their soil to the earthball where indeeth we shall calm decline, our legacy unknown" (79. 16–17). The earwig provides Earwicker with his surname, while also being associated with Shem, in a context suggesting that the earwig is not too different from a solitary worm or a hair louse: "Criniculture can tell us very precisely indeed how and why this particular streak of yellow silver first appeared on (not in) the bowel, that is to see, the human head, bald, black, bronze, brown, brindled, betteraved or blanchemanged where it might be usefully compared with an earwig on a fullbottom" (164. 25–29). Shem provides a variation on the paternal earwig since he is responsible for singing and writing lyrical poetry ("pure lyricism of shamebred music" [164. 15–16]). Naturally, Shaun as Jones will accuse him of perverting the proper values associated with space: "Of course the unskilled singer continues to pervert our wiser ears by subordinating the space-element, that is to sing, the *aria,* to the time-factor" (164.32–34). The opposition between life and death and time and space finds a concrete outlet when producing a fantasy of penetration through the ear (Professor Jones clearly becomes Freud's biographer here). One witnesses a generalization of this primal fear in the *Wake:* "Tiffpuff up my nostril, would you puff the earthworm outer my ear" (509. 28–29). Or again: "Come here, Herr Studiosus, till I tell you a wig in your ear" (193. 13).

The fantasy could easily tie up with Stephen's fantasy of poisoning his readers through their ears (as with the King in *Hamlet*) in the Library scene of *Ulysses:* "They are still. Once quick in the brains of men. Still: but an itch of death is in them, to tell me in my ear a maudlin tale, urge me to wreak their will" (*U,* 9. 336–38). This urge is translated as "the itch in his egondoom" (*FW,* 343. 26) in the *Wake,* a rich phrase that links the ego and the id of Freudian theory with the "itch" to write that displaces authority. The kingdom of the old subject's autonomy is "doomed" in Joyce's variation on Freud's *Wo Es war, soll Ich werden* – both the future and itchy *Ich* are haunted by "qwehrmin" (343. 22). The "tragedoes of those antiants" (343. 22–23) comes from the fact that one cannot shut one's ear. This is the sad fate of the human body and also of the whole of Europe, recurrently presented as the "earopen." "It falls easily upon the earopen" (419. 14), as Shaun says after he has recited the poem which concludes the fable of the Ondt and the Gracehopper. But he resists symptomatically the idea that all these "shemletters" (419.19) and "anaglyptics" (419. 19) have been written by his brother Shem.

The central fable of the Ondt and the Gracehopper uses "entymology" (417. 4) too systematically to just allude to it. I would need to read the whole passage closely, which cannot be done here for reasons of space – or time. To rush through a complex tangle of arguments, I would just like to say that I now tend to approach the text by way of Nabokov's *Ada*, a novel which pays homage to Joyce's great "poem" of the night,[23] and forcibly links insects and incest. At one point the children play at anagrams with the word "insect" and come up with: "Dr Entsic was scient in insects . . . 'Nicest!' 'Incest,' said Ada instantly" (*Ada*, p. 71). Young Ada loves bugs, beetles, caterpillars, moths, butterflies, grubs. She goes beyond Molly Bloom's motto of "I love everything that flows" when she asserts triumphantly: "*Je raffole de tout ce qui rampe* (I'm crazy about everything that crawls)" (*Ada*, p. 49). At that time, she has not yet been "perverted" by her brother (she still thinks he is a first cousin) who introduces her to incestuous sexual games. The same scene takes place in *Finnegans Wake* and Earwicker betrays himself at one point when he admits to "having belittled myself to my gay giftname of insectarian" (358. 7–8). The "old offender" is obviously "humile, commune and ensectuous from his nature" (29. 30–31). The story of Honophrius at the end of the book would provide a good example of the generalized incest linking all family members (572–73). It would also include the "fornicolopulation" (557. 17) of characters like "Formio and Cigalette" (563. 27). Joyce would have us rewrite *Alice in Wonderland* (translated into Freudian terms by Empson's reading in *Some Versions of Pastoral* [1935]) – "we grisly old Sykos who have done our unsmiling bit on alices" (115. 21–22)) and turn the eponymous heroines plural into a singular name: "A Louse in Wonderland." – "Pou!" (415. 26), what a terrible pun!

As we have seen with Stephen's hallucination, like lice, letters are wont to multiply and "plultiply" (405.1). They share fundamental properties with lice: both entail a proliferation of almost invisible signs that threatens to engulf any truth, origin, or meaning. The materiality of the letters is indissociable from a living body, which finally allegorizes the ideality of the great Letter carried by all the characters in the *Wake*. Bridging thus the gap between biology and language, I wish to address a related issue: the question of the divisibility or indivisibility of the letter, a property which may or may not be connected with the letter's materiality. This discussion has violently opposed Derrida to Lacan and more recently Gasché to Zizek, for instance.[24] I have to acknowledge that in this one instance, I believe the Lacanian position to be unassailable (which may pose another type of problem). Lacan posits that a letter, even cut, divided, torn into small fragments, will nevertheless remain the letter it was, while Derrida stresses the possibility of endless division and absolute loss. Besides, for Lacan, the letter always reaches its destination, for as soon as it is read – and we would not even mention it had it not been read – the person who has it becomes its addressee. Derrida, on the other hand, stresses the materiality of disappearance, of total obliteration, at least as a possibility, against the ideality of a self-regulating economic circuit. It is not a coincidence that Lacan should refer to "interrupted circles" and "cut worms" in his seminar on the "Purloined Letter." He annotates his own text in an interesting way:

Cut a letter in small pieces, and it remains the letter it is – and this in a completely different sense than *Gestalttheorie* would account for with the dormant vitalism informing its notion of the whole.[9]

Footnote[9]: This is so true that philosophers, in those hackneyed examples with which they argue on the basis of the simple and the multiple, will not use to the same purpose a simple sheet of white paper ripped in the middle and a broken circle, indeed a shattered vase, not to mention a cut worm.[25]

One page later, Lacan adds a crucial reference to *Finnegans Wake* when commenting on the unsuccessful attempts by the Paris police to find the letter hidden in the Minister's apartment:

And to return to our cops, who took the letter from the place where it was hidden, how could they have seized the letter? In what they turned between their fingers what did they hold but what *did not answer* to their description. "A letter, a litter": in Joyce's circle, they played on the homophony of the two words in English.[26]

Another footnote sends us to *Our Exagmination round His Factification . . .* without any precise reference – but we recognize here the famous "Litter to Mr. Germ's Choice" penned by Vladimir Dixon (who, for a long time, was thought to be a thin disguise for Joyce himself). I might add that Joyce's version of the Lacanian Moebius strip running through "Penelope" and through the endless circulation of *Finnegans Wake* cannot avoid a moment of cut, which finally entails a segmented – albeit Nietzschean – self-devouring snake. Joyce escapes from any kind of "dormant vitalism" by adding merely: "let it sleep, do not wake it up (27. 22–23)," like the sleeping giant on the hill of Howth.

How could I conclude without cutting the worm, or undercutting my previous argument? I have followed the evolution that stretches "from zoomorphology to omnianimalism" (*FW*, 127. 13–14), coming perilously close to identifying lice with an allegory of the Fall or of Life. Such an allegorization may well have been in Joyce's mind when he multiplied allusions to the role of lice in the "Fall." One of the titles for Anna Livia's mamafesta is: "*Measly Ventures of Two Lice and the Fall of Fruit*" (106. 21). The main consequence of my reading qualifies the structuralist idea (exemplified by Lévi-Strauss or Barthes) of an absolute opposition between nature and history that should warn us against any possible "naturalization" of historical or social productions. Barthes, especially in *Mythologies*, saw as the reactionary consequence of myth a transformation of history into nature. This is almost what *Finnegans Wake* does – Joyce makes a myth out of history, a history which repeats itself, telling over and over again the same old stories – but with an important difference: he never forgets the constitution of a new language, understood as the promise of a new social bond.

As with Vico's monumental *New Science*, one should not miss the more insistent motif hidden beneath the programmatic assertion of endless cyclical repetition. Like Vico, who bases his historiography upon the wisdom of one people, the Italian nation (whose philosophy is probably, according to Vico of course, more ancient and noble than that of Greece), Joyce bases his own universal story on a dominantly Irish history. If *Ulysses* was clearly "an epic of two races" (*LIV*, 271), the Irish and the Jewish races always engaged in a fruitful dialogism, the *Wake* is an epic of all races, which entails that it is based on a specifically Irish topography, a basically Anglo-Irish idiom, and Irish paradigms of tradition and anecdote. Joyce manages in this way to bypass a universalist discourse, and founds his own discourse of tolerance on the singularity of one nation – after, that is, its idiom has been broadened so as to accept the whole "earopen." This is what I will call "hospitality."

Rather than simply naturalizing history, Joyce more conspicuously transforms nature into living and disseminating language. It is not only that language follows some fundamental laws of transformation, but also that his imagination of nature creates endless differences. Nature seen in its biological and zoological aspects allows for all sorts of teratologies. Therefore, Joyce's history of Ireland, his post-colonial and post-nationalistic politics, cannot be dissociated from a weird, denaturalized zoology of language. In more optimistic moments, Joyce seems to believe in the possibility of creating a new Europe almost overnight, through a lingua franca based on English grammar and the grafting of a few other lexicons onto this syntactic and narratological grid. In less optimistic moments, Joyce seems to suggest that language is a pure process of creation, destruction, and regeneration, a process that he can only mimic, distort, or speed up in his invented idioglossary. The common point between both positions is that the notion of "imagined communities" relies above all on a shared language. This is why Joyce's critique of nationalism which was explicit in *Ulysses* has to be implicit in *Finnegans Wake*. His universal history never leaves the confines of Dublin and its suburbs, while he keeps returning to the traumatic scene of the "birth of a nation" – in a passage describing the electric radio apparatus given to Earwicker in order to "capture" all the messages coming from the whole world: "Whyfor had they, it is Hiberio-Miletians and Argloe-Noremen, donated him, birth of an otion that was breeder to sweatoslaves, as mysterbolder, forced in their waste" (309. 11–13). *Finnegans Wake* appears closer in tone and spirit to Gabriel Garcia Marquez's *Hundred Years of Solitude* or Salman Rushdie's *Midnight's Children*. Which is not so much to ascribe it to the genre of "magical realism" as to describe a common mixture of folklore, national history, mythical paradigms, all structured by the theatricalization of a wild and loose oral tale.

In these novels, an archetypal family bridges the gap between private and public realms, and sends us back to the same and different Heraclitean stream: "The untireties of livesliving being the one substrance of a streambecoming" (*FW*, 597. 7–8). It is no use trying to enter the stream with the hope of delousing oneself: even if one never swims twice in the same river, it carries along its own life-affirming vermin. Having read Joyce, we too have been bitten by the bug. We have learned to live with bugs and viruses not only in our organisms but also in our computers, these bugs remaining halfway between our bodies and our hypertextual encyclopedias: "In the buginning is the woid, in the muddle is the sounddance and thereinofter you're in the unbewised again" (*FW*, 378. 29–31). Joyce answers his own desparing prayer to darkness with another prayer couched in the impure bog Latin of Wakese: "*Taurus periculosus, morbus pedeiculosus. Miserere mei in miseribilibus!*" (466. 31–32). In the plain English of an Irish bull (if you are not sure what this means, here is how to identify an Irish bull: if you see seven cows in a field, the one that is full of lice is an Irish bull) this gives: "Dangerous bull, lice disease. O pity me among the lousiest of all!"

CHAPTER SIX

The egoist vs. the king

The Irish provinces not England and her tradition stand between me and Edward VII.

James Joyce, *The Trieste Notebook.*[1]

THE EGOIST AND THE KING

The second issue of *The Egoist* dated January 15, 1914 mentions James Joyce for the first time through the pen of Ezra Pound, who was more or less officially its literary editor. Pound and Joyce had started corresponding just one year earlier, when following Yeats's suggestion, Pound had requested texts, any text the Irish exile would deem fit to send for publication. His first letter reveals that Pound may have been slightly ironical about the magazine's gender politics (it begins with the declaration: "I am informally connected with a couple of new and impecunious papers ['The Egoist' which has coursed under the unsuitable name of 'The New Freewoman' 'guère que d'hommes y collaborent' as the Mercure remarked of it"])[2] but not sanguinely opposed to its ideology. However, the first text sent by Joyce for *The Egoist* was not literary (he had immediately replied to Pound's offer by mailing his poem "I hear an army" which duly found its way into the *Imagistes* anthology) but a political tract, a pamphlet on censorship. Under the title of "A Curious History," Pound echoes Joyce's recapitulation of the incredible series of hardships he endured when attempting to publish *Dubliners*. Pound quotes a letter by Joyce (already published in two newspapers only: *Sinn Fein* [Dublin] and *The Northern Whig* [Belfast]) detailing the harrowing incidents that prevented the publication. Joyce's letter puts the main emphasis on the reaction of the British censors to his having portrayed Edward VII in an unflattering light.

In December, 1909, Messrs. Maunsel's manager begged me to alter a passage in one of the stories, "Ivy Day in the Committee Room," wherein some reference was made to Edward VII. I agreed to do so, much against my will, and altered one or two phrases. Messrs. Maunsel continually postponed the date of publication and in the end wrote, asking me to omit the passage or change it radically. I declined to do so, pointing out that Mr. Grant Richards, of London, has raised no objection to the passage when Edward VII. was alive, and that I could not see why an Irish publisher should raise an objection to it when Edward VII. had passed into history.[3]

There, Joyce found a confirmation of his grim views of Irish subservience, which is why he could jot down the remark I have used as an epigraph in the *Trieste Notebook* ("The Irish provinces not England and her tradition stand between me and Edward VII"). Taken in isolation, the sentence could suggest pro-British feelings; Joyce is of course pointing to the specific moral "simony" of the enslaved Irish, a simony that could be measured: even if Joyce had paid one hundred pounds, the minimum sum required to sue a publisher for breach of contract in court, he had been warned that he would not get a verdict in his favor because of the possible slur to the late king.

Joyce explains in his letters to the press that he then decided to approach the king himself, and accordingly wrote to King George V, to whom he sent the incriminating story. George's secretary simply wrote back to acknowledge this: "The private secretary is commanded to acknowledge the receipt of Mr. James Joyce's letter of the 1st instant and to inform him that it is inconsistent with the rule for His Majesty to express his opinion in such cases."[4] The king refused to take part in a literary dispute fraught with crucial political issues.

The offensive passage is the discussion in "Ivy Day" in which Mr. Henchy "buries" Parnell and extols the British King for being "just an ordinary knockabout like you and me." Edward VII is described as "fond of his glass of grog" and "a bit of a rake, perhaps" but all in all "a good sportsman." The English king is the "jolly fine decent fellow" who reappears in the "Circe" episode of *Ulysses* dancing and singing: "On coronation day, on coronation day, / O, won't we have a merry time,/ Drinking whisky, beer and wine!" (as we shall see shortly).[5] The political satire seems rather mild, and aimed more at the Irish politicians who capitalize on Parnell's name while welcoming British capital. The king's visit to Ireland allegorizes a general betrayal and loss of values; it is also intimately connected with Joyce's personal saga: Edward VII visited Ireland between July 21 and August 2, 1903; just a little later Joyce's mother died, on August 13, 1903. Her cancer had forced her son to come back hurriedly from Paris, and he spent the last weeks of her comatose sickness reading the newspapers with anger and frustration, and participating in the meetings of the Irish Republican Socialist Party.[6]

The king's name remains as the key symbol of an empire which has reduced Ireland to a secondary nation. As Joyce had already noted in the 1907 article he wrote in Italian for the Triestine *Piccolo della Sera*, Ireland had not only always betrayed leaders like Parnell, it had also willingly submitted itself to a double oppression: "Ireland, weighed down by multiple duties, has fulfilled what has hitherto been considered an impossible task – serving both God and Mammon, letting herself be milked by England and yet increasing Peter's pence (perhaps in memory of Pope Adrian IV, who made a gift of the island to the English King Henry II about 800 years ago, in a moment of generosity)."[7] I will return to this Biblical tag in my last chapter.

Pound observes a discretion in his "Note" that could call up the king's own reticence, since he merely notes that Joyce is "an author of known and notable talent." However, the next issue of *The Egoist* provides his real answer to the blockage by censorship: on what is exceptionally dated Monday, February 2nd, 1914 (on the same page of the magazine, one reads: "*Published the 1st and 15th of each month*"), thus making a noticeable effort to have the appearance of the review coincide with Joyce's thirty-second birthday on February 2nd, the third issue of *The Egoist* begins the serialization of *The Portrait of the Artist as a Young Man*.

We can compare this with Pound's article on Joyce for *The Egoist* in February 1917 (Pound had also reviewed *Dubliners* for the readers of *The Egoist* in July 1914). Pound salutes the publication of Joyce's novel, whose obvious worth and appeal confirm his earlier praise of the author. However, the king is still present as an interlocutor:

Members of the "Fly-Fishers" and "Royal Automobile" clubs, and of the "Isthmian," may not read him. They will not read Mr. Joyce. *E pur si muove.* Despite the printers and publishers the British Government has recognised Mr. Joyce's literary merit. That is a definite gain for the party of intelligence. A number of qualified judges have acquiesced to my statement of two years ago, that Mr. Joyce was an excellent and important writer of prose.[8]

This 1917 review ushers in the important comparison with Flaubert, which was to stamp Pound's general view of Joyce for a long time. Can one say with Joseph Kelly that Pound's critical effort aimed at "universalizing" and thus depoliticizing Joyce? In the section called "Joyce the Egoist" of his *Our Joyce: From Outcast to Icon*, Kelly voices a damaging criticism: "The effect of all of Pound's commentaries on Joyce's reputation was to place Joyce in this small coterie of artists. He made Joyce one of the chief parts of this cosmopolitan, international literary machinery. The success of such a project required the destruction of Joyce's reputation as an *Irish* writer, and so Pound ignored Ireland."[9] Kelly adds that such a depoliticization runs counter to Dora Marsden's political articles in *The Egoist*.

However, if we focus on the issues of the same period, when Pound pays homage to Joyce's new novel, it is a slightly different picture that emerges: while Dora Marsden is engaged in a study of very abstract philosophical notions like "The Constitution and Origin of the 'Image' in Imagination" – this is the title of her lead article for the following issue in April 1917 – it is at that time Pound who looks much more political. In the issue in which he pays homage to Joyce's new novel, he prints a second protest about the suppression of Dreiser's works in the United States ("Dreiser Protest") followed by a list of writers and political luminaries who have signed the protest. Pound's somewhat vehement accusations mixing mangled foreign words and personal diatribe ("*O patria mia, vedo le mura e gli archi* as usual, and the cowardice of a servile democracy, also as usual, and the pusillanimity of America's popular writers, also as usual, and the inactive timidity of America's 'elder generation of *literati*,' also as usual, and my contempt for these national characteristics remains unaltered – as usual"[10]) are offset by Dora Marsden's refusal to commit herself (she writes after the first Dreiser protest in October 1916 that she "takes no responsibility for the expression of the above personal views"[11] – and decides to print a protest against Pound's first Dreiser article, a letter by an unnamed "Member of the Authors' League of America" who tries to remain neutral and balanced but expresses the idea that American patriotism and common sense will eventually triumph. Thus, when Pound compares Joyce with Flaubert, it is not at all to treat Joyce as an international esthete who would embody for him the values of high Modernism; on the contrary, Pound keeps repeating that, like Joyce, Flaubert was a serious political writer – which is not a quality he finds among contemporary English or Irish writers. Pound's deliberate "de-Irishing" (to quote Kelly) is therefore completely political: he shows that it is only by taking some distance that a "diagnosis" can be brought to bear on the Irish issue.

I doubt if a comparison of Mr. Joyce to other English writers or Irish writers would help to define him. One can only say that he is rather unlike them. *The Portrait* is very different from *L'Education Sentimentale*, but it would be easier to compare it with that novel of Flaubert's than anything else. Flaubert pointed out that if France had studied his work they might have been saved a good deal in 1870. If more people had read *The Portrait* and certain stories in Mr. Joyce's *Dubliners* there might have been less recent trouble in Ireland. A clear diagnosis is never without its value.[12]

This is why one cannot agree with Kelly's conclusion that "Pound had no use for Joyce so long as he was an Irish writer presenting a chapter in the moral history of his country to general readers in Ireland and abroad."[13] A more careful delineation of what the term of "audience" entails will therefore be necessary (I will return to this point in a later chapter) but before, an accurate examination of Joyce's links with "his" king, in an historical and cultural context determined by his being an exile, living abroad in Italy and Switzerland, and also having to measure his worth by universal models or masters, is inevitable.

JOYCE, AN EDWARDIAN BY DEFAULT

This ideological discussion forces us to return to issues of literary and cultural classification, and I will then proceed enthymemically to high-light the absurdity of certain historical categories. By "enthymeme," I allude to the trope which figures so prominently in the "Aeolus" episode of *Ulysses*, a trope also prominent in Aristotle's *Rhetorics*, since it reproduces the formal structure of a syllogism while presenting a sophism, or a questionable half-truth.[14] In fact, enthymemes provide a good rhetorical equivalent of the workings of ideology. According to Virginia Woolf and basic historical divisions, Joyce should be defined as a "Georgian" writer (major). According to Wyndham Lewis in the thirties and more recent critics whose approach is related to "cultural studies," Joyce can be categorized as a late "Victorian" (minor). Therefore, the truth should be found somewhere in the middle, and Joyce may be called an "Edwardian." To qualify this pseudo-syllogism, my contention is that Joyce can appear as an "Edwardian" indeed, but only in a very literal sense, so as to bridge the gap between his personal biography, his Irish background, his decision to freeze his political struggle in 1904, and his immersion in the spirit of the times heavily marked by egoism. Joyce will become an "Edwardian" if and only if one can equate "Edwardianism" with egoism, an egoism that leaves the solitary Irish writer in an unequal fight against the most powerful sovereign of the times. In many ways, Joyce came to see himself as engaged in a personal war he was waging against the English king, in a symbolic struggle which could not but be symptomatic, with a touch of paranoia and grandiosity from which his daughter would not be immune.

If we now turn toward Woolf's famous remarks on the "new" spirit which had just been born at the end of 1910, Joyce qualifies as a Georgian: "I will suggest that we range Edwardians and Georgians into two camps; Mr. Wells, Mr. Bennett and Mr. Galsworthy I will call the Edwardians; Mr. Forster, Mr. Lawrence, Mr. Strachey, Mr. Joyce, and Mr. Eliot I will call the Georgians."[15] The ironical cascade of "Mrs." corresponds to the fictional framework suggested by the title: a real Edwardian writer – Arnold Bennett, whose main writings were published before 1911 – faces a feminine character, who embodies the spirit of the age. This age drastically changed in 1910: "in or about December 1910 human character changed" ("Mr Bennett and Mrs Brown," p. 70). Woolf's date, taken quite literally, cannot refer to the death of King Edward, which occurred as early as May 1910, a fact which has been noted by most commentators. However, it can neither strictly be assumed to allude to the famous Post-Impressionist Exhibition which started in November 1910 at the Grafton Galleries. The first of the two exhibitions organized by Roger Fry in London at the Grafton Galleries started on November 8, 1910 and ended on January 15, 1911. It is true that Virginia Woolf visited the first exhibition, "Manet and the Post-Impressionists," in December, in which case her remark means above all: my character, my "ego" changed in December 1910. The very precision of the date can nevertheless evoke the eight months that elapsed between the replacement of King Edward by King George and the beginning of a new decade – eight months which are indeed quite sufficient for the half-aborted or at least premature birth of the "modern" spirit in early 1911.

Woolf wishes to identify the change in mentality by which we usually define "Modernism" with the Georgian period, while the first decade of this century (1901–10), so conveniently identified with the reign of Edward VII, would merely have seen the stammering of a new generation, still caught up in the antiquated ideas and ideals of the Victorian age. Joyce, Eliot, and Lawrence stand on one side of the divide, and smile with the wide aggressive grin of *Les Jeunes*, whereas Wells, Bennett, and Galsworthy still wave at us coyly from behind the fence. But what of Conrad and Hardy, Forster and Ford, Yeats and Shaw? Most commentators are prone to underline the artificiality of these distinctions, to the point that a study of the Edwardian age has it end in 1919.[16] It seems, accordingly, that Modernism recedes further back into the endings of the Victorian age.

However, another version of "high Modernism" inspired by feminism would insist upon defining it as a male reaction to a Victorian literature that was highly feminized. The analysis has been made in Huyssen's groundbreaking essay on "Mass Culture as Woman: Modernism's Other" in *After the Great Divide*.[17] If one situates Joyce from the point of view of the very vocal proponents of a "male" and "hard" Modernism, then Joyce is less a Georgian – a new term which would already sound negative for Pound and Lewis – than a very late Victorian, or, to be more precise, a late Symbolist (but this term entails an important geographical displacement). In the British context, Pound and Lewis often oppose the "men of 1914" to the "Georgians" – by which they generally stress the difference between parochial British writers and an internationalist, cosmopolitanism, and radical avant-garde limited to the "Vorticists" and the group of artists and writers gathered in *Blast*. Lewis's attack on Joyce published in the first issue of *The Enemy* in January 1927 contains the most coherent argument in favor of Joyce's belated Victorianism:

The nineteenth-century naturalism of that obsessional, fanatical order is what you find on the one hand in *Ulysses*. On the other, you have a great variety of recent influences enabling Mr. Joyce to use it in the way that he did . . . It is like a gigantic Victorian quilt or anti-macassar. Or it is the voluminous curtain that fell, belated (with the alarming momentum of a ton or two of personally organized rubbish), upon the victorian scene. So rich was its delivery, its pent-up outpouring so vehement, that it will remain, eternally cathartic, a monument like a record diarrhoea. No one who looks *at* it will ever want to look *behind* it. It is the sardonic catafalque of the victorian world.[18]

Such a view was also voiced by Pound after his *Egoist* period and in a tone which became shriller during the thirties. It is clear that both Pound and Lewis saw British culture as predominantly feminine; this is why they needed to associate it with the derogatory term of "Victorian." Victoria was a queen, after all, and as as a queen she would easily embody old-fashioned ideals, leading Pound to a neat lumping together of her royal dignity with all the ills of an age that would send its youth to die in trenches:

> For an old bitch gone in the teeth,
> For a botched civilization.[19]

One might say that on the contrary, Joyce never looked down on a feminized Victorian culture he would elect as an adversary, precisely because he saw his adversary as a male king. Unlike Lewis and Pound, Joyce considered his fight uneven, it is true, but as a man to man's boxing match, as is were.

Meanwhile, after Pound had read *Ulysses* in installments he could adapt Joyce's metaphor from "The Holy Office" to a novel he perceived as achieving the catharsis of all the ills of the nineteenth century, a welcome purge of the Victorian body politic. Even as he praised *Ulysses* for the readers of *The Dial*, he took pains to point out that Bloom's mind was made up of the remnants of a dead culture: "Bloom . . . is the man in the street, the next man, the public, not our public, but Mr Wells' public . . ."[20] More recently, the Victorian aspect of *Ulysses* has been stressed by such critics as Cheryl Herr, who in her *Joyce's Anatomy of Culture*,[21] shows how much Joyce's mind was indeed full of the trivia of nineteenth-century popular culture. This has obviously to do with the surface realism of *Ulysses*, its naturalism even, its extensive use of news-papers cuttings, advertisements, local and topical gossip, all the trap-pings that in the end recreate so convincingly the Dublin of 1904.

This world had almost disappeared when Joyce was busy reconstruct-ing it from memory – and with the aid of maps and of Thom's *Directory* in Trieste, Zurich, and Paris. A retrospective referential illusion would have us take this world for a given, whereas it is indeed a construct – which makes it all the more interesting. In this sense, *Ulysses* remains indeed an Edwardian document, since it presents us with one of the most systematic explorations of the world of 1904 that are available to us, which is why it still gathers so many "Edwardian" readers (those who treat it as a literary Baedecker with which to roam the streets of Dublin). A comparable time-lag between the moment of the publication of *Ulysses* (1922) and of the historical period evoked (1904) applies in the case of *Finnegans Wake*: published in 1939, this nightmare of a universal history is nevertheless situated in Ireland and refers to the Dublin Easter Rising of 1916 as much as to the Civil War which marked Ireland's inde-pendence.

Can Joyce thus be called an "Edwardian" just because of the massive presence of the Edwardian world and mentality in *Ulysses*? He would if he had died in 1911, which would mean that he would be considered as a minor Irish poet, the author of excellent short stories evincing the influence of naturalism, a disciple of Flaubert, Maupassant, and Ibsen. His untimely death would be construed as having prevented the com-pletion of what should have been his masterpiece: a complete system of esthetics based on Aristotelian definitions. As we have seen in a previ-ous chapter, Joyce never completed his treatise, nor found fame as a poet although he tried with some obstinacy. But if an historical cate-gory such as "Edwardianism" has some sense, it cannot merely serve to oppose an "early Joyce" and a "later Joyce" in terms of publication dates. One idle speculation would be to posit that *A Portrait of the Artist as a Young Man* is Edwardian, while *Ulysses* would be Georgian. My contention is on the contrary that Joyce displaces these English categories by shifting them and pushing them closer to strategies he discovered with French writers.

JOYCE'S MODERNISM AS PRINCE'S PAEAN:
SYMBOLISM FALLING ASLEEP

As Woolf implies, Modernism developed new stylistic strategies not just because of a "linguistic turn" that affected modern philosophy (say from Vico to Heidegger) and culture in general, but more fundamentally so as to depict and create a new type of subjectivity. If we go back to the culture Joyce explicitly referred to as his own source of stylistic inspiration, we can see that he does not call it "Victorian" but "Symbolist," or more precisely, at the cusp between Mallarmé's gentle art of indirection and Oscar Wilde's more pointed wit founded on a systematic inversion of homely truisms. As Buck Mulligan remarks in *Ulysses*, "We have grown out of Wilde and paradoxes" (*U*, 1: 554), which is more an ambivalent admission of belatedness than a claim of maturity. The first illustration I will give of this culture Joyce tried to recapture in his novels is the novel from which Joyce took the concept of "interior monologue," Dujardin's *The Bays are Sere*.

Les Lauriers sont coupés is the French title of the 1887 slender novel from which Joyce allegedly derived his idea of interior monologue. Did Dujardin really start *ex nihilo* the tradition of "stream-of-consciousness technique" or "silent monologue"? Joyce repeatedly acknowledged his debt to Dujardin, perhaps to hide more important debts to prestigious authors such as Tolstoy (as his brother Stanislaus suggested). This has triggered the totally unfounded rumor (still current in many encyclopedias and students' guides) that most of *Ulysses* has been written in the mode of interior monologue. After the publication of *Ulysses*, Dujardin dedicated *Les Lauriers sont coupés* to Joyce by identifying him with a "Jesus" who literally resurrected him, and Joyce reciprocated by dedicating *Ulysses* to Edouard Dujardin, "*annonciateur de la parole intérieure*" while signing: "*le larron impénitent.*" Confirming that he was ready to bring about a serious reevaluation of this neglected *fin-de-siècle* novel, Joyce did not hide an important literary debt. In the wake of *Ulysses* and Valéry Larbaud's enthusiasm, Dujardin's Symbolist novel was republished in

1924, and reinscribed in the prehistory of Modernism at the place it deserved. Dujardin himself became one of the first French Joyceans when he published his *Interior Monologue* in 1931, and finally survived Joyce by eight years. However, the modernity of this novel, still apparent today, allows us to understand the bridge between Symbolist novels and what can be called properly Modernist writing.

In the opening paragraph, a young man appears in the middle of a Paris crowd:

For from the chaos of appearances, amid periods and sites, in the illusion of things being begotten and born, one among the others, distinct from the others, yet similar to the others, one the same and yet another, from the infinity of possible existences, I appear . . . Paris, on a bright evening of setting sun, the monotonous noises, the pale houses, the foliage of shadows; a milder evening; and the joy of being someone, of walking; the streets and multitudes, and, stretching far in the air, the sky; all around, Paris sings, and, in the haze of shapes perceived, softly it frames the idea.[22]

The slightly blurred and impressionistic passage could come straight from *Mrs. Dalloway* – while evoking the diffuse unanimism of the "big city" one finds in the rare descriptive passages dealing with Dublin in Joyce's *Dubliners*.[23]

It is not sure, indeed, whether Dujardin's narrative technique is the most ideally suited to allow for a reconstruction, even subjective, of everyday life in a big city. The novel's beginnings are inauspicious, since, given the perspectivist mode of narration, the least movements become difficult to describe. Here is how Prince gropes his way up the stairs of a friend who plays the role of his confidant:

Here's the house I have to go into, where I shall find someone; the house; the entrance to the hall; let us go in. Night is falling; the air is mild; there is a cheerfulness in the air. The staircase; the bottom steps. Supposing he's left early? he sometimes does; but I want to tell him about the day I've had. The first floor landing; the wide, well-lit staircase, the windows. I've confided in him, in this decent friend of mine, about my love affair. (*Bays*, p. 3)

This awkward passage looks more like the kind of mistake that Joyce would have wanted to avoid, not imitate! However, as soon as the novel progresses a little, it manages to impose its own sense of rhythm. More than the first city novel postulating a new subjectivity, *The Bays are Sere* may be called the first Wagnerian novel (Dujardin is often alluded to as having introduced Wagner to Mallarmé, whose "Mardis" (Tuesday salons) he regularly attended, and he is remembered as the editor of the monthly *Revue Wagnérienne* which, launched in 1885, lasted until 1888).

In a wonderfully complex scene a barrel-organ tune is reproduced with its bars of music and becomes entwined with Prince's thoughts as he takes a leisurely stroll down the Boulevards. The passage blends various types of music and modulates desire in a roller-coaster rhythm of tumescence and detumescence; the popular song of "I love you more than my turkey-cocks" generates the leitmotiv of "I love you more," which leads to a frenzied erotic fantasy until it is cut by "I've my lecture tomorrow" (*Bays*, pp. 47–49). This paves the way for Joyce in his use of musical analogies in the "Sirens" episode of *Ulysses*, and also more generally shows him how to play on leitmotives as structuring devices that allow him to strengthen the density and cohesiveness of his novel. Valéry Larbaud has noted that almost all the formal inventions developed in *Ulysses* were already to be found in Dujardin's novel. Just like Bloom watching the "silk flash rich stockings white" (*U*, 5: 130) of a beautiful lady getting into a hansom when a tramcar interposes its heavy bulk, at one point, Prince glimpses an exciting red-haired woman in the street when a friend unduly demands his attention; like Stephen glancing rapidly through Mr. Deasy's letter in "Nestor," one follows Prince as he surveys his diary and a series of letters written to him by Léa (*Bays*, pp. 33–45), a convenient device that allows us to get a recapitulation of their meetings and slow courtship. In contrast to the already noted stiffness of some parts of the narrative, these formal inventions are made unobtrusively, graciously, almost "in passing" as it were; it is true that they are all controlled by a pervasive irony.

Irony and eroticism are indeed the two outstanding qualities of *The Bays are Sere*, and Joyce could not fail to have been attracted by this original blend. Daniel Prince, the hero and first-person narrator, is a delicate but by no means unsexed suitor of a *cocotte*, Léa d'Arsay, who clearly takes advantage of him, and by yielding small favors piecemeal manages to get considerable sums of money from the young student, who relies on his family stipends to make ends meet. The novel takes place on the very night when Prince has decided that Léa has to pay back in kind, and the main irony derives from the fact that she appears all too willing while he is embarrassed by his scruples and romantic notions about "pure" love. For instance, at one point, to put her suitor more at ease, she pretends to fall asleep in his arms. A rather torrid evocation of her tender body follows ("it is her body's perfume I can sense in the deep essence of the mingling flowers; yes, her woman's being; and the profound mystery of her sex in love; lecherously, daemonically, when virile mastery of fleshly impulse surrenders to a kiss, thus the terrible, bitter, blanching ecstasy rises" (*Bays*, p. 55). This also calls up the cheap erotic novels in which the "Sweets of Sin" – elevated to a pure artform by the Victorians – produce these verbal gems ("Her mouth glued on his in a luscious voluptuous kiss while his hand felt for the opulent curves inside her deshabillé" *U*, 10: 611–12) that *Ulysses* so masterfully parodies. And then, in a telling anticlimax, it is Prince himself who dozes off ("she sleeps; I feel sleep coming over me; I half close my eyes . . . there . . . her body; her breast swells and swells; and the sweet scent mingled . . . fine April night . . . in a while we'll go for a ride . . . the cool air . . . we're going to leave . . . in a while" (*Bays*, p. 55) – only to be woken up by Léa's taunting "congratulations, my dear" (*Bays*, p. 56)!

This technique will be exploited to satiety by Dorothy Richardson in *Pilgrimage*; Richardson is never tired of describing Miriam Henderson's thoughts when she is about to fall asleep ("They grimace . . . Is there any-where where there are no people? . . . be a gipsy. . . There are always people"[24]). The spaced out dots become a signature and punctuate Miriam's consciousness, endowing it with an obsessively ruminating power that makes the volumes of *Pilgrimage* so slow and dreamy. Because the technique of the interior monologue has to be sustained systemati-cally both in *Pilgrimage* and in *The Bays are Sere*, any sexual banter will have either to reveal deep pockets of ignorance or generate dramatic irony. Whereas Miriam is still innocent of the wicked ways of the world, Prince's words are always betraying him, his actions appear at odds with his discourse and show how paralyzed he is by a romantic "respect" that hides petty calculations about the sums he is able to spend for Léa. Alternating between noble schemes and miserly bartering, the call of flesh imposes itself while he muses naively: "renunciations, goodbye to the renunciations, I want her!" (*Bays*, p. 78). In the end, having finally surrendered all the money he had with him, Prince leaves without our knowing whether the leavetaking is final or for a few days. Léa's "honor" is still intact, but if Prince thinks he'll "to the woods no more" we know that this is as true as the song. This is how they part: "gone for ever, the possibilities of love between us . . . Pale and unforgettably beautiful, my friend stretches out her hand to me.// 'Goodbye.' //'Goodbye.' // She gives a friendly smile; on her breasts the lights glimmer, blonde and noc-turnal" (*Bays*, p. 79).

A similar suspense or lack of resolution in terms of the plot reigns at the end of *Ulysses* – we cannot tell what will happen on June 17 (will Molly Bloom continue her affair with Boylan or will Leopold Bloom insist on having his breakfast in bed, thus reinstating the male rule that has gone awry?) leaving the real transformations to occur at the level of symbols, images and metaphors. At the same time, a technique that consists in leaving a character to expose herself or himself through speech foregrounds the function of the invisible yet all powerful "arranger" who organizes the musical and ironical montage. Paradoxically, the more "freedom" is granted to a character, the more dependent he or she will be upon the hidden puppet master! This principle works as much for *The Bays are Sere* as for *Ulysses*, a novel in which the invisible and godlike "arranger" ends up being identical with the increasing stylistic autonomy of each "episode." When Léa laughs at Prince's clumsiness and delusions of respectability, we laugh at both, seeing her for what she is, and then we may be led to look for similar moments of blindness in our lives. Even the awkwardness and naiveté that characterize the style of the first pages I have alluded to can be blamed on Prince's own immaturity rather than on the author's lack of art.

Mallarmé was quick to perceive the novelty of Dujardin's "discovery" – much as Eliot was to do later when he coined the term of "mythical method" for *Ulysses*. Mallarmé thanked Dujardin for the new novel in a letter of 1888:

I can see you have set down a rapid and dancing mode of notation whose sole aim . . . is to express, without misapplication of the sublime means involved, an everyday life that is so crucial to grasp (*le quotidien si précieux à saisir*.) So there is here less a happy result of chance than one of those discoveries we are all tending towards in our different ways.[25]

Le quotidien si précieux à saisir – this sketches a whole program for a Modernism intent on catching up with modernity. The new Modernism is determined by a deeper psychological realism aiming at describing the experience of life in great cities with their countless chance encounters and a lyrical sense of the fleeting beauty of such "trivialities" – a program quite similar to that of Joyce's "epiphanies."

THE EGOIST'S MONOLOGY

Can interior monologue, which as a literary genre is contemporaneous with the emergence of a new ego, be held responsible for this awareness of a different subjectivity? Obviously not once and for all, since Woolf, for instance, manages to achieve exactly the same type of effect – the creation of a new and inclusive subjectivity – in *Mrs. Dalloway* without having to resort to what she would probably see as a crude type of unmediated psychological impressionism. When Peter Walsh falls asleep in

Regent Park after a first abortive visit to Clarissa Dalloway, he amuses himself by following a young woman almost to her door and then dozes off on a bench in the sun. Woolf never abandons a third person narrative ("he thinks" is simply used in the present) but deploys a poetic wealth of images to call up the "dark woods" of sleep and its oneiric world ("Such are the visions which proffer great cornucopias full of fruit to the solitary traveller, or murmur in his ear like sirens lolloping away on the green sea waves, or are dashed in his face like bunches of roses, or rise to the surface like pale faces which fishermen flounder through floods to embrace"[26]). The almost cloying /f/ alliterations betray a regressive backsliding into a subconscious realm, while the phrase "Such are the visions" will be repeated to evoke what Peter sees or hears – and we do not need the fiction of seeing everything through his eyes or thinking with his mind.

Besides, even such a devout practitioner of interior monologue as Joyce never called up sleep better than when Bloom is caught falling asleep in a passage that cannot fall under the heading of "interior monologue" – since in the catechism of "Ithaca," it is simply the novel's language that falls asleep by itself. Bloom, like Peter Walsh, is indeed a "traveller" who rests. We know that, a "weary" Bloom rests: "He has travelled."

With?

Sinbad the Sailor and Tinbad the Tailor and Jinbad the Hailer and Whinbad the Whaler and Ninbad the Nailer and Finbad the Failer and Binbad the Bailer and Pinbad the Pailer and Minbad the Mailer and Hinbad the Hailer and Rinbad the Railer and Dinbad the Kailer and Vinbad the Quailer and Linbad the Yailer and Xinbad the Phtailer. (*U*, 17: 2321–26)

Joyce's stylistic genius is on display when he first creates this childlike incantation marked by a nursery rhyme-like litany which he then subtly distorts to let the work of sleep come through. No need here for the fiction of some unifying consciousness; it all happens in a purely textual dialogue.

What then of Molly Bloom's interior monologue? Here comes the ineluctable objection: isn't Molly famously stretched in her bed, rethinking her whole life and the entire novel that has come to a close but not to a conclusion? Molly's situation can be advantageously compared with that of the opening of Proust's *Recherche*. Whereas the Proustian narrator goes to bed early so as to wake up suddenly without knowing where he is, and thus changes his self as his surroundings whirl in his mind, or becomes the characters of a book just finished before falling asleep, Molly is depicted in a moment of "ideal insomnia" (she thinks a few

times: "goodbye to my sleep for this night anyhow" [*U*, 18: 925]; She
even tries to count sheep: "let me see if I can doze off 1 2 3 4 5 what kind
of flowers are those" [*U*, 18: 1544–45]), which can suggest that the whole
monologue is the vast expansion of an effort to fall asleep – a way of
counting sheep by using a more creative discourse, in fact. Just as Proust's
wonderfully crafted prologue is a hymn to the lability of the self, or to
the selflessness of whoever reads (or writes), similarly Molly unravels
herself as she muses.

The main difference lies of course in the fact that Marcel's sleepy
ruminations introduce the reader to the whole series of volumes, while
Molly concludes a novel without adding much more than a few details
to the impressive array of "facts" we have already gleaned about the
characters. However, both Proust and Joyce need these two superfeta-
tory chapters, an "Overture" and a coda, to make their reader(s) become
a part of their book. More paradoxes preside over this transformation,
since in both cases it presupposes a previous reading:

And half an hour later the thought that it was time to go to sleep would awaken
me; I would make as if to put away the book which I imagined was still in my
hands, and to blow out the light; I had gone on thinking, while I was asleep,
about what I had just been reading, but these thoughts had taken a rather peculiar turn; it seemed to me that I myself was the immediate subject of my book:
a church, a quartet, the rivalry between François I and Charles V.[27]

Proust's emphatic insistence on one of the secrets whose full significance
can only be disclosed at the very last pages of the book ("I myself was
the immediate subject of my book") is clearly played out in *Ulysses* too,
less in the sense that Joyce repeats, as we have seen, "Molly Bloom, *c'est
moi*" than in the sense that he forces all his readers to come to the same
identification. *Madame Bloom, c'est nous!*

Marcel's serial awakenings marked by a loss of the old and stable ego
thus correspond to Molly's ideal insomnia (an insomnia that will then be
postulated as the condition of the ideal reader of *Finnegans Wake*) – a
wakefulness through which Molly can tease out the numerous contradictions of her psyche and her teeming inconcilable desires. She both wants
her lover(s) – not only Boylan, since an idealized Stephen replaces him
in her fantasies – and her husband back and with her, and she wants to
go back to the beginning and erase everything, she wants to sing and be
silent. She is, as Joyce wrote in a letter, obscene, amoral and mythical but
her lyricism is such that she becomes the "prehuman" and "posthuman"
embodiment of earthly desires and not merely the limited allegory (in
the medieval sense) of femininity.

The chapter's obscenity is remarkable for a time when the mere apparition of the word "bloody" could send a printer to prison. While she is so full of contradictory and mobile desires, her center is indeed her body – even if her only bodily "action" in this episode is to leave her bed to reach the chamber pot after having discovered that her period has come. "O how the waters come down at Lahore" (*U*, 18: 1148) is the apt Biblical reference that allows her to conclude the book on such a hymn to desire and femininity. Molly concludes magnificently a long journey through styles, but thanks to her amazing monologue, Joyce becomes his own rereader, the author being given birth again and again to by the constant revisions and refractions of his own language. The consequence of Joyce's steady "progress" from one style to the other is that the author is forced into a paradox: as we have seen with Molly, he has to "become" the character, who is set on the stage dramatically and left on her or his own, while turning at the same time into the character's transcendent Other, the "God of the creation" that has been elaborated. In psychic terms, this entails relinquishing all control to the character, but being invested in a parallel increase of control of language and style. Or, in other words, he is constantly caught up between hysteria and paranoia, between the pleasure taken in a feminine dissolution of the self, and the "male" desire to control if not reality at least the language that describes it. As Stirner had already demonstrated in *The Ego and His Own*, the culmination of egoism into absolute knowledge in a Hegelian mode entails a complete fading of the subject who then becomes one with a language through which the Other speaks.

ALL THE KING'S MEN – OR WHAT IS THE GENDER OF EGOISM?

Let us then return to Woolf's sense that "human character" had changed in 1910. She clearly hints that *her* character changed that year. If it is true that the old "ego" has died, it may have been replaced with a new ego that has turned into a system, an exploitation, an ideology, "egoism." Modernism, as we have seen, can be defined as the age of egoism – an idea to be found in Dora Marsden's two journals, but also among other women writers. Thus Dorothy Richardson opposes a feminine "egoism" to a masculine "selfishness":[28] "For the essential characteristic of women is egoism. Let it at once be admitted that this is a masculine discovery. It has been offered as the worst that can be said of the sex as a whole. It is both the worst and the best. Egoism is at once the root of shameless selfishness and the ultimate dwelling place of charity." Clearly, Dorothy Richardson had followed the transition from *The New Freewoman* to *The Egoist* and she too would agree that Clara Middleton, Meredith's feminine egoist who finally learns from a male society how to achieve her own sexual, moral, and political independence, is both a Victorian and an Edwardian heroine.

Indeed, Miriam Henderson, the main protagonist of *Pilgrimage*, will strike the reader, after a few thousand pages of her reveries, as slightly egocentric. Richardson's definition of female egoism can be read as a vindication of her novelistic sequence: it is worth listening to Miriam's musings because this can lead the reader to a deeper truth. Men's egoism has nothing to do with female egoism: "their egoism is as nothing to the egoism of the womanly woman, the beloved-hated abyss, at once the refuge and the despair of man."[29] She describes the perversion of feminine "egoism" into "selfishness" by a desire to imitate and emulate men. And Richardson continues with a lyrical and impassioned praise of this paradoxical female egoism that transforms itself into its opposite: "For the womanly woman lives, all her life, in the deep current of eternity, an individual, self-centered. Because she is one with life, past, present, and future are together in her, unbroken . . . Only completely self-centered consciousness can attain to unselfishness – the celebrated unselfishness of the womanly woman."[30]

Woolf refused to share this optimistic view of a positive female egoism and emphasized the critique of what she calls "egotism" in the novel that owes most to *Ulysses*, *Mrs. Dalloway*. The term is used when Clarissa hears from Peter Walsh the confession that he is in love with a much younger woman living in India. "But the indomitable egotism which for ever rides down the hosts opposed to it . . . this indomitable egotism charged her cheeks with colour; made her look very young; very pink."[31] In this context, when Clarissa feels slighted, egotism appears almost positive: it signals the reawakening of passion, if only through a gnawing feeling of dispossession. Is egotism the right term here? Yes, in the sense that Woolf introduces a sly denunciation of this irrepressible desire to be at the center of our world, no matter how often our illusions may be buffeted or destroyed – as in this instance when Clarissa discovers that she is not the sole source of romantic projections for her old flame Peter.

Later, it is Mrs. Dalloway's "anti-self," the rather ludicrous figure of Miss Kilman, who is similarly accused of being egotistical: "'I never go to parties,' said Miss Kilman, just to keep Elizabeth from going. 'People don't ask me to parties' – and she knew as she said it that it was this egotism that was her undoing; Mr. Whittaker had warned her; but she could not help it."[32] The egoistic "imp of the perverse," as Poe would say, her self-defeating urge to express her wish to remain at the center proves to be her undoing: she loses Elizabeth, who decides to leave and take a walk on her own. Even Sally, Clarissa's old friend, and a much more refined character, is not immune from such a defect: "She had the simplest egotism, the most open desire to be thought first always, and Clarissa loved her for being still like that."[33] Part of the plot of *Mrs. Dalloway* consists in Clarissa's discovery that by the grace of empathy, she can break through her own social bubble and reach to people who suffer and die – like Septimus, who clearly functions as the symptom precipitating (quite literally) all the failings of post-war British society.

Woolf returned to this critique of egotism in *A Room of One's Own* with a more gendered twist: egotism has become identified with an ideology of wholeness. Thus "it is fatal for anyone who writes to think of their sex. It is fatal to be a man or woman pure and simple; one must be woman-manly or man-womanly."[34] She develops the Coleridgean theory of an "androgynous mind" in her fiction with *Orlando*. Orlando, as a mythical character, explodes the old ego with his/her bisexual and transgenerational powers of inclusivity. This is why Woolf sees male or female egotism as a mistake. For her, one of the worst defects of the male Modernists is their "egotism": "The first-class carriage that takes you to the best hotel in Brighton – that's true of Arnold B[ennett] though not quite true of Wells. Still, there's a wordliness about them both. What's it all for? – as Henry James said. But the worst of Joyce &c. is their egotism – no generosity or comprehensiveness."[35] Woolf has technique in mind much more than personal attitude, but she proves that technique is inseparable from a sense of personality or "ego."

The limited praise Woolf meted out in "Mr. Bennett and Mrs. Brown" to the triumvirate of Wells, Bennett and Galsworthy is for the fact that they seem to respect the decorum required by their medium, which is not the case with Joyce: "Mr. Joyce's indecency in *Ulysses* seems to me the conscious and calculated indecency of a desperate man who feels that in order to breathe he must break the windows."[36] Here, artistic egoism is combined with the radical innovation of a "Modernism" which destroys the still useful conventions elaborated by an older generation, and which is too confident in the pedagogical quality of the new work. The Modernist seems to say contemptuously: if you cannot teach yourself how to become the book's contemporary, then you are not fit to be a contemporary – and you still live as a Victorian, without knowing it.

The main issue is the alleged lack of compassion for the "common reader" that struck contemporaries (and Woolf above all) as the main sign of their being "modern," and we will have to explore the issue of this "new reader" in some detail. For Joyce, his own struggle with the new and old reader started as a confrontation with censorship. The long and infuriating history of the delayed and thwarted publication of *Dubliners*, whose "scrupulous meanness" implied for Joyce the recurrent use of "bloody" – already a great sin for the British censor – and of some political allusions has been alluded to earlier. As a symptom, it merely confirmed for Joyce the irredeemably "provincial" status of Ireland.

PROVINCIALISM THE ENEMY

The figure of the British king is very useful for Joyce since it allows him to create a nexus of images defining the absurdity of all oppression while providing an easy "center" as a target for political satire. This is why in "Circe," Stephen echoes Stirner's idea that one is only free when one can "own oneself" completely. Thus, pointing to his head, he says: "But in here it is I must kill the priest and the king" (*U*, 15: 4436–37). When we reach this explosion of anarchistic and egoistic solipsism, a passably drunk Private Carr overhears the remark and waxes patriotic: "What's that you're saying about my king ?" (*U*, 15: 4446–47 and 4566). Carr's violence proves that no privacy obtains when one speaks of "killing the king" – and his furor culminates in a series of expletives: "I'll wring the neck of any fucking bastard says a word against my bleeding fucking king" (*U*, 15: 4598–99). This is clearly an escalation in linguistic outrage after the mild oaths of *Dubliners*, which is why, summoned in such a gentle manner, the king appears in person:

(Edward the Seventh appears in an archway . . . In his left hand he holds a plasterer's bucket on which is printed Défense d'uriner. *A roar of welcome greets him)*

EDWARD THE SEVENTH
(slowly, solemnly but indistinctly) Peace, perfect peace. For identification, bucket in my hand. Cheerio, boys. *(he turns to his subjects)* We have come here to witness a clean straight fight and we heartily wish both men the best of good luck. Mahak makar a bak. *(he shakes hands with Private Carr, Private Compton, Stephen, Bloom and Lynch)*
(General applause. Edward the Seventh lifts his bucket graciously in acknowledgment.) (U, 15: 4449–65)

By deriding the pretense of impartiality and British "fair play" (it is clear that the king wants a fight, whereas Bloom is still trying to prevent it)

Joyce pokes fun at one of the most enduring Victorian ideologies. Besides, although Stephen makes it plain that he does not acknowledge this king as his king, he replies to Private Carr's menacing entreaties by reverting to the philosophical perspectivism of egoism that is being exploded: "I understand your point of view though I have no king myself at the moment" (*U*, 15: 4469–70). However, Stephen reverses both the ideology of nationalism and the Christian model of self-sacrifice when he explains that he does not want to die for his country, and prefers to let his country die for him. This is repeated in front of Bloom in "Eumaeus," when Bloom displays a peculiar but real "patriotism," asserting that he is "as good an Irishman" as the nationalist Citizen, and that he has plans according to which "all creeds and classes" would have a "comfortable tidysized income" of around "£300 per annum" (*U*, 15: 1132–35). This confirms the "prophetic" side of Bloom who dreams of a utopian future for Ireland. On the other hand, the Stephen one meets late at night in *Ulysses* does not seem to have progressed or learned much since his first flight away from Dublin at the end of the *Portrait*. However, *Ulysses* has already dethroned the young Artist and replaced him with a "responsible" "citizen" – who also happens to embrace the "androgyny" (at least in "Circe") that Woolf saw as indispensable for a creative mind.

One might conclude that Stephen's decision to kill the Priest and the King in his own mind amounts to the first radical step in the direction of exile – an exile that becomes identical to a textual suicide. Such a suicide by disappearance corresponds to the major shift in the novel when it abandons the "father and son" motif in the quest, as well as all the echoes from the *Bildungsroman* or *Künstlerroman* structures. If the second half of *Ulysses* does not merely announce the death of the Priest and of the King, but the death of the Artist, it is in the name of the birth of language (not yet of the reader, as Roland Barthes would have it). Thus the entire period from the first "Portrait of the Artist," Joyce's juvenile confession rejected in 1904 by the editors of *Dana* because they found it too opaque, to the strange disappearance of Stephen who fades away in the night of Dublin, leaving Molly and Leopold Bloom facing each other, can be called Edwardian. But the new *Ulysses* which starts rereading itself, thanks to the page-proofs first of the *Little Review* and *The Egoist*, then thanks to Darantiere's large *placards*, has to be seen in a different light, opening a new space of writing that, for want of a better word, we can identify with "modernity." However, the elimination of the Artist from the general composition of *Ulysses* does not prevent a return of the same theme in *Finnegans Wake*, although in a more parodic mode.

This is the mode which dominates in "Circe": the king has become a clown, a jovial and moronic simpleton, whereas the most offensive insults are put in the mouth of his staunchest supporter. Joyce pays off an old debt from Zurich with "Private Carr" – the British official whose fateful intervention makes him such an amusing character in Stoppard's *Travesties* – while opening up the recurrent scene in which a man writes to the king in order to correct some wrong-doing or mistake. This archetypal fantasy returns with alarming frequency in the letters Lucia wrote to her father in the early thirties, but this can be attributed to her paranoid state. *Finnegans Wake* uses the incident in itself and gives it a central function. The Earwicker family seems to distinguish itself by an urge to write or carry a letter whose addressee or main subject is a "majesty" whose gender varies.

The reader will never be told exactly what the letter contains, but one answer among many is given by the childlike language of the "Nightlessons" of II, 2: "All the world's in want and is writing a letters. A letters from a person to a place about a thing. And all the world's on wish to be carrying a letters. A letters to a king about a treasure from a cat. When men want to write a letters. Ten men, ton men, pen men, pun men, wont to rise a ladder. And den men, dun men, fen men, fun men, hen men, hun men wend to raze a leader. Is then any lettersday from many peoples, Daganasanavitch? Empire, your outermost" (*FW*, 278. 13–23). The allegorical letter which is being written by ALP in order to defend HCE from false accusations and slanders is sent to a sovereign (whatever the letter says, it always begins with "Dear Majesty") who controls an "Empire." Even when the "subjects" try to enlist the sovereign in their murky battles, they cannot be trusted when banded together in a crowd intent upon "raising a leader" (as we shall see in connection with Beria in chapter 11).

Ellmann and other biographers have shown how much Joyce was using his own daughter's delusions as to the possibility of getting access to the King of England. In 1935, Lucia wrote to the King of England about her father, a letter beginning with "Majesty"[37] which is clearly repeating her father's 1911 letter. The transformation of the incident into dark comedy should at least not lead us to conclude, like Lewis and Pound, that *Work in Progress* was purely interested in linguistic experimentation and therefore completely apolitical. As we have seen, Joyce's strategy when addressing the "crazy" predicament of a divided Ireland and a Europe slowly but surely becoming engulfed in another world war was to use his family and especially his daughter's psychosis (with recurrent elements of paranoia, often implying a "direct" relation to the highest person in power, like the Pope or the king, who both figured prominently in Lucia's delirious associations) in the construction of a new language.

One could compare the attitude of Wells reviewing *A Portrait of the Artist as a Young Man* in 1917 to Joyce's attitude concerning Thomas Hardy a decade later. Wells immediately recognized the novel as a classic and he wrote that its claims to literature were "as good as *Gulliver's Travels*" (quite a far cry from Pound's parallel with Flaubert at the same time). On the whole, Wells was struck by the novel's political orientation and the evocation of the "political atmosphere in which Stephen Dedalus grows up." Noting rather naively that the treatment of religion as a repressive force would not apply to a "boy's experience who has been trained under modern conditions," he also underscores the general anti-English feeling which dominates in Joyce's novel: "everyone in this Dublin story, every human being, accepts as a matter of course . . . that the English are to be hated. There is no discrimination in that hatred, there is no gleam of recognition that a considerable number of Englishmen have displayed a very earnest disposition to put matters right with Ireland . . ."[38] This testimony to the political power of Joyce's quasi-autobiography never hints that Stephen rejects political commitment in order to assert his artistic career above all the rest. In a way, Wells may read the novel more correctly than readers who conclude that there is complete identification of the author with the "hero."

When asked to write a tribute to Thomas Hardy, who had just died, Joyce declined to send a contribution to a special issue of the *Revue Nouvelle* published in February 1928, protesting his incompetence and his ignorance, but praising Hardy's integrity "in a period when the reader seems to content himself with less and less of the poor written word and when, in consequence, the writer tends to concern himself more and more with the great questions which, for all that, are settled very well without his aid."[39] Here we would find again an apolitical Joyce who restricts his domain of competence to his language and to his nation – he leaves Hardy's encomium "to critics of his own country" – and Wells did not fail to write his own. This would confirm the picture presented by Wyndham Lewis in *Time and Western Man*, when he describes how Joyce turns into a "writing-specialist" who is only interested in problems of literary technique. In love with his own "enjoyable virtuosity," he never tries to express any idea, since he is only interested in how to present ideas. To this artistic indifference, Lewis opposes the "creative intelligence" which "today" is "political."[40]

However, this attitude is based on a misunderstanding of what appears as the political nature of *Finnegans Wake*, a text which situates both the Irish civil war and its emancipation from British rule and the end of colonialism in a world-wide context. The problems posed by the birth of the Irish Free State are compared with the return to a Babelian situation, while the archetypal family which Joyce posits in order to organize his linguistic germinations function as a structural grid upon which he embroiders endlessly. This universe is indeed a post-colonial world in which English is taken as the dominant vehicular language, while a Britain which loses its colonies one after the other is superimposed on the fate of the ancient Irish kings slowly divested of their power by successive waves of invaders. Indeed, in presenting this linguistic philosophy as his own brand of Modernism, Joyce can be inscribed among those who believe in a "time-philosophy" and who affirm the typically Edwardian value of "Life" as opposed to "Art." But Lewis's perspective, with its ambiguous political position (he condemns Futurism and Fascism as applied Bergsonism just a few years before praising Hitler's classical genius) leaves him alone against all the other Modernists.

Joyce's "egoistic" stance leaves him poised between two worlds, the old Victorian world which has never completely died away, and the shadowy world of the future which he hopes can be "ear-open" more than "European," to use a recurrent pun of the Wake. Joyce believed that his book was prophetic, and thought that the Finno-Russian war of 1940 was a confirmation that the "Finn again Wakes."[41] In 1940 as in 1909, Joyce never doubted the importance of his own work (no more than his own importance). Thus when he was jotting down the sentence about the "the Irish provinces" standing between him and Edward VII in 1909, after one of his two visits to Dublin that year, only one year before the death of the English king, Joyce was clearly aware of his own status in the European world of letters, and of the value of his texts as political tools. The word to stress is therefore not "Irish" but "provinces" – or, as Pound wrote in *The New Age*, "Provincialism the Enemy."[42] In this polemical essay, Pound states once again his loathing of the Irish problem and sees the creation of the new in the arts dependent upon a synthesis between London and Paris. After a few slurs on Ulster and Belfast – "the 'outer world' not only has no sympathy, but is bored, definitively bored sick with the whole Irish business" (*Selected Prose*, p. 172) – Pound concludes with a utopia in which London and Paris would be one: "A lumping of Paris and London into one, or anything which approximates such a lumping, doubles all the faculties and facilities. Anything which stands in the way of this combination is a reaction and evil. And any man who does not do his part toward bringing the two cities together has set his hand against the best of humanity" (p. 173).

Like Pound, Joyce had clear ideas about the ideal capital from which one can attack provincialism as an error or a terror. If, however, the preparatory notes to *Exiles* show that Joyce was entertaining dreams of making Dublin a capital just like Ibsen's Christiana, he never believed he would be the king or even "unacknowledged legislator" of his world (as Pound tended to do) – a world defined by exile rather than sovereignty. Joyce was satisfied with being a "producer" working with lots of "anticollaborators," an "engineer" devising the software necessary to make the universal word-machine function hypertextually. But like Shem, Joyce could boast that "he would wipe alley english spooker, multaphoniaksically spuking, off the face of the erse" (*FW*, 178. 6–7) – inventing a new Anglo-Irish language, which speaks in and out of seventy or so different idioms in order to radically abolish the "King's English."

CHAPTER SEVEN

The conquest of Paris

Yet the past assuredly implies a fluid succession of presents, the development of an entity of which our actual present is a phase only. Our world, again, recognizes its acquaintance chiefly by the characters of beard and inches . . .

James Joyce, "A Portrait of the Artist" (1904)

The men care for their hair like women; this is a reproach brought against the effeminate Paris by Hector and Diomed.

Giambattista Vico, *The New Science*[1]

One focus of this book is an investigation of the overdetermined links between Joyce and the Parisian avant-garde of the late twenties, of his often tortuous negotiations between an international Modernism and an ethical sense he kept of his being above all an Irish writer in exile. I have to admit that an earlier investigation had been motivated by a wish to ascertain whether Joyce's decision to stay in Paris at the time of the completion of *Ulysses* had been no more than a strategic move, or whether he had indeed found a congenial atmosphere of artistic experimentation.[2] I would now like to investigate whether Joyce did not so much wish to present himself as a "Parisian" as to identify himself more subtly with Paris, the Trojan hero and archetype of the seducer in the Greco-Roman world – for Vico, as I will show in chapter 9, the prototype of the arch-villain because he breaks the most fundamental law, the unwritten law of hospitality. This would displace the well-known analysis of Joyce as an ironical Don Juan, a self-portrayed seducer in front of a slyly resisting Amalia Popper at the time of the Trieste *Giacomo Joyce* (written in 1914), to a slightly later stage, corresponding with the move to Paris of the twenties.[3]

My question would combine two motifs, which both intertwine biographical and textual elements; on the one hand what could be called the "conquest of Paris," recapitulating Joyce's skillful tactics aiming at ensuring an international recognition (this part could be entitled: *A Successful Career* – to call up the title of Joyce's first play, a manuscript which he decided to destroy), and on the other hand a more complex conquest of femininity, which would encompass Helen, Penelope, and a city in which, paradoxically, feminized men become successful conquerors of women. As I will try to show, the rape of Helen by Paris can be translated as the "rape of Lutetia" or the conquest of Paris. The first strategy has now been acknowledged as central to most Modernist writers, all quite conscious that they could only succeed if they were to create their own audiences. The second strategy belongs more specifically to Joyce, and to his particular version of seduction. Joyce might well have guessed that the best way to ensure one's immortality was not to storm through the ruined palace of universal culture as Pound seems to have done with his *Cantos*, but to identify with a feminized culture that is digested and recreated by anastomotic absorption. His readers then will have to imitate this complex negotiation and thus transform, if only marginally, themselves.

The best starting point for any account of the important yet minor role played by Paris as a person and not a place in *Ulysses* would be Stephen's remark in *Scylla and Charybdis*: "Paris: the wellpleased pleaser" (*U*, 9: 268). The epigram seems to identify Paris with Mr. Best, as he tries to please both Eglington and Stephen. Stephen hints that Best's obsequious manners just betray a smug and thin veneer of French sophistication. The scene takes place during the discussion about Shakespeare in a context in which Best quotes "French" readings of *Hamlet* through Mallarmé, and AE decides to leave the library, no doubt unable to stand Stephen's peroration any longer.

Stephen concludes that he will put on his "best French polish" in order to convince at least Mr. Best, who has so far defended a neo-Mallarmean position. His silent remark on Paris the "wellpleased pleaser," with its insinuation of narcissistic gratification, is far from flattering. But we need to go back to its first occurrence in "Proteus" to understand its true meaning: "Faces of Paris men go by, their wellpleased pleasers, curled *conquistadores*" (*U*, 3: 215). By the striking elision of "their," Stephen has reduced the portrayal of typical Parisian lovers – rising from the beds of their wives' lovers' wives – to mere whiskers, or more precisely *favoris* (sideburns or sidewhiskers). The reduction is accompanied by a shift from the plural to the singular, from a possessive to an article: "Paris: *the* wellpleased pleaser." The consequence of this shift is to force us to identify Paris the Trojan hero and Paris the French capital.

It is no coincidence that "Scylla and Charybdis" should go back to the memories of Paris developed in "Proteus," since we learn in this episode that Stephen elaborated his theory of paternity while he was walking in Rue Monsieur le Prince. Indeed the *favori(s)* image also anticipates the role of suitor associated with Boylan in connection with Molly Bloom as unfaithful Penelope. We begin to comprehend the logic underlying these themes when they are connected with Stephen's ironical self-portrait as a failed Paris, when his mother's cancer prevented him from completing his Paris stay as a student in 1903: *"Prix de Paris:* beware of imitations. Just you give it a fair trial. We enjoyed ourselves immensely" (*U,* 3: 483). Far from identifying Stephen with an unrepentant Paris, this stresses his limitations as frustrated student and ineffective lover: not even a staunch francophile like Mr. Best, Stephen is merely a secondbest Best, as it were. If the outcome of the fateful seduction of "Helen, the runaway wife of Menelaus," as Mr. Deasy calls her (*U,* 2: 391–92), by Paris has been the Trojan war and the destruction of the proud Ionian city at the hands of Greek "barbarians" (if one may apply to the Greeks a term they usually reserved to non-Greek speakers), this nevertheless can be seen as a logical outcome of a "fair trial" between three goddesses. When the golden apple of discord given by Aphrodite to the elect of the mortals is transformed into a more sizeable gold of an exotic Eldorado, we realize that the "conquistadores" have come from the other camp.

The mention of Greek "barbarians" recurs in Stuart Gilbert's *James Joyce's Ulysses: A Study* – in a footnote which was probably suggested by Joyce himself, as most footnotes in this essay were. It compares the Achaeans with the Vikings who invaded Ireland: "Like the Viking berserks who conquered the Irish 'saints and sages,' the Achaeans were far less cultured than the aborigines, educated by Phoenician intercourse, whom they ousted. In fact, Helen was quite excusable for preferring the *savoir vivre* of Paris to the Nordic crudity of the austere Menelaus."[4] Moreover, another footnote complicates the issue by showing that the Danes, obviously aware of their shortcomings, would go to Paris to acquire some taste of refinement: "Egypt . . . was to the Achaeans what Paris was to the Danes and is still to northern and western races, an arbiter of elegance . . . An old chronicle tells that the Danish nobles 'sent their sons to Paris to prepare themselves not only for the ecclesiastical career, but also to gain a knowledge of mundane affairs.'"[5] In this context, it is fitting to note that Stephen has brought back to northern Dublin unmistakable signs like a "Latin quarter hat" (*U,* 1: 519) and a taste for black tea. One can ask all the more urgently how it happens that the Trojan Paris should not appear in any scheme of "correspondences" for *Ulysses*: this disappearance is all the more suspect as his name recurs regularly in the text.

Was Paris an all-too civilized seducer who brought doom to his own homeland, or was he, as Vico suggests, not only effeminate, but also the arch "enemy" of the main "law" of hospitality: "Thus Paris was the guest, that is to say the enemy, of the royal house of Argos, for he kidnapped noble Argive maidens, represented by the (poetic) character of Helen."[6] However, for Vico, Paris who was perhaps a shepherd, is seen as more refined than Menelaus who, like most heroic natures, remained "gross and wild": "Menelaus, though on Helen's account he stirs all Greece to war against Troy, does not show . . . the slightest sign of amorous distress or jealousy of Paris, who has robbed him of her and is enjoying her."[7]

Joyce, who knew his Dante by heart, could not identify with the Greek side that easily. Indeed, Canto v of the *Inferno* presents Paris and Helen as very close to one another (evincing admiration for those who have "lost their lives for love" in a direct echo of the first line of the poem, with the surprising use of "nostra vita"), whereas it is in Homer's *Odyssey* that Telemachus, looking for help, sees Helen and Menelaus happily reunited.

> ". . . See Helen, for whose sake so many years
> of evil had to pass; see great Achilles,
> who finally met love – in his last battle.
>   See Paris, Tristan . . ." – and he pointed out
> and named to me more than a thousand shades,
> departed from our life because of love.[8]

Meanwhile, it is not until Canto XXVI (thus much further from Limbo and closer to Satan) that we meet Ulisse, an aged and doomed hero brought down by his wish to explore the world beyond the gates of Hercules. For Dante, love as a sin is more amenable to epic transfiguration than hubristic curiosity and unbounded epistemophilia. And as with Lacan, it is always the big Other who has the last word: "so that our prow plunged deep, as pleased an Other, / until the sea again closed – over us."[9]

Stephen's pun on *favoris* hardly suggests that he identifies with Paris in his turn; one first reason is that he does not seem to have "whiskers" to boast of, since the very presence or absence of any beard on Stephen's face is open to discussion. We cannot forget that the whole action of the *Odyssey* appears to have been triggered by the fact that Telemachus has come of age, this being made manifest when he grows a beard. The ·

opening of the epic shows Telemachus' just fury when he realizes that his fortune is being wasted by the suitors' continual feasting in his palace. Then, after Odysseus has returned and is ready to take his revenge on the suitors, Penelope herself quotes her husband's last words before taking leave of her and going to the Trojan war. Odysseus had left her some freedom at the precise point reached by the narrative:

> And when you see that my son is growing a beard,
> Marry whom you may wish to and leave your own home.[10]

This is repeated in the next book, in the famous disclosure of Penelope's dream to a still disguised Odysseus:

> My son while he was yet childish and weak of mind
> Would not let me marry and leave my husband's home;
> But now that he is big and has reached the measure of youth,
> He implores me to go home again out of the hall,
> Chafing at the property that the Achaeans consume.[11]

Thus the presence of a beard on Telemachus' face proves that he has "grown to bearded manhood" or "grown to early manhood," as the Homeric phrase goes, and is now ready to play an active role in the complex domestic and political economy of Ithaca, that is to confront the suitors. His growing beard inverts the tapestry woven and unwoven at night by Penelope: one could even say that as much as the discovery of Penelope's ruse, it is the presence of this beard that precipitates the action, forcing it toward some crisis and resolution.

Thus the presence or absence of hairs, whiskers, beard, or mustache on Stephen's face should take on a crucial importance in a novel which opens so unambiguously with a magisterial scene of shaving. Why then do we not see Stephen shave along with Mulligan, whereas he "suffers" him to use and drop his own handkerchief to wipe a razor? Would the novel be immediately ended if we were to witness a reciprocal shaving of the two young men on the tower?

One first reason one could adduce is that in the first episodes, Stephen is still deprived of any real body, as Joyce explained to Budgen and in his "schemes." Stephen is also obviously allergic to any mixture of water and foam which would call up his mother's bile. Besides, his specific instrument is the "steelpen" and not the razor or lancet wielded by Mulligan, who nevertheless calls him "kinch, the knifeblade" (*U*, 1: 55). The only scalpel Stephen can make use of is that of his sharp mind (a mind which needs a brother as "whetstone" to "unsheathe" its "dagger definitions," to link two different passages of "Scylla and Charybdis" [*U*,

9: 997 and *U*, 9: 84]). With a mind and a pen, one can indeed rather add beards to faces, not erase or shave them: we know from *A Portrait of the Artist as a Young Man* that Stephen was fascinated by a character still found in *Finnegans Wake*, Balbus, the bearded Roman of strange graffiti on urinal walls. This curious mixture of themes encountered here derives from the common root linking "beard" and "babble," leading back to an original Viconian insight which conjures up bearded giants mumbling and stumbling through a wild *silva* of original woods. These etymological "barbarians" are still in need of a no less bearded Zeus who will thunder and castrate, forcing them to shave and start having families, religions, laws, in brief laying the foundations of society.

As Stephen is clearly not yet ready for such an optimistic view of human progress toward collective spirit, we can therefore easily imagine a rather unshaven young poet parading through Bloomsday. Indeed, Stephen's beard must have grown to more than a stubble when he reaches Bloom's house. This may be why we have to wait until the "Ithaca" episode to be given useful advice on the advantage of shaving by night – in a passage which suggests that Bloom shaves a face that we know to be decorated by rather thick mustaches (at least in Joyce's famous drawing[12]) while everything remains suspended in the void of a conditional modalization:

What advantages attended shaving by night ?

A softer beard: a softer brush if intentionally allowed to remain from shave to shave in agglutinated lather: a softer skin if unexpectedly encountering female acquaintances in remote places at incustomary hours: a cleaner sensation when awaking after a fresher sleep since matutinal noises, premonitions and perturbations, a clattered milkcan, a postman's double knock, a paper read, reread while lathering, relathering the same spot, a shock, a shoot, with thought of aught he sought though fraught with nought might cause a faster rate of shaving and a nick on which incision plaster with precision cut and humected and applied adhered: which was to be done. (*U*, 17: 277–87)

What takes place here is a strange scene of shaving as writing, or writing as shaving. In fact, no actual shaving takes place, but the onomatopoeic force of language is so great that most readers will imagine such a scene, a little like Stephen's aborted visit to the Gouldings in chapter 3. The hallucinated textual shaving followed by a "nick" creates its own temporality, between another morning to come and "now," when we are privy to what has to be taken as Bloom's musings unless it is Joyce who muses along with his character.

This passage evokes one of the first actions to happen on June 17 – although it could also never materialize. And while we are busy entertaining idle thoughts of nought or aught, the text has already swiftly shaved itself, cut itself, and cured itself. The only trace of the deed consists in this adhering plaster that is almost invisible, like a textual sign of remorse. The evolution of *Ulysses* consists in a move from an "initial style" in which one could still wonder why Stephen does or does not shave (the psychological narrative doubling a mythical model) to a "late style" which rewrites youthful cries of *Non shaviam!* into a metamorphic and totally autonomous language which uses Bloom's cheek as a mere pretext, in order to continue its tongue-in-cheek latherings.

The motif of seduction is also crucially present: more than the fear of a nick or incision, the real reason for shaving at night is the always possible, even if unexpected encounter with female acquaintances. Bloom – if we can still call "Bloom" this place of text or body which offers us a cheek to lather and shave – Bloom is a Dublin Paris always ready to answer the trial of Venus, just as Molly imagines at one point that she will shave her pudenda in order to excite men and gain more power. But she also knows where women get mustaches from ("only thats what gives the women moustaches" [*U*, 18: 1358]), she muses when dreaming of having oral sex with Stephen Dedalus).

Would then Stephen agree with Antisthenes in awarding the palm of beauty to a mustached Penelope closer to Duchamp's notorious Mona Lisa he entitled "L.II.O.O.Q" (so as to suggest a strong and unpateresque libido), and not to Helen "the wooden mare of Troy in whom a score of heroes slept" (*U*, 9: 622–23)? The "beardless Shakespeare" called up in "Circe" had also probably thought of this issue, much as Duchamp did when he reissued the original portrait of Mona Lisa without any facetious intervention, and called it the "shaved version." Whereas Martin Cunningham, who owns a respectable beard, is systematically compared with Shakespeare in the first episodes, yet when Bloom and Stephen seem united for the first and perhaps last time (at least in such a neat imaginary superposition), they see themselves in the brothel mirror in front of "the face of William Shakespeare, beardless" (*U*, 15: 3822). Traditionally, Shakespeare is depicted with just a trace of beard under his mouth, and with a mustache, but never with a regular beard.

This is perhaps why Joyce started growing a beard in Zurich, some time around 1919, as many photographs show. My impression is that this new beard, covering up mustache, whiskers, and goatee corresponds both to the seduction attempt on the person of Martha Fleischmann, and to the radical change in the orientation of *Ulysses* – a change which took place in 1919, when the "first part" of the book had been reached with the completion of "Scylla and Charybdis," and when Joyce started moving from Stephen's "early manhood" to Bloom's invisible mustache.

As Ellmann explains, quoting conversations with Vela Bliznakoff in 1954 and 1956, Joyce was subject to bouts of depression when struggling with the completion of his novel in Zurich. In those moments, Nora could not persuade him to wash or shave. She had to enlist Vela, a beautiful young woman, who had been Joyce's student in Trieste and had also come to Zurich, to plead with him. Face to face with Vela, Joyce apparently agreed to shaving and washing more systematically.[13] Ellmann situates these scenes around 1915; by 1919, Joyce had found another solution by growing a rather large beard. Why indeed should he renounce a strategy that allowed him to engage in seductive ploys with attractive young females?

An unshaven Joyce need not betray only a sick or depressive position. The bearded Joyce, described either as having a ginger-colored goatee (possibly auburn in color, like Christ's beard) or a dark beard (which can be seen in Budgen's painting, reproduced in the 1960 edition of *James Joyce and the Making of Ulysses*, and whose presence is confirmed by Budgen's description in his book) is seen to be closer to a libidinous Satan, whose seductive power attempts to exert itself in Zurich. It is tempting to contrast this painting with a strange portrait of Freud which Max Oppenheimer, alias Mopp, the Austrian expressionist painter, made around 1909, at a time when Freud had of course never shaved, and which depicts a beardless Freud – a Freud who looks suspiciously like Jacques Lacan![14] The portrait had been made at Paul Federn's instigation: Federn wished to offer it as a present when Mathilde, Freud's eldest daughter, married. Federn, a friend of Freud who was to move to the United States, had been Edoardo Weiss's analyst. Edoardo Weiss, one of the leading Triestine analysts and also brother of Ottocaro Weiss, Joyce's close friend during the Zurich years, admitted that he had been troubled by the painting which was hanging in Federn's office, so that in the end Federn got rid of it.

Psychoanalysis has indeed a lot say about the link between hairy signs and sexual power. Let us note two conflicting versions of the role of the beard. Traditionally, it has been associated with manhood and virility. Lytton Strachey captures this age-old association in a pleasantly written page:

Michelet has a wonderful passage in his introduction to the history of the Renaissance on the position of God the Father in the Middle Ages. He was deserted, he says, worshipped, forgotten. No altar was raised to Him, no shrine; the vows and the prayers of men were turned towards the Son, and the Saints, and the Virgin Mary. What is more the Father had no beard. Unlike the Ormuz of the Persians, the Jehovah of the Jews, the Zeus of the Greeks, the soft and melancholy God of the Middle Ages was "imberbe," was hardly a man, was unendowed with generative force. With the Renaissance, indeed – for so we may continue the allegory – the beard of God sprouted for a moment into a magnificent growth; and so we see it in the Sistine Chapel depicted by the hand of Michael Angelo. But today? What can we say of the Father's beard, the generative force of the World? It is gone, it is vanished, it is shaved! And that rounded chin, that soft repletion of flesh and fat, is it not more hateful than ever was the bristling and curling hair? More base, more vile, more loathsome, more incomparably lewd?"[15]

Lytton Strachey may well be projecting his own fantasies in this passage, and disclosing the hidden rationale for his personal choice of always wearing a long and abundant beard; he nevertheless captures a strong connection between beards and virility that Joyce also echoes in various texts as well as in his use of Homeric parallels. *Finnegans Wake*, full as it is of references to beards, mustaches, sideburns and goatees, is cautious about the equation between pilosity and virility: "and to try to analyse that ambo's pair of braceleans akwart the rollyon trying to amarm all of that miching micher's bearded but insensible virility and its gaulish moustaches, Dammad and Groany, into her limited (*tuff, tuff, que tu es pitre!*) lapse . . ." (*FW*, 291. 21–25).

We have conversely the curious example of another famous exile, Karl Marx, who as he sensed that his life was at an end, sick and depressed, took a last tour of Europe, and finally went to Algeria in quest of warmth. Under the scorching sun of Africa, Marx consented to the sacrifice. As he writes to Engels on April 28, 1882 (James Joyce was then barely three months old): "I have done away with my prophet's beard and my crowning glory."[16] This leads Wheen to describe Marx in the last chapter of his biography as "the shaven porcupine."[17] Marx died in 1883 indeed, but he had taken the precaution of having a last photograph of himself taken in Algiers as a fully bearded man. The myth had to remain intact.

If we examine a number of Joyce photographs around the time he was finishing *Ulysses*, they show variations, that, if they are not as dramatic as Marx's own, are quite regular. One of the most assertive goatees to be seen adorning Joyce's chin appears in the series of drawings

Wyndham Lewis made in 1921 (Lewis had described Joyce as wearing a "small gingerbread beard").[18] In Trieste in 1915, in Zurich in December 1918, and in Paris in the famous series with Sylvia Beach in 1920, there is only a mustache, the chin is beardless (*JI*, 32, 33, 37). On the other hand, one can see a full beard in Zurich, 1919, as I have already mentioned (*JI*, 27), a little beard in Paris in the early twenties (*JI*, 40–43), or a very small goatee in Bognor in 1923 and in Ostend in 1924 (*JI*, 35, 50). Throughout the late twenties and early thirties, watching Joyce's chin is like being confronted with an objective hallucination: it appears and disappears at will, an almost invisible beard is often present as a mere trace, demurely covering the slightly cleft indentation of the chin that rounds off the face, or hanging loosely like individualized stray hairs, as one can see in Augustus John's 1930 drawings (*JI*, 72). It looks as if the hesitation about the beard had been resolved by 1931: Joyce's chin is consistently *glabrous* while not totally *imberbe* when he is captured with Nora in London during their hurried marriage ceremony. He is beardless when Lipnitski and Freund photograph him in Paris in the middle and late thirties. One can assume that he had by then decided to stay in Paris, a capital that had become his refuge, while taking the symbolic step of officially marrying: this is a Viconian allegory.

Joyce is therefore Paris only insofar as he takes up the destructive function of a hero who is no great fighter but wards off an untimely demise thanks to the help of the goddess of love (who shrouds Paris and carries him away to Helen at the beginning of the *Iliad*). This is why the scene of "not-shaving" conjured up in "Circe" also confirms the surety of Bloom's hand, his "operative surgical quality" added to his reluctance "to shed human blood even when the ends justified the means" (*U*, 17: 293–94). *Ulysses* would thus be signed by the hero who embodies the most exact opposite of a Homeric Odysseus bent on exacting full revenge on the suitors. *Ulysses* can be seen as the book of a strange anti-Ulysses, a cunning and seductive hero, whose true signature is just disclosed at the very end only, when we reach the famous triad: "Trieste–Zurich–Paris." One has simply to read slowly the name of the last two cities, and say aloud (both in German and French): ". . . Ich – Paris!"

CHAPTER EIGHT

Joyce's transitional revolution

Joyce's decision to stay in Paris was no doubt connected with the impression derived after a few years of having found there not only a safe haven but also a place where *"les jeunes"* would listen to him respectfully, look to him as a pioneer, and accept to "book their berths" with him. This can be attributed in great part to the positive influence of Eugène Jolas. Joyce's relation to Eugène Jolas can be understood as much in terms of overlapping egos as determined by their parallel trajectories in philosophy, politics, and esthetics. The movement that led to their collaboration needs to be precisely historicized, as the waning of a certain type of "happy avant-garde" with the turn from the twenties to the thirties. It could also be recontextualized from the vantage point of the present, now that the last century's main literary achievement has been identified as *Uysses*. However, let us not be swayed too quickly by the Modern Library's vote, since we cannot ignore that Jolas and his associates had long ago announced the death of the novel: "The Novel is dead / Long live the novel" – a proclamation to be found at the end of *transition* no. 18 (November 1929, no p.). The manifesto-like tract vigorously asserted "The novel of the future will take no cognizance of the laws imposed by professors of literature and critics." Like Jolas, Joyce believed one should bypass the old "literary genres" and focus on the only political and esthetic issue that mattered, the creation of a "new language."

"WORK IN PROGRESS" AND THE "MAN FROM BABEL"

Jolas begins *transition* no. 15 with an editorial essay entitled "Super-Occident" that takes stock of the crisis in values (both economic and spiritual) brought about by the Crash of 1929. While rejecting what he calls Eliot's "intellectual treason," his conversion and turn to conservatism, he surveys the intellectual and artistic movements around him and finds that he cannot identify with any of their programs: he sees

Surrealism as groping toward the spirit, the Bauhaus praises pure functionality, proletarian art apes bourgeois philistinism, fascism has perverted the Nietzschean utopia, and so on. Wishing he could recreate a new individual able to blend the particular and the universal, the conscious and the subconscious, he notes: "But before this development is possible, a continuous subversive action will have to take place" (*transition* no. 15 p. 13) which leads him to the postulation of a revolution: "Never has a revolution been more imperative" (p. 15). But, whereas one might expect some kind of political plan to follow – he has already explained how an earlier anarchism had been overcome ("Anarchism was one phase of our development, but we know now that it belongs to another age" [p. 14]) – the next sentence restricts starkly the domain of application of such anarchism to the Word: "We need the twentieth century word. We need the word of movement, the word expressive of the great new forces around us . . . The new vocabulary and the new syntax must help destroy the ideology of a rotting civilization" (p. 15). And then he launches into a long diatribe against journalism and bad popular literature that culminates in one of the worst cases of purple prose: "The art of the future must be conceived as a universal art, with regional autonomy. We want the most complete decentralization in life and in expression, while, at the same time, working for the new humanity, which will, as always, be biologically monistic, but evolutionary in manifestations, totalistic and autochthonous" (p. 16).

In case the reader has not grasped his meaning, Jolas returns with a more dispassionate rhetoric to the same series of ideas in his editorial notes at the end of the same issue. There he seems to make amends for his earlier position and stresses "real life" issues: "Literature alone does not suffice. We also have to meditate about the motives and directions of our being. We must seek the new conditions of life around and within us, in order to avoid becoming esthetes of a dying decade. We must plunge into philosophy and social sciences, while we form the things of our creative vision" (*transition* no. 15, p. 187). Here, to sum up, it seems that while Jolas begins expressing the most durable elements of his system, he is trying to blur the boundaries between categories that we, today, tend to keep separate – Modernism and the avant-garde on the one hand, Modernism and Romanticism on the other hand.

In the same "Notes," Jolas claims that the ambition of his journal and friends – seen as friends who can now show their "collective power" – is to express "the new mythology of our epoch" (*ibid.*). But, even more clearly this time, he refuses any alliance or compromise with Michael

Gold's *New Masses* and reiterates his condemnation of "proletarian phi-listinism" (p. 188). It seems that one can see in these remarks as well as in the famous "Proclamation" of the "Revolution of the Word" in the fol-lowing issue a simple return to the "Earliest System-Programme of German Idealism" of 1796 – a parallel that can be confirmed by the systematic appeal to Blake's famous "Proverbs of Hell."[1] In this joint dec-laration – no one is sure who actually wrote the program (probably Hegel) and it is to be found among Hölderlin's, Schelling's, and Hegel's collected works – the three poets and philosophers who had been together at the Tübingen *Stift* state that they can only be useful for the German people if they create a "new mythology": "we must have a new mythology, but this mythology must be in the service of the Ideas, it must be a mythol-ogy of *Reason*." The anonymous author adds: "The philosophy of the spirit is an aesthetic philosophy" and claims already that poets are the "unacknowledged legislators of the world": poetry must become again what it was before, "*the teacher of mankind*," "for there is no philosophy, no history left, the maker's art alone will survive all other sciences and arts."[2]

Now, while Jolas is continually alluding to Joyce and taking his *Work in Progress* as the best realization of such a "new Mythos," how can we rec-oncile his unrelenting Romanticism with Joyce's well-known distaste for Romanticism?[3] Should we change our view of Joyce's radical opposition to Romanticism, or admit that he simply did not wish to antagonize his publisher-friend by voicing too clearly his doubts? Besides, Joyce's anti-Jungism clashes with the concept of the universal and collective mythos. But the main issue I would like to reopen is that behind the possible dis-agreement about a collective mythos there is a firm agreement that the foundation of any mythos is to be found in a logos understood as full verb and word.

Jolas and the contributors to *transition* and also *Our Exagmination . . .* are fond of quoting Ogden's and Richard's linguistic theories. This is the case of John Rodker, in *Our Exagmination . . .* when he sends his reader to *The Meaning of Meaning* in order to illustrate how the mind invents "hybrid formless onomatopoeic" to express certain feelings.[4] *The Meaning of Meaning* is a groundbreaking work that starts by refuting de Saussure's theory of the sign as being too "philological" – too far from "things" (therefore not "verifiable" scientifically) and too close to the logic of one language, namely French.[5] After having given their own def-inition of meaning as a triangular arrow linking Symbol, Thought, and Referent (*MM*, p. 11), the two authors devote their second chapter deals to the classical conception of "the power of words" in order to examine the most important myths of language. They discuss at length Mauthner's nominalism (a strong influence on Beckett and Joyce), Hugo's mystical conception of the *Verbe* as God, and finally provide an example of how language works even when it means almost nothing. They imagine that if a writer (not too far from Lewis Carroll's *Jabberwocky*) was to say: "*The gostak distims the doshes*" (*MM*, p. 46) one could still make relatively good sense of it – thanks to the prevalence of grammar (one could say "*the goshes are dimmed by the gostak*"). This is in a nutshell what takes place with Joyce's "synthetic" language. Like Ogden, Joyce believes that meaning percolates through our activities into the world of symbols we inhabit. Language is more a "mode of action" or a "gesture" than an expression of thought – a view confirmed by Malinowski in his appendix to *The Meaning of Meaning*. If Joyce's own linguistic theories owe more to Jousse and Saussure taken together than to Ogden and Richards, it is clear that Ogden's and Richard's psychological pragmatism finds its way into the *Wake*, at least when reformulated as a theory of generalized mime: "lead us seek, lote us see, light us find, let us missnot Maidadate, Mimosa Multimimetica, the maymeaminning of maimoomeining!" (*FW*, 267. 1–3).

It is curious to see how much Jolas and Gilbert relied upon Ogden's and Richards's basic definitions when they launched the idea of a "Revolution of the Word." For instance, in *transition* no. 18 (pp. 203–205), Gilbert's "Functions of Words" starts a discussion of the loaded term of "Revolution," in which he tries to distinguish strongly the symbolic from an emotive function of language. "The Revolution of the Word" aims at promoting the secondary, non-utilitarian function of language, so as to address the *aura*, the "light vapour which floats above the expression of the thought" (p. 204). A true revolutionary is one who will compose a personal "syntax," not merely in the linguistic sense, but in the etymological sense of "setting things together." As soon as expression is privileged over communication (as the Manifesto insists it should be) then this new "syntax" can explore the "dream world" and create a new vision, therefore a new reality.

We will see how Ogden fits into the general picture of avant-gardism later; his hidden and pervasive influence suggests that all the essays in *Our Exagmination . . .* ought to be read together, anonymously almost, as if they had all been written by one single author. They recreate the voice of *transition*, a review marked by its reverence for Joyce who stands out as the only indisputable "authority" all contributors agree upon.

THE CRITICAL LEGACY OF TRANSITION

Suzette Henke has "revisited" the essays contained in *Our Exagmination . . . in Classics of Joyce Criticism*, and in doing so she has acted like most Joyce scholars, ironically dismissing the collection as a series of "critical anomalies," as critical pieces that only deserve to be kept in the museum of early and misguided efforts.[6] Most Joyceans have felt authorized to such an attitude by the master himself, who seems to mock himself and his "disciples" above all – especially when he reintroduces them into his book as the "twelve deaferended dumbbawls of the whowl abovebeugled to be the contonuation through regeneration of the urutteration of the word in pregross" (*FW*, 284. 19–23). Henke also notes that Beckett's essay is the only introduction that has survived and is regularly anthologized – probably more for Beckett's reputation than for his explanations of Joyce, she suggests. "Those decentered disciples sent on a 'wilgoup's chase across the kathartic ocean' (*FW*, 185.6) foundered in a nexus of undecidability but made valiant efforts to resist the centrifugal force that marginalized their critical enterprise" (Henke, "Exagmining Beckett & Company," p. 61).

I believe on the other hand that this collection still remains the best introduction we have to the *Wake*, above all because it does not attempt to impose a grid and it remains systematically attentive to the way the "Word" functions in all its dimensions. It is a perfect pedagogical tool in that it seizes deftly and with a variety of discourses the "poetic" and "musical" aspects of the text that have been rarely studied (if at all) by Joyce specialists of the following generations. The collection is also carefully constructed as an introduction: one can notice that the chronological order of publication has not been respected, since Beckett's piece – published last, since the *transition* issue (no. 16/17) in which it is found announces the publication of the whole volume of *Our Exagmination . . .* – comes first. It is clearly meant as a general introduction to the collection as well as to the *Wake*. One of the earliest pieces, by Elliott Paul on "Mr. Joyce's Treatment of Plot" (*transition* no. 9), is paradoxical indeed since it was published in 1927, that is twelve years before the publication of the book itself! Besides remarking on the circular structure of the work, Paul provides in fact an introduction to the problem of characterization in the *Wake* that attempts at going beyond the recurrent litanies on "distortion and creation of words" (*Our Exagmination . . .* p. 131). The curious collapsing of "plot" with "characters" could be read in a positive light – as if apart from a few archetypal motifs such as the "Fall," Joyce's epic had not really created a "story" but merely a matrix of stories – in which time and space are indeed elastic since "the characters are composed of hundreds of legendary and historical figures, as the incidents are derived from countless events" (*Our Exagmination . . .* p. 134). Clumsy and vague indeed as these pages are, they nevertheless convey the pleasure of discovery and enjoyment of a new type of writing clearly defined as a new "polyphony" (p. 136) that however baffling, always respects the syntactical structures of English. The avant-gardism of the "apostles" never pushes them into a position of "radical break" with the past and with usual language, as was the case for instance of the French reception of Joyce in the seventies with *Tel Quel*.

Above all, the collected pieces in *Our Exagmination . . .* give us a concrete sense of the creation of a new reader. John Rodker's essay is perhaps the best in that respect especially when he sees the main achievement of Joyce as a "complete symbiosis of reader and writer" in *Work in Progress* (p. 143). Joyce will echo later with: "His producers are they not his consumers? Your exagmination round his factification for incamination of a warping process" (*FW*, 497. 1–3). I will return to this aspect shortly, while pointing out that the work of the *transition* critics did not stop with this volume. Important insights were added in later issues. For instance, in *transition* no. 18, Michael Stuart writes a wonderful essay on "The Dubliner and his Dowdili: Notes on the Sublime" (pp. 153–61) that stresses the function of the Sublime in the *Wake*. And a little later, Jolas's valediction entitled "Homage to the Mythmaker" (in the last issue of *transition*, no. 27) discloses an important "fact" or fiction: he writes that Issy might be an "adopted daughter" (p. 170), a notion that has never been taken seriously by any other critic, and that might bring a new element to an ongoing biographical debate focusing on the role of "incest" in the *Wake*. More importantly perhaps, all these later *transition* critics stress the links between Joyce's esthetics and Romantic theories of the Sublime from Longinus to Burke, from Kant to Schlegel (who is quoted by Jolas in *transition* no. 27, p. 175). Put together, these insights embody exactly what Ginette Verstraete has called the "feminine sublime"; a better understanding of *Finnegans Wake* is gained when one moves beyond the confrontation between Kant and Hegel and uses the model provided by Schlegel's esthetics.[7] This "feminine sublime" would then encompass beauty, ugliness, and their fusion through a sense of derision.

THE PLAIN READER BE DAMNED

I would like to provide another type of historical contextualization by showing how *transition* could fit in a general map of Modernism – if the term can still be thought relevant. By the end of the 1920s, the term "Modernism" had gained critical acceptance, and critics like Graves and Riding had produced their celebrated *Survey of Modernist Poetry*,[8] an influential work published, by a curious coincidence, at the same time as *transition* was launched in Paris. If both *transition* and *A Survey* were published in 1927, thus launching the last wave of Modernism or what has been called late Modernism, it might be rewarding to focus on one central critical tool, the concept of the "plain reader," especially if we take Jolas's 1929 "Proclamation" about the "Revolution of the Word" seriously, with its strident conclusion: "The Plain Reader Be Damned!"[9] Jolas and his friends (among whom were Stuart Gilbert, Hart Crane, and Kay Boyle) were no doubt unequivocally responding to what they saw as the timidity of the British, who seemed to be obsessing about the "rights" of an hypothetical "plain reader."

There was another writer (published only once in *transition*, no. 19/20, 1931), Charles Duff, who seemed to follow directly Graves and Riding's ideas about Modernism. He published an essay that was meant to provide the exact opposite – if not the antidote – to *Our Exagmination . . .* Duff dedicates his *James Joyce and the Plain Reader* (1932)[10] to the plain reader in a telling admission of ingenuousness: "DEDICATED / WITHOUT MALICE TO / THE PLAIN READER." The mention of "without malice" aims at mediating between the excess of a purely "Parisian" avant-garde and a more conservative Irish or British audience. Duff provides a rapid summary of *Anna Livia Plurabelle* and other passages from *Work in Progress* published in *transition*, with the announcement that Joyce had embarked on an "intellectual and spiritual ocean of almost infinite possibilities" (*JJPR*, 20). Then the survey stops, and Duff feels the need to answer to a basic objection, voiced in the name of the plain reader. The reply comes from an appeal to the reader's intelligence: "I believe the plain reader to be more intelligent than the majority of reviewers think he is, or than he suspects himself" (*JJPR*, 20). The idea recurs throughout this short introduction to Joyce's major works, until the end, when Duff concludes with another examination of *Work in Progress*, which he describes as "an item flung at the heads of critics, a breed very heartily detested by Joyce" (*JJPR*, 71–72).

By a curious literary populism, the a thor and the "plain readers" are seen to communicate directly, provided that the latter are helped not by professional critics but by an enlightened and sympathetic "guide," who, although self-appointed, provides a convenient and easily comprehensible Baedeker. Duff multiplies asides that mark him off as a brilliant amateur, unlike Stuart Gilbert, who is indirectly faulted for being too pedantic:

> I had read the book [*Ulysses*] twice with enjoyment, and, I believe, some understanding, before I bothered to look closely at the Homeric clothes-line upon which that huge heap of dirty Dublin linen is spread out before us. We may well leave it for learned commentators to amuse themselves with, and assume that the plain reader need not worry too much about it. If he cannot appreciate the book without it, he will never do so with it . . . (*JJPR*, 34–35)

This position, not far from that of someone like Ezra Pound, keeps a robust appearance of undeniable common sense. Gilbert's book on *Ulysses* is damned with faint praise when it is presented as "the best substitute for the original" (*JJPR*, 75). This Parthian shot confirms the idea that obtains throughout: a plain reader should be able to read the text without erudite glosses. On the other hand, autobiographical elements and basic plot summaries are deemed sufficient to enlighten the reader.

Duff surveys Joyce's works in order to emphasize that Joyce has always been interested in depicting all the layers of the human mind. He notes links between Joyce's experiment and various explorers of the human psyche (Joyce is favorably compared with Plato, Aristotle, Shakespeare, Goethe, Freud, and Loyola, for "he knows his Freud and – his Loyola" [*JJPR*, 55]) to show that he does this better than any of his predecessors. If, on the one hand, "there is nothing new about attempts to deal with mind-states; literature is full of them" (*JJPR*, 55), Joyce's "extraordinary resourcefulness in the employment of language" and his "elimination of the mental 'censor'" enable him to "plumb and chart depths of human psyche that were well known to exist, but were avoided with fear by his predecessors" (*JJPR*, 56).

At this point, it becomes clear that the concept of the plain reader used by Duff owes less to Graves and Riding than to C. K. Ogden's pragmatic linguistics. Duff quotes Ogden's *A.B.C. of Psychology* to point out that consciousness cannot be delineated strictly from the unconscious or preconscious minds. Joyce's work aligns itself with scientific models ("His art has achieved more than science or theology in presenting those depths" [*JJPR*, 56]) while literary criticism is also subservient to harder sciences like experimental psychology:

Experimental psychology is still in its infancy, but it is to a well-developed literary branch of the science of psychology of the future we must look chiefly for
guidance in regard to the later phase of Joyce's art, if we are to avoid the stu-
pefaction which is so often the companion of appreciation resulting from our
merely emotional reactions. Until the science of psychology is well advanced,
literary criticism generally must remain what it is – improvisation or guesswork.
(*JJPR*, 58)

The turgid style, worthy of a Shaunian Professor Jones, betrays a stylistic and conceptual uneasiness: this type of positivist scientism seems to
provide a common discourse, the promise of a future truth creates a *doxa*
that ought to be shared by "plain readers" and "plain critics" alike.

BABEL AND DEBABELIZATION

Duff's 1932 attempt is not very far from C. K. Ogden's experiment of the
same year, when he translated the last four pages of *Anna Livia Plurabelle*
into Basic English, "the International Language of 850 words in which
everything may be said" and published the result in *transition*. As Ogden
proudly announced: "the simplest and most complex languages of man
are placed side by side."[11] Indeed, the translation is surprisingly successful, for apart from a few conceptual rewritings ("Well, you know or don't
you kennet or haven't I told you every story has an end" thus becomes:
"Well are you conscious, or haven't you knowledge, or haven't I said it,
that every story has an ending") the rhythm is generally well conveyed.
The piece ends on: "Night now! Say it, say it, tree! Night night! The story
say of stem or stone. By the side of the river water of, this way and that
way waters of. Night!" (*In Transition*, p. 139). Like Duff, Ogden wants to
prove that Joyce is indeed doing very complex things with simple means.
He also demonstrates that since one cannot translate proper nouns or
the rhythm given by a still normal grammar, the verbal inventions are
not as important as most detractors would have it.

C. K. Ogden published in 1931 a revealing book, *Debabelization*,[12]
whose subtitle adds: "With a Survey of Contemporary Opinion on the
Problem of a Universal Language." The tone of this essay is often facetious, as when Ogden imagines that if the Soviet Union were to follow
the project of a universal language called *Novial*, it would be called *Sovial*
(*D*, 15). By deriding other projects, he stresses that English should
become the basis of a new universal language, otherwise one merely
adds "to the existing Babel." Since English has the best features that
mark it off as a grammatical and semantic basis, Ogden's project of the

"universalization of English" is not very different from Joyce's poetic experimentation with several languages.

If we are content merely to assume its adoption with the necessary phonetic modifications, we have *Anglic*. If we prefer to imagine that it will gradually absorb other languages in virtue of its adaptability, flexibility, and analytic simplicity – taking what it needs *from all*, we get what may be called *Pasic*: a foretaste of such a language may be found in the later work of James Joyce. (*D*, 15–16)

However, *Basic* (with its eight hundred words) is to be preferred if English is to succeed as a language used by the whole world in a purely instrumental fashion.

In view of the recurrent reference to artificial languages in *transition*, it is important to remember that Ogden does not advocate the use of a "synthetic" language like Ido or Esperanto, but wishes to adapt and simplify an existing language. His other model is Chinese, and he notices that Chinese has produced a language of great complexity of thought and evocative power without having "cases, modes, tenses, and a complex system of derivations" – whereas Esperanto has all of these (*D*, 104). Chinese, however, is inferior to English because it is not technical or accurate enough (*D*, 132), an idea which is often enacted in *Finnegans Wake*, as when the archdruid Berkeley is made to explain the meaning of the book in a sort of Anglo-Chinese pidgin: "pidgin fella Balkelly, archdruid of islish chinchinjoss . . . pidginfella Bilkilly-Belkelly say patfella, ontesantes, twotime helmhaltshealing, with other words verbigratiagrading from murmurulentous till stridulocelerious in a hunghoranghoangoly tsinglontseng while his comprehendurient, with diminishing claractinism, augumentationed himself in caloripeia . . ." (*FW*, 611. 5–32).

THE NEW READER

Joyce was not only pleased with efforts like Duff's or Ogden's, but also incorporated them into the very substance of *Finnegans Wake* – just as he did with the attempts of his twelve "apostles" of *transition*. In many ways, despite its deliberate obscurity, the *Wake* continues the vindication of the plain reader's rights while exploring the night-world and the pure word. In a 1974 essay, Manfred Pütz was one of the first critics to return seriously to Paul's concept of the productive role of the reader in *Finnegans Wake*.[13] When Pütz, working from a German reader-response theory, started limning the elusive contours of a figure that is created by the text ("A reader figure haunts the pages of the *Wake* – a figure not to be confused with the actual reader, but rather a creation of the author analogous to the author-persona" ("The Identity of the Reader," [p. 387]) he was concerned with the difficulty of identifying a single and stable figure. Pütz has shown very accurately how Joyce would build up a contradictory image, never hesitating to blur gender and age along with the most basic characteristics of the reader. What stands out, on the other hand, is that most chapters engage with a number of fictional addressees who can be teased or praised, cajoled or made fun of.

The appellations vary from "Ladigs and jointuremen!" (*FW*, 228.35) to *"looties and gengestermen!"* (350. 8–9) or "ladies upon gentlermen and toastmaster general" (462.2), but on the whole the book constantly creates the illusion of an illocutionary dramatization of its utterances. These figures cannot be subsumed by the actual characters speaking to one another but clearly imply an imagined reader who is being addressed by a real or fictional author. In fact, through the creation of this illocutionary function, very often the reader becomes the writer, or conversely. For instance, the admonition: "But how transparingly nontrue, gentlewriter!" (63. 9–10) can be construed as a more or less direct address to a "gentle reader" in the bantering mode so often used by Sterne or Defoe. Thus the recurrent appeal to "you reder!" (249.13–14) cannot be dissociated from the constitution of a composite figure joining "lay readers and gentilemen" (573.35). We should not forget the important function of a "lay reader" (the layman who reads from the Bible during an Anglican service) or of a "lay psychoanalyst" (a "non-doctor" according to Freud's work of 1926.[14]). Both initiated exegetes and "lay reader" thus contribute together to the production of the text's meaning.

In the Letter episode, the narrator addresses the issue of Anna Livia's readers and rejects the idea that she is not simple and direct: "But how many of her readers realise that she is not out to dizzledazzle with a graith uncouthrement of postmantuam glasseries from the lapins and the grigs" (112.36–113.2). Anna Livia's nudity is equivalent to stressing a meaning accessible to a lay reader: "she feel plain plate one flat fact thing" (113.5). After order has been reestablished among the unruly audience ("Mesdaims, Marmouselles, Mescerfs! Silvapais!" [113. 11]), ALP reiterates that her story boils down to a few basic elements: "Yet it is but an old story, the tale of a Treestone with one Ysold" (113.18–19). All this should of course assuage the lingering doubts of those readers who have lost confidence: "You is feeling like you was lost in the bush, boy? You says: It is a puling sample jungle of woods" (112. 3–4). The point in

Finnegans Wake is not to find one's way out of the dark forest; one should accept being lost and even enjoy the feeling of a wandering progression through a night of the soul, a state of non-knowledge that Jolas had explored before Joyce (as we have seen in chapter 4).

In *Ulysses*, Joyce had postulated the reconciliation of the Citizen and the Artist while leaving to an uneducated female voice the "last word" of his book. In his arduous progression through *Work in Progress*, Joyce's creation of an ideal audience has first and foremost a defensive function: the "common or neuter" reader is less educated than critics might wish, yet he or she will read the book and derive "lots of fun" from it. By the thirties Joyce, who had already decided to base his new epic on an Everyman (Here Comes Everybody) wished to make the "new reader" – whose forerunner could have been Eugène Jolas – an integral part of his narrative structure. We will then have to grasp how this "new reader" paves the way to the concept of an "ideal reader" linked to the strategic location of a world capital in which all the languages of humanity can be spoken. After all, Babel was a city, and Babylon one of the world's first capitals.

CHAPTER NINE

Hospitality and sodomy

After he woke me last night same dream or was it? Wait. Open
hallway . . . That man led me, spoke. I was not afraid. The melon
he had he held against my face. Smiled: creamfruit smell. That was
the rule he said. In. Come. Red carpet spread. You will see who. (*U*, 3:
365–69)

IRISH HOSPITALITY

Why is it at times easier to recreate the atmosphere of Joyce's Dublin in
places such as Zurich, Paris, Philadelphia? It cannot just be that there
are more James Joyce pubs in these cities than in Dublin or that the
Bloomsday celebrations have turned into mass-produced tourist attrac-
tions! Is it because as readers we enjoy our *imitatio Joyci* when following
a familiar paradigm of exile and displacement? Or is it because, as Terry
Eagleton pointedly notes, Joyce's compliment to Dublin is incredibly
backhanded? Here is what Eagleton has to say about the internationalist ethos of Modernism:

Joyce's compliment to Ireland, in inscribing it on the cosmopolitan map, is in a
sense distinctly backhanded. The novel celebrates and undermines the Irish
national formation at a stroke, deploying the full battery of cosmopolitan modernist techniques to re-create it while suggesting at the same time with its every
breath just how easily it could have done the same for Bradford or the Bronx.[1]

While the prospect of rewriting a *Ulysses* set in the Bronx will surely
tempt aspiring graduates from creative writing seminars, Joyce himself
very soon perceived the ambivalence of his own position.

Quite early in his career, he became aware of a tension between the
cosmopolitan pattern he wanted to write down as the symptom of
culture and a national or provincial reality that tenaciously resisted the
virtuoso deployment of the most varied technical skills. On a purely personal level, the guilt generated by this ideological tension made him

believe that he could not be "faithful" to Dublin (or the Dublin of his youth), no matter how hard he tried, because he could not shake off, please, or tame his literary superego. More curiously, the main feature of Dublin Joyce felt he could not adequately convey or represent was its "hospitality," that is, in fact, its openness to strangers. A well-known passage from a letter to Stanislaus expresses this idea very well:

Sometimes thinking of Ireland it seems to me that I have been unnecessarily harsh. I have reproduced (in *Dubliners* at least) none of the attraction of the city for I have never felt at my ease in any city since I left it except in Paris. I have not reproduced its ingenuous insularity and its hospitality. The latter "virtue" so far as I can see does not exist elsewhere in Europe. I have not been just to its beauty: for it is more beautiful naturally in my opinion than what I have seen of England, Switzerland, France, Austria or Italy. And yet I know how useless these reflections are. For were I to rewrite the book as G. R. suggests "in another sense" . . . I am sure I should find again what you call the Holy Ghost sitting in the ink-bottle and the perverse devil of my literary conscience sitting on the hump of my pen.[2]

Grant Richards had indeed reproached Joyce – among other things – for his negative attitude to Dublin, which is why the same letter immediately mentions "Two Gallants," which presents an authentic "Irish land-scape" "with the Sunday crowds and the harp in Kildare street and Lenehan" (*LII*, 66*)*. It is symptomatic that Joyce should choose the story that announces *Ulysses* most in order to defend his ability to evoke the city. Lenehan entirely anticipates the urban odyssey enacted by Bloom and companions; he embodies what Poe and Baudelaire had called the "man of the crowd," the idle *flâneur* of urban modernity who moreover accepts to become the "companion" for one night of a parodic anti-hero, Corley, whose "exploit" consists in forcing the young cleaning woman he has just seduced to steal from her employers and hand him a gold coin. The "Irish landscape" we discover in the story is accordingly mediated by Lenehan's concerns with time and money. "The problem of how he could pass the hours till he met Corley again troubled him a little. He could think of no way of passing them but to keep on walking" (*D*, 50). What Lenehan exemplifies for us is the pleasure taken in random urban explorations; his mood finds adequate reflection in the streets ("[he] felt more at ease in the dark quiet street, the sombre look of which suited his mood" [*D*, 50]), which end up providing a new intimacy through facades and exteriors, as Walter Benjamin had noted in the case of Baudelaire's Paris.[3] However, the pleasure taken in the exploration of Dublin does not blunt the sharpness of Joyce's scalpel; he denounces clearly the perverted gallantry of the two men, whose attitude betrays once more the prevalent simony: like all Dubliners, they survive by exploiting weaker people and their own values are indissociable from an overarching economic and moral prostitution.

Joyce's earlier admission of human failure and literary remorse concerning his home city may have suggested to Flann O'Brien the picture of an aged Joyce who, having miraculously survived the war, is hiding in Dalkey in order to realize his main ambition, the redaction of a theological treatise denouncing the "reckless" invention of the Holy Ghost by the early Church Fathers.[4] The letter was written from Rome in 1906, when Joyce was completing the original plan for his collection of short stories. In the same letter, he expresses his admiration for Griffith's political program – as the editor of *Sinn Fein* was then advocating the boycott of British goods, a new scheme of education and national service, above all the creation of a national banking system. If, as we have seen, Joyce resists only two theses of the *Sinn Fein* program having to do with race and language (he resists the advocacy of "racial hatred" on the one hand and the return to Gaelic on the other), he can triumphantly assert his patriotism when he jokingly says he helped the importation of Irish tweeds to Italy. The rather cryptic reference to the Holy Ghost and his "perverse devil" can be made sense of in the context of what Stanislaus has to say about his brother's "perversity" (never too far from "egoism") in his *Dublin Diary*. It seems that Joyce obeys a strange compulsion to criticize in spite of his love, to debunk what he fundamentally admires, just because he thinks he owes it to himself as a writer, as a future great writer who competes not only against Irish contemporaries such as Russell or Moore, but against Flaubert, Maupassant, Ibsen, and even Shakespeare.

The nostalgia one can easily detect in this letter was probably due to the culture shock experienced by Joyce during his short Rome stay. It was while in Rome that he drafted *Exiles* – whose preparatory notes contain interesting allusions to a marital crisis – and also that he planned "The Dead," a late addition to *Dubliners*. The writing of "The Dead" partly fulfills the self-imposed task of "making amends" for the rest of the stories, as Richard Ellmann expressed it in his biography.[5] The last story deals directly with the two related issues of hospitality and betrayal, which appears indeed as the perversion of hospitality. The terms "hospitable" and "hospitality" are employed systematically in the story, no less than six times during the speech Gabriel delivers to thank his aunts for their annual dinner. The word also comes as the first of the headings reviewed by Gabriel while he mentally rehearses his speech. "He ran over the headings of his speech: Irish hospitality, sad memories, the Three Graces, Paris, the quotation from Browning" (*D*, 192). This is the outline of the speech as prepared by Gabriel before he has been startled by Miss Ivors's brusque accusations. He then inflects the gist of the speech so as to respond to her ironical remark that he is a "West Briton":

He would say, alluding to Aunt Kate and Aunt Julia: *Ladies and Gentlemen, the generation which is now on the wane among us may have had its faults but for my part I think it had certain qualities of hospitality, of humour, of humanity, which the new and very serious and hypereducated generation that is growing up around us seems to me to lack.* Very good: that was one for Miss Ivors. What did he care that his aunts were only two ignorant old women? (*D*, 192)

Among the multiple ironies that run parallel in these sentences, one can notice that it is the new militant tone that makes Gabriel change his quotation from Browning – he fears it will sound too intellectual – from a "thought-tormented music" to a "thought-tormented age." Gabriel's objective alliance with "ignorant women" he seems here to despise has to be toned down during the actual performance: had he kept the phrase "on the wane," he would have all too readily announced not only their disappearance but his own! The italicized paragraph I have just quoted expands into almost one page in the real speech, which develops the opposition between spaciousness and brittle intellectuality, warm-hearted tradition and sweeping Modernist critique. Gabriel sides with tradition against a nationalist Modernism, and for him, "hospitality" almost becomes synonymous with "humanism." Can we therefore say that Joyce has paid his old debt with Dublin when he puts these words in Gabriel's mouth? Not really.

First, we cannot forget that Gabriel's position will change considerably at the end of the story – he will eventually accept the idea of setting out "on his journey westward" (*D*, 223), so as to reconcile himself with a deeper past he had previously no notion of, even when he was praising traditional values. Then, we know that he cannot become so easily identified with the smugness of a neo-Victorian "praiser of the past," with a conservative humanism accusing the younger generation of being too stridently aggressive. What he seems to be arguing for is a truce between the warring factions, for hospitality, like literature, should be "above politics" (*D*, 188). The family gathering, also open for friends and pupils of the three musical hostesses, which might well take place on the day of the Epiphany, ideally ought to unite everyone. Since "hospitality" is not only a synecdoche for the whole set of family values praised by Gabriel, but entails a performative operation (it asserts itself through Gabriel just when it is enacted in the ritual dinner), it is no wonder that Miss Ivors decides that she has to leave the house at once. This puts Gabriel in an awkward position:

Gabriel hesitated a moment and said:
– If you will allow me, Miss Ivors, I'll see you home if you really are obliged to go.
But Miss Ivors broke away from them.
– I won't hear of it, she cried. For goodness sake go in to your suppers and don't mind me. I'm quite well able to take care of myself. (*D*, 195)

Gabriel pretends to believe that he cannot be the cause of her abrupt departure since she has gone laughing, but later comes to a better realization: "It shot through Gabriel's mind that Miss Ivors was not there and that she had gone away discourteously" (*D*, 203). Whereas earlier he was anxious about finding her among the audience ("It unnerved him to think that she would be at the supper-table, looking at him while he spoke with her critical quizzing eyes. Perhaps she would not be sorry to see him fail in his speech"[*D*, 192]), he now finds more confidence in the idea that he can berate her in her absence. All this suggests clearly that Gabriel both wishes to exclude her from the gathering and to take her as an example of rudeness, of the brash new spirit he condemns. "Hospitality" begins fissuring itself, and needs an alien, a *xenos*, as a butt to satirize and criticize in order to rejoice in its fake universality. Gabriel is thus portrayed as the liberal intellectual who is caught up between the values of the past he cannot completely make his – there is a forced and histrionic quality in his praise of tradition, which is visible in his use of pseudo-epic similes, a point I shall return to – and the growing militancy in a period of impending troubles he cannot cope with. Like the Hegelian *schöne Seele*, Gabriel's beautiful soul sways and swoons too quickly, betraying his own alienation, his gnawing sense of failure, his restless uneasiness.

The "hospitality" he extols as a major political or cultural value is indeed fraught with tensions and ambivalences. This is why he can begin his speech with a bold image playfully suggesting victimization: "Ladies and Gentlemen. It is not the first time that we have gathered together under this hospitable roof, around this hospitable board. It is not the first time that we have been the recipients – or perhaps, I had better say, the victims – of the hospitality of certain good ladies" (*D*, 202). As anthropologists and explorers concur, there is never far, indeed, from the position of the guest to the role of the sacrificial victim, a point which is crucial to understand why Stephen Dedalus refuses Bloom's hospitality.

The guest is a victim because he cannot refuse the consequences of an opening of privacy to strangers – and the consequences can be momentous, as the example of Paris shows. This is why Gabriel then sees himself – through a negation – as an unwilling Paris who cannot choose between three goddesses or three graces: "I will not attempt to play to-night the part that Paris played on another occasion. I will not attempt to choose between them. The task would be an invidious one and one beyond my poor powers" (*D*, 204). Symptomatically, Gabriel projects in this fantasy the very part he has played so far: that of someone who refuses to choose. This ultra-polite attitude should have been expected, after all, from the Trojan hero who chose Aphrodite over the other two divinities, with the tragic outcome that we know: the seduction of Helen, awarded as a prize, the war of Troy, utter destruction for the city and Priam's family.

However, refusing to choose is already a choice, and Gabriel appears as a would-be Paris who not only cannot choose but also fails three times in three decisive encounters with women. He fails with Lily, the caretaker's daughter, when he cursorily alludes to marriage and is "discomposed by the girl's bitter and sudden retort" (*D*, 179). He fails with Miss Ivors, who seems in fact to enjoy his company and teases him out of admiration, hoping that he and Gretta will join her group of friends. And he finally fails in understanding his wife's mood at the end of the story – simply because, in his complacent conceitedness, he cannot imagine that she could have had another love-story prior to their meeting. The three issues that bring such discomfiture could be aligned with the three goddesses Paris had to choose among. Hera, the goddess of marriage, could have been invoked by Lily if she had "gone to her wedding" with her young man (*D*, 178). Athena, the goddess of reason and also of politics would be Molly Ivors's tutelary divinity. And Aphrodite, the goddess of love, must have nodded while Gretta had to obey her family's order and leave Galway, thus condemning poor Michael Furey to an untimely death. Her understatement is even more powerful than Gabriel's lame prying:

– I suppose you were in love with this Michael Furey, Gretta, he said.
– I was great with him at that time, she said. (*D*, 220)

Gabriel's illusion of mastery – he thinks he might be in a position to compare and choose from the "Three Graces of the Dublin musical world" (*D*, 204) – is completely overturned when he realizes that he was the object of a similar comparison: "While he had been full of memories of their secret life together, full of tenderness and joy and desire, she

had been comparing him in her mind with another. A shameful consciousness of his own person assailed him" (*D*, 219–20). He then sees
himself as a "nervous well-meaning sentimentalist," "orating to vulgar-
ians and idealising his own clownish lusts" (*D*, 220). As we have seen, a
sentimentalist according to Meredith, quoted by Stephen in *Ulysses*, is
someone who "would enjoy without incurring the immense debtorship
for a thing done" (*U*, 9: 550–51). This bitter self-evaluation may look
unfair for Gabriel, who seems obsessed with tradition and pays homage
to the rituals of old-age, but it captures quite well the idealizing mechanism he has fallen prey to in his dealing with his wife. Moreover, in spite
of his paralyzing sense of secondarity, Gabriel only pays lip-service to
tradition. His escapism looks toward a modern Europe as a way out of
his country's archaic feuds, which explains his desire to flee to France,
Belgium, or Germany ("partly to keep in touch with the languages and
partly for a change" [*D*, 189]). Much in the same way as he longs to be
outside in the park full of snow when he mentally rehearses his speech
("How cool it must be outside! How pleasant it would be to walk alone,
first along the river and then through the park!" [*D*, 192] – whereas we
know that he dreads the proximity of the snow and fears colds), he
praises Irish hospitality at the same time as he confesses distaste for his
own country: "O, to tell the truth, retorted Gabriel suddenly, I'm sick of
my own country, sick of it!" (*D*, 189). Gabriel constantly praises what he
betrays in thought and deed, flying away from Irish politics to go vaca-
tioning abroad and writing for more prestigious British newspapers than
the local ones. There is some dramatic irony in the fact that he praises
the past just before being engulfed by a darker and unknown past.

Thus we discover that "hospitality," like "exile," is never a simple
notion in *Dubliners*. As we can guess with Eveline, she is wrong to stay in
Dublin, for she has chosen paralysis against life, but she would have been
equally wrong in following Frank, who would probably have turned her
into a prostitute at the first opportunity. *Dubliners* is replete with failed
exiles, like Little Chandler or Bob Doran, who because they never find
the courage to "pay the price" finally opt for a slow inner death. Joyce,
on the contrary, knew that he had paid the full price for his literary and
economic exile. Part of the price was, as we have seen, that he had to
become a "Paris" in order to conquer the French capital, a city he never
fully inhabited as a citizen.

Stephen too opts for exile in *Ulysses*, but while he thinks: "He has the
key. I will not sleep there when this night comes. A shut door of a silent
tower, entombing their blind bodies . . . Take all, keep all" (*U*, 3: 276–79),

he nevertheless seems to be haunted by the previous night's dream, a premonitory dream of hospitality: "After he woke me last night same dream or was it? Wait. Open hallway . . . That man led me, spoke. I was not afraid. The melon he had he held against my face. Smiled: cream-fruit smell. That was the rule he said. In. Come. Red carpet spread. You will see who" (*U*, 3: 365–69). This dream may be taken to announce his encounter with Bloom in the brothel, and hint of Molly's "melons" or buttocks that are very much in Leopold's mind. However, Stephen abides by his firm decision to wander in the city as a homeless exile (a decision which forces him to reject two possible shelters, his own house and the Tower) for most of the day and part of the night. This is why his refusal of Bloom's hospitality is all the more unaccountable.

One would have to distinguish between types of hospitality, Bloom's Jewish sense of hospitality being different from a purely "Irish" type with its attendant betrayals and political intrigues, or from a "French" type which would imply "lascivious" encounters leading to "French trian-gles." We know that the autobiographical basis for *Ulysses*, meant origi-nally as another story for *Dubliners*, consisted in some help offered by a near-stranger, a certain Mr. Hunter, after a meaningless fight, just as in the scene that closes "Circe" (*JJII*, 162, 230). Hunter was supposed to be Jewish and it took Joyce several years of meditation and his having been immersed in a more cosmopolitan culture to tease out the implications of this fact or rumor. One can therefore claim that *Ulysses* is a great novel of hospitality because it demonstrates the impossibility of hospitality. After Leopold Bloom and Stephen meet, their encounter produces the mirage of hospitality glimpsed by Stephen ("Open hallway . . . That man led me, spoke. I was not afraid") but eventually leads to a final dis-juncture.

The first episode describing the meeting itself is "Oxen of the Sun," in which, for the first time, Bloom and Stephen are sitting at the same table. It is no accident that this should take place in a maternity hospi-tal. It is fitting to note that "hospital" and "hospitality" both derive from Latin "*hostis*," meaning "stranger" as guest or "stranger," as enemy: the antithetical meanings of "hostility" and "hospitality" stem from the same root, in a complex tangle that lies at the foundation of social insti-tutions, as we shall see with Vico's philological and historical synthesis. There would be an antithetical and pluralized law at work, as Jacques Derrida has pointed out in *Of Hospitality*.[6] It is from within the hospital that Stephen can lay down what could be called – to quote from a novel by Pierre Klossowski, *Les Lois de l'hospitalité* – the "laws of hospitality."

Stephen drunkenly extemporizes on Beaumont and Fletcher, called by Dixon "Beau Mount and Lecher," and recirculates the phrase used by Buck Mulligan about the Elizabethans when he admits that they shared "but the one doxy between them and she of the stews to make shift with in delights amorous for life ran very high in those days and the custom of the country approved with it" (*U*, 14: 358–60). He concludes with a parody of the Bible and of Nietzsche's Zarathustra: "Greater love than this, he said, no man hath that a man lay down his wife for his friend. Go thou and do likewise. Thus, or words to that effect, saith Zarathustra" (*U*, 14: 360–63).

Joyce distorts John's gospel, since he had written "life" and not "wife" (John 15: 13). One needs to read closely the entire passage with all its parodic overtones that rewrite relationships between "foreigners" and Irish people, all dominated by a perverted sexual law – what better way to talk about colonial oppression? Pierre Klossowski's strange series of novels that take "hospitality" as their theme can help us understand this logic.[7] The main "law of hospitality" posited in the novels has been written down in a document, a kind of charter, that Octave has pinned to the wall above the bed he reserves for his guests – a text commented on at some length by Derrida. To paraphrase it, the host "actualizes the potentialities" of his guests when he offers his wife to them, a wife who literally becomes "*maîtresse de céans*" (the mistress of the house) when she turns into everybody's "mistress."[8] Such a plot might sum up in a rather brutal manner the triangles linking Leopold Bloom, Molly Bloom, and Stephen Dedalus. The "Ithaca" episode, in so far as it provides a systematic reformulating of most of the novel's themes, also contributes to a re-examination of this ambivalent and loaded root.

When Bloom prepares cocoa for Stephen after their joint entrance into 7, Eccles Street, the catechistic narrator insists on the special privilege granted to Stephen by Bloom: "What supererogatory marks of special hospitality did the host show his guest?" Bloom does not use his special mustache cup, Milly's gift for his birthday. After this question and answer, Bloom and Stephen become respectively "host" and "guest." While sharing the same cup, as it were, Stephen acknowledges this sign of hospitality: "His attention was directed to them by his host jocosely, and he accepted them seriously as they drank in jocoserious silence Epps's massproduct, the creature cocoa" (*U*, 17: 367–70). Hospitality neutralizes privilege and, to welcome, creates a space in between words, which needs a "jocoserious silence," halfway between derision and respect. Acknowledgment is indeed at stake a little later when we learn that if neither Stephen nor Bloom alludes to their racial differences, they remain aware of them in this complex tangle: "He thought that he thought that he was a jew whereas he knew that he knew that he knew that he was not" (*U*, 17: 530–31). This is why we reach the very curious, almost baffling moment, when Stephen, in order to thank Bloom for his hospitality, intones the scurrilous anti-Semitic ballad of Little Harry Hughes. Bloom first smiles when he can check that his window remains unbroken, unlike in the story depicted, and then betrays some misgivings about intolerance and fanaticism. However, Stephen's aim, although in relatively poor taste, has been to stress the reversibility of the roles of "guest" and of "victim." The Gentile boy who has been killed by the Jew's daughter becomes in his words the "victim predestined" who "challenges his destiny" and allows himself to be immolated, all the while "consenting" to the sacrifice (*U*, 17: 833–37).

The antiphonal narrative of "Ithaca" follows a very curious logic at this point, in order to superimpose the image of Milly Bloom and that of the cruel Jew's daughter. In spite of the lurking undercurrent of symbolic aggression in Stephen's song, Bloom utters the proposal of hospitality: "To pass in repose the hours intervening between Thursday (proper) and Friday (normal) on an extemporised cubicle in the apartment immediately above the kitchen and immediately adjacent to the sleeping apartment of his host and hostess" (*U*, 17: 931–34). The topographical precision renders the proximity of guest, host and hostess all the more risky, especially when we discover that "the way to daughter led through mother, the way to mother through daughter" (*U*, 17: 944–45). This leaves us with a nagging question: where is Milly's bedroom? If it is, as we may surmise, under or above her parents' room, and left empty by her stay in Mullingar, why is not Stephen asked to sleep there? Then, Bloom asks another "inconsequent" question, thus creating a real *non sequitur*, when he asks Stephen if he had known Mrs. Sinico. Stephen's "monosyllabic negative answer" prepares for his real refusal a second later: "Was the proposal of asylum accepted? // Promptly, inexplicably, with amicability, gratefully, it was declined" (*U*, 17: 954–55). The phrasing exactly duplicates the description of Bloom's refusal to have dinner with the Dedaluses in 1892 (to be true, the invitation had been tendered not by Simon Dedalus, but by young Stephen, who was ten then): "Very gratefully, with grateful appreciation, with sincere appreciative gratitude, in appreciatively grateful sincerity of regret, he declined" (*U*, 17: 475–76). The language mimics Bloom's profuse politeness, while also calling up Stephen's brusque disclaimer, when he has to confess to

Eglington that he does not really believe his own theory about Shakespeare: "Do you believe your own theory? // – No, Stephen said promptly" (*U*, 9: 1065–67). This promptitude or haste in disclaiming links between the subject and either subjective discourses or social commitments seems to be a fundamental male paradigm. Bloom and Stephen appear more linked by this joint preference for freedom over entanglements than connected by any "mystical paternity."

The series of refusals, denials, dissociations would force us to go back to a very obscure center in Joyce's works, or rather a corner – the missing fourth corner of a parallelogram known as a "gnomon" according to Euclid's geometry and the narrator of "The Sisters." Fritz Senn has rightly identified it as any "form characterized by incompletion."[9] It is as if the principle of light and clear, radiant manifestation that we usually identify with epiphanies had to disclose an exactly doubling opposite in a principle of darkness, or darkness made visible: this would be the connection between the gnomon's interplay of shadows and the general economy of the family and society that could be called simply "Joycean sodomy."

JOYCEAN SODOMY AND HOSPITALITY

There are a few allusions to sodomy in *Dubliners* (Stanislaus Joyce once referred in a letter to the "Sodomite" he and his brother had met one day and who was the model for the "pervert" who masturbates in front of the two boys in "An Encounter"), but with *Ulysses*, the central paradigm is provided by the parable of Sodom in Genesis 19, less because of the luxurious wickedness of the inhabitants of the city, but because the narrative accounting for the destruction of Sodom stresses that the main transgression the Sodomites were guilty of was not just homoerotic lust, but a denial of the sacred law of hospitality: the two angels who reach the city are welcomed by Lot, who sits at the gate as a living embodiment of hospitality. When he insists that they come to his house, and prepares a feast for them, he is surprised by the crowd, who insists upon having sex with the strangers. In an excess of charity, Lot even offers his two daughters, who are still virgins at the time, hoping to deflect their lust! These daughters will later repay the compliment and abuse an all too charitable father, making him drunk and taking him as an unwitting genitor in order to start a new branch of the family – incest being condoned once the fundamental rules of hospitality have been obeyed through and through. This seems to sketch the scene of a primal family always assailed by doubts over incest, sexual potency, and symbolic transmission that is repeatedly adumbrated in *Finnegans Wake*.

The best approach to the sexual issue underlying the question of hospitality in *Ulysses* lies in keeping alert to the strong undercurrent of homosexual images alongside the Freudian pairing of paternity with incest repression. If the numerous and tantalizing allusions to Lord Douglas's famous phrase of "the Love that dare not speak its name"[10] do in fact allude to Bloom or Mulligan, then the question of "homosexuality" or "sodomy" cannot be dissociated from a more general discussion of incest. Joyce's ambivalent stance on the issue of homoeroticism – which makes it difficult to pinpoint a tentative ideology of resistance or deviance in his works – always tends to reinscribe itself in the question of triangular desire originating in the family romance. Desire thus understood invokes the cultural dimension of paternity and maternity, but without the ideological anchor of nature taken as the norm of sexual propriety.[11]

Thus, whereas Aquinas's theory of incest defined as "avarice" is instrumental in helping Stephen qualify what could be broadly called a Freudian thesis, Joyce does not use Aquinas's scale of values (in which sodomy is not too harshly viewed)[12] when he lets Stephen oppose all perversions to the almost unthinkable transgression constituted by male homosexual incest, an incest linking father and son in a "love" taken so literally as to prove the lack of a divine love from the Father to all His metaphorical sons. Such an unthinkable limit allows Joyce to define *a contrario* the absolute law regulating proper and improper sexual exchanges: "[fathers and sons] are sundered by a bodily shame so steadfast that the criminal annals of the world, stained with all other incests and bestialities hardly record its breach. Sons with mothers, sires with daughters, lesbic sisters, loves that dare not speak their name, nephews with mothers, jailbirds with keyholes, queens with prize bulls" (*U*, 9: 850–54). Typically, Stephen prefers to quote from classical myth than to allude directly to the "new Viennese school," and in such a way that the centrality of Lord Douglas's loaded "love that dare not speak its name" remains ambivalent, since, in the context, nothing testifies to the exclusion of the father-and-son relationship.

Yet the rest of the paragraph posits such a paradigmatic impossibility of male homosexual incest. Stephen, being cruelly aware of his mythical ancestor's invention, which enabled Queen Pasiphae to enjoy intercourse with a bull, cannot but accept a difficult heritage; Daedalus used all his genius in the deployment of *ignotas artes* that smack of perversity.

This is also why Simon Dedalus's first name scrambles up the name of Minos, the king who had built a labyrinth in order to hide the fruit of such an unnatural coupling, the Minotaur. If we take the figure of the labyrinth as an allegory of critical interpretation, we shall not erase the obscure nexus around which it revolves.

When the "Circe" episode returns to this *locus classicus*, it is once more through Stephen's voice in what appears to be merely a drunken extemporization but could also come from the deeper layers of his unconscious. Stephen says: "Queens lay with prize bulls. Remember Pasiphaë whose lust my grandoldgrossfather made the first confessionbox . . . And Noah was drunk with wine. And his ark was open" (*U*, 15: 3865–69). With these words, Stephen manages to shock even Bella, who replies: "None of that here. Come to the wrong shop," as if the type of perversion Stephen alludes to was to remain beyond the limits of an "honest" brothel. Stephen's "perverted transcendentalism" implies a complex interaction between Greek myths and Christian rites; their conjunction does not fail to take Irish history in a vice, as it were, since the old and proud families of the Ascendancy can claim to descend from some animal in Noah's ark, as befits an episode prone to evoke bestiality in all its aspects, with the difference that here this ark sounds suspiciously like an arse.

Joyce will ultimately follow Stephen's suggestion in *Finnegans Wake* when he shows how the two brothers unite as Buckley in order to shoot and/or sodomize the Russian general. *Ulysses* always offers the possibility of mocking variations on its own central myths, as if the voice of the Nameless One who narrates the Cyclops episode was one of the masks left ready for the reader. If, indeed, "jewgreek is greekjew" in *Ulysses*, then the perversion of the two positions culminates in snide suggestions of homosexuality and incest, suggestions that spare absolutely no one in the novel.

The main filter through which homosexuality is less designated than suggested is Douglas's phrase "Love that dare not speak its name" – a phrase apparently attributed to Wilde by Stephen when he dismisses Mulligan's offer of friendship ("Staunch friend, a brother soul: Wilde's love that dare not speak its name. His arm: Carnly's arm. He now will leave me" (*U*, 3: 450–52). In *Ulysses*, on the whole, it is "love" in general that dare not speak its name, as the controversy about Gabler's reintroduction of the "word known to all men" into his edition has shown. It is as if the name of love was never easy to utter, let alone define. And when Aquinas defines love, in a passage of his *Summa*, as "wishing someone's good,"[13] he also takes pain to show how one can wish one's own good as well as someone else's and lists among the causes of love "similarity": *similitudo* can cause love to be born out of a pleasure in closeness and near identity such as the species can provide. As Aquinas notes shrewdly, too much similitude can also provoke another extreme, namely hatred. Thus one should resist the temptation to name too crudely the "sin." In this respect, one can take as a model Joyce's main authority, Wilde. One of the few texts of his that are directly quoted in *Ulysses* is the famous "platonic dialogue" on Shakespeare, *The Portrait of Mr. W. H.* – another "Portrait of the Artist" as a young homosexual. This is the interpretation that was most commonly given to Wilde's essay, an interpretation that reappears in Mr. Best's rather jumbled version: Shakespeare would have written his sonnets for a young man he was in love with (in Wilde's own terms): "He felt, as indeed I think we all must feel, that the Sonnets are addressed to an individual – to a particular young man whose personality for some reason seems to have filled the soul of Shakespeare with terrible joy and no less terrible despair."[14]

Let us emphasize that, during the discussion in the library, Stephen mocks Mr. Best's dilution of Wildean paradoxes and sneers at his "tame essence of Wilde" (*U*, 9: 532). The "real" essence of Wilde would indeed appear wilder, less tractable, less amenable to genteel banalities. Space would not suffice to present a systematic study of Wilde's essay, but following Lawrence Danson's lead, I wish to focus on the curious strategy his narrative unfolds. As Danson writes, "Wilde creates a daisy chain of converts and skeptics to tell his story, and the resulting self-subverting narrative enlists a tale of scholarly detection in the service of the indeterminate."[15] The narrator hears from his friend Erskine how Cyril Graham, a beautiful friend fond of acting and cross-dressing, has identified the W. H. of Shakespeare's dedication as a certain Willie Hughes. When Erskine remains unconvinced by the theory, Cyril adduces a portrait of Willie Hughes. Erskine quickly finds out that this is a cheap forgery. Hearing that Cyril Graham has subsequently committed suicide, the narrator (but not Erskine) is ready to believe in a theory that is powerful enough to force someone to die for it. He writes a letter to Erskine stating his own belief, but he curiously loses this belief in the very act of writing the letter, which, however, convinces Erskine once more of the truth of the Willie Hughes theory. Erskine then announces that he, too, is ready to commit suicide if this can prove the theory valid. When the narrator rushes to him, Erskine is already dead; but it turns out that this was the result not of suicide but of consumption. The vertiginous series of assertions and negations whirling in a breathtaking succession problematizes the very notion of belief in any given theory.

It seems therefore that the last person to have been converted to this theory (or perverted by it) is Stephen – when he confirms Eglinton's suspicion that he does not believe his own theory about Shakespeare. Stephen's refusal to assume the full paternity or responsibility for a theory we have witnessed him rehearse at length is homologous to the Wildean caveat. As Danson writes: "Any attempt to stop the play of Wilde's narrative and say what it is *really* about will either demonize or neuter it."[16] Like Wilde, Joyce knows that imputations of sexual perversion often reveal more about those who proffer them – much as the Marquis of Queensbury's curious slip of the pen accusing Oscar Wilde of being a "posing so*m*domite" can be read as "son-domite" thus betraying the presence of his own son behind the scandal.[17]

Before drawing the full consequences of such a hermeneutic principle, let us return to one of the most crucial introductions to Joyce's fiction, the beginning of "The Sisters" in *Dubliners*. This story has received all the attention it deserves, yet something remains unsaid in the famous "sin" linking the young narrator and the old paralytic priest. An exchange takes place during the boy's dream: the boy sees himself partaking of a smile that suggests a perverse communion. "I too was smiling feebly, as if to absolve the simoniac of his sin." The anaphoric /s/ sound stresses the contagion of a sin which also suggests "sodomy" (it could almost be rephrased as: "as if to absolve the sodomic of his son") – at least in the Dantean mode of Canto xv, when Dante and Virgil meet Brunetto Latini. Brunetto's true role and place have still to be ascertained: he was not generally taken as a homosexual yet appears among the Sodomites and calls Dante "my son" twice in the canto (xv. 31 and 37), whereas Dante confirms the paternal function he has played for him, stressing the "dear, good paternal image" he has kept of Brunetto (xv. 83–84).[18]

It would be tempting to see in the repressed term of "sodomy" the fourth or missing corner of the "gnomon" evoked by the boy in the first paragraph of the story. I have already evoked the esthetic paradox or dichotomy that has often been overlooked: if the notion of epiphany calls up a "shining forth," a luminous revelation, the gnomon contains an ana-phanic counter-principle that hints of a dark and incomplete disclosure. It is fitting here that sodomy should be seen as "visible darkness" and never fully emerges out of its dim casket or closet. Sodomy would thus appear as the arch-sin, precisely because in its inception it just describes a city in which human relations are perverted, without bringing a clear accusation against male homoeroticism.

Let us return once more to Chapter 19 of Genesis; I have described the sin committed by the inhabitants of Sodom as a transgression against the sacred law of hospitality. The Sodomites are the Bible's Lestrygonians, as it were, who sexually cannibalize any stranger coming their way. Why, indeed, is Lot so eager to offer his two virgin daughters in a desperate effort to protect the angels from the mob's lust? By a further dramatic irony, the same daughters he was ready to sacrifice in an extreme instance of charity, once they have fled the destruction of Sodom with him, will take advantage of his sleep in the cave and have him engender two sons, thus starting the lines of Moabites and of the Ammonites – two tribes who will later become fierce enemies of Israel (Genesis 19: 31–38). If such a paternity remains unconscious (Lot being drunk repeats Noah's drunkenness of Genesis 9: 21), the consequence of Sodom is another transgression, an incest apparently condoned by the Bible and by history.

In the context of *Dubliners*, "sodomy" seems fitting to provide a name for Dublin's paralysis or "hemiplegia," that could thus be renamed "Dubliny." The rain of fire that destroys Sodom and Gomorrah also provides the Sodomites of *Inferno* with a punishment neatly designed by the *contrapasso*. Bloom rightly situates these cities next to the Dead Sea and connects them not with male homoeroticism but with an exhausted female organ: "Brimstone they called it raining down: the cities of the plain: Sodom, Gomorrah, Edom. All dead names. A dead sea in a dead land, grey and old. Old now. It bore the oldest, the first race . . . Dead: an old woman's: the grey sunken cunt of the world" (*U*, 4: 221–28). Female sterility stamps the mark of Sodomite sin, not male homoeroticism, according to Bloom at least. This is why, as I have contended, one should read *Ulysses* as a novel describing the necessity and the impossibility of hospitality: if Stephen had accepted Bloom's offer of a shelter during the first hours of June 17, 1904, he would not only have accepted him as a surrogate (or "symbolic") "father," but would have had to conform to one of the many developments foreseen by his host – of which marrying Milly or becoming Molly's new lover would only be two (and heterosexual at that) of all the other possible outcomes. Stephen cannot accept any more than he can return to the Tower; both male tempters, Buck Mulligan and Leopold Bloom, perform a sodomite variation on simony in offering him a substitute family (necessarily perverse in some way) and a last attempt to accept life in Dublin.

A more radical exile than a stay in a nearby cave (accompanied or not by tempting young females) is required of him. In *Ulysses* as in "The Sisters," the only solution is the abrupt discontinuity of leavetaking, which triggers the work of mourning of the young boy, or accounts for the "inexplicable" way in which Stephen refuses Bloom's hospitality. This is how Joyce manages to posit a paternity that is neither "real" (since Simon Dedalus is still present) nor "symbolic" (or Homeric, Bloom forcefully fitted in Odysseus' shoes), but that plays with distance, absence, and alterity in order to avoid the trap of perversion. What is the core of this curious relation that borders on lack of relation? The problem can be put as different ways of avoiding any love that would testify to some corruption, and to replace it by a mystical or saintly attitude. This seems to define the nexus of what Stephen calls "original sin" in connection with his discussion of Shakespeare. Shakespeare is driven by an urge to create, possibly in order to blind himself to truth, since he is always already dispossessed of whatever he may produce. This derives from his first defeat, his having been seduced too early by a more mature woman, his future wife. "No later undoing will undo the first undoing. The tusk of the boar has wounded him there where love lies ableeding ... There is, I feel in the words, some goad of the flesh driving him to a new passion, a darker shadow of the first, darkening even his own understanding of himself" (*U*, 9: 459–64).

Stephen's demonstration is quite cunning in that it links the role of femininity in Shakespeare's "undoing" to an original reformulation of the definition of "original sin" in the Maynooth Catechism. Such an "undoing" is literally another form of paralysis (etymologically, "untying"), while Shakespeare could appear here superimposed on James Flynn. Original sin entails the male sharing of a knowledge akin to a contagious disease, yet which paradoxically weakens the understanding of the disease. This opens onto the specifically Joycean notion of a "gnomon" linking simony and sodomy. Something resists comprehension in the transmission of an unnamable sin chaining father and son together but in an absolute void. The central element to be stressed here is obscurity, not the precisely homoerotic factor (which is always to be avoided at any cost) in and of the structure.

It took many years before Joyce could simply face the fact that what he was exploring was precisely the obscurity that surrounds sin and paternity alike. He had also meanwhile to resist an impulse to name it all too clearly. This can be seen in the shifting evaluation of Oscar Wilde's transgression. In a letter from August 19, 1906, Joyce writes about Wilde's *Picture of Dorian Gray*:

I can imagine the capital which Wilde's prosecuting counsel made out of certain parts of it. It is not very difficult to read between the lines. Wilde seems to have had some good intentions in writing it – some wish to put himself before the world – but the book is rather crowded with lies and epigrams. If he had had the courage to develop the allusions in the book, it might have been better. (*LII*, 150)

This proves that in 1906 Joyce still clings to a romantic notion of an author faulted for "not daring" to speak the name of the perversion he describes, still hesitant to "come out," as it were. His wit and epigrams are mere disguises for a truth that ought to be exposed fully. Only three years later, in the paper written in Italian for the *Piccolo della Sera*, Joyce has become more sophisticated, more wary of naming this "truth." He quotes the famous statement Wilde gave as a defense of his only novel to the *Scots Observer* and then generalizes boldly:

Everyone, he wrote, sees his own sin in Dorian Gray (Wilde's best known novel). What Dorian Gray's sin was no one says and no one knows. Anyone who recognizes it has committed it. // Here we touch the pulse of Wilde's art – sin. He deceived himself into believing that he was the bearer of good news of neo-paganism to an enslaved people . . . But if some truth adheres to his subjective interpretations of Aristotle, to his restless thought that proceeds by sophisms rather than syllogisms, to his assimilations of natures as foreign to his as the delinquent is to the humble, at its very base is the truth inherent in the soul of Catholicism: that man cannot reach the divine heart except through that sense of separation and loss called sin. (*CW*, 204–05)

The Italian context cannot suffice to explain this extraordinary reversal of Wilde's explicit values; while treating him as a crypto-Catholic, Joyce seems indeed to be speaking about himself. Whereas Wilde spent all his life denying any validity to the sense of religious transgression the religious sense returns as the full repressed it was. In fact, by naming his "sin" just "sin" (and not "sodomy" for instance), Joyce suggests that the sin, if it is to keep its full value, cannot be reduced to a sexual content. The sin's meaning is produced by an interpretation that performs what it identifies. The "picture" is thus indeed a mirror for the reader who projects his or her fantasies. And the entire piece on Wilde moves tellingly from a meditation on Wilde's proud "titles" (Oscar Fingal O'Flahertie Wills Wilde, later transformed by Joyce into "Fingal Mac Oscar Onesine

Bagearse Boniface" [*FW*, 46.20]) by which he was addressed during the trial, to an acceptance of the final role selected for himself by the Irish dramatist: that of a fallen Christ. He also represents the "dishonored exile" (*CW*, 201) whose death in Paris in 1900 not only marks the end of the *fin-de-siècle* era, but also heralds a new period – in which young Irish esthetes attempt to "grow out of Wilde and paradoxes" (*U*, 1: 554) and yet remain, as Mulligan's phraseology suggests, bound up in Wilde's sophistic and enthymemic network.

Wilde looms large in *Finnegans Wake*, in which he seems to have replaced another victim of Irish and English hypocrisy, Parnell. Both Parnell and Wilde used self-defeating tactics and exemplify the central predicament of the great man turned into scapegoat, be it in the field of politics or esthetics. Indeed, Wilde almost perversely attracted doom by interfering in a bitter struggle between a father and a son (the Marquess of Queensbury and Lord Alfred Douglas). The lopped-off corner of a symbolic gnomon would be an adequate figure limning their post-oedipal rivalry. Like Meredith's *The Ordeal of Richard Feverel* – with its opposition between a "system" of education and misguided spontaneity – "Wilde's love that dare not speak its name" (as if Douglas's phrase had been attributed by Stephen to Wilde, through the calculated indecision of the genitive) is clearly based upon "a history of Father and Son."

I have already alluded to Queensbury's misspelling of "sodomite" as "somdomite." This misspelling led Wilde to take the fateful decision of suing for libel. In his "For Oscar Wilde posing somdomite," it seems that Queensbury expressed anger at the fact that Wilde was a mere "poser,"[19] while betraying his rage in front of his own son. During the trial, Wilde's first mistake was to lie about his age, declaring he was thirty-nine when he in fact was forty-one; he thus was forced to appear in doubt about his own age and to expose his own negation: "I have no wish to pose as being young. I am thirty-nine or forty."[20] In *Finnegans Wake*, where Wilde becomes one of the central characters, Joyce stresses the general intermeshing of culpability in order to universalize sodomy: "We've heard it aye since songdom was gemurrmal. As he was queering his shoolthers. So was I. And as I was cleansing my fausties. So was he. And as way ware puffing our blowbags. Souwouyou" (*FW*, 251.36–252.3). This relatively transparent sentence affirms the catholicity of reciprocal sinning. Sodom still defines the Wildean sin, but the fall of this particular city becomes part of the universal comedy whose Viconian coordinates make it inseparable from the way civilization needs the social construction of family and the law to survive.

Such an assertion of communal transgression nevertheless seems deprived of any tragic character, as when Shaun accuses Shem of all possible sins and states that he will finally tackle directly "the malice of your transgression" (*FW*, 189.3) by diving with his brother and their female audience into a universal fountain of life and sin, "while we all swin together in the pool of Sodom?" (*FW*, 88 23–24). This "swin" is ineluctably linked to the difficulty met by all the jurymen in the *Wake*, when they try to dissociate the accusations of sodomy from the pandemic incest in the Earwicker family. Sam Slote has shown how an entry in notebook vi.B.2 refers to the strange suspicions about Wilde's father, a renowned otologist, when he was accused of having chloroformed and raped a patient: "HCE names/ – chloroformed /incest."[21] This reappears as another accusation against HCE when he is thought to have drugged and abused Issy. The irony is that both in Doctor Wilde's case and in Earwicker's trial, their wronged wives come up to offer the strongest defense of their husbands' morality.

Wilde is thus an arch-sodomite for Joyce not only because of the homosexuality that emerged with many lurid details during his trial. He is heir to a suspicious doctor who founded the Royal Victoria Eye and Ear Hospital in Dublin, and whose name had already been translated once: as Oscar Wilde's son narrates it, the origin of the name was Dutch and was translated as "builder": "A certain Ralph Wilde from Durham was supposed to have crossed over to Ireland and have settled as a builder in Dublin. This is apocryphal. My ancestor's name was unquestionably de Wilde, and its Dutch pronunciation puzzled the simple Irish folk, with the result that 'de Vilde' very soon became 'the builder'."[22] A passage in the *Wake* seems to allude to this incident, mentioning the "charnelcysts of a weedwastewoldwevild when Ralph the Retriever ranges to jawrode his knuts knuckles" (*FW*, 613.19–22). It is relatively easy to admit that Wilde also falls into the great category of doomed "masterbuilders," precisely because his name – and his works – confirm the link between sin and son, and also between the building of Dublin and Biblical sodomy.

Despite Joyce's adherence to the anti-homoerotic prejudice of his time, he does not actually condemn (or endorse) a sodomy that becomes tantamount to the arch-sin, precisely because it is never reducible to transgressions such as those a tribunal might define. Joyce's purgatorial and comic sense of sodomy locates it primarily in language; sees it indissociable from the web of slander and gossip that always needs fresh butts to feed its endless discourse. All this noise barely hides a fundamental unspeakability. *Finnegans Wake* is built on this paradox and constructs the only adequate linguistic equivalent for such a collective obsession. Its material is offered by obscene jokes, tall tales such as those of the Norwegian captain or the Russian general, family narratives such as the father's encounter with a young man in Phoenix Park where privates are wont to masturbate and sexy girls to urinate – all of which hinges on the omnipresence of guilt. A guilt that never denies sexual division, since it relies upon it, but transgresses infinitely all other boundaries so as to force all readers to admit a common legacy of sin which makes us all "sons of the sod": "To say too us to be every tim, nick and larry of us, sons of the sod, sons, littlesons, yea and lealittlesons, when usses not to be, every sue, siss and sally of us, dugters of Nan! Accusative ahnsire! Damadam to infinities!" (*FW*, 19.26–30).

HOSTIS AND THE ENEMY

In the context of this discussion of sodomy and hospitality, the question one might want to ask at the end of *Ulysses* – "Where will Stephen sleep?" – can appear idle. First of all, why should one assume that Stephen must sleep? Already described as a "noctambulist," he clearly follows in the steps of Milly's "somnambulism" (*U*, 17: 929–30). He is not just the future author of *Ulysses*, rather one of the future "anti-collaborators" of *Finnegans Wake* – his "ideal insomnia" preparing him well for the function of "ideal reader" (120.13 14) inscribed in the very text. In a later chapter, I will return to the analysis of the functions of this "ideal reader," a reader whose being is predetermined by a concept of hospitality. Before sketching this new figure, I would like to insist upon the importance of hospitality in the structure of *Finnegans Wake*.

Finnegans Wake is largely based on Vico's *Scienza Nuova*, a treatise that elaborates a theory of universal history from mainly philological insights into various languages. Vico's standpoint is systematically anti-Cartesian, since he believed that men could never reach any truth about substance, matter, movement, and infinity, issues that should be left to God who created the world, but that they could know what they had created themselves, namely language, stories, culture, laws, cities, monuments, civilizations. Like Kant, but with a different slant, Vico refutes both dogmatism and skepticism by the principle of certitude which stems from my knowing what I have achieved by myself. *Verum* and *Factum* momentously merge for the pragmatic subject of knowledge and action. Moreover, if abstract knowledge of metaphysical notions has to be replaced by documents, historical data that remain particular to a language, a place, even a few tutelary divinities, one can surmise that Providence merely functions as a unifying myth in Vico's system, and that the real point of departure for his historiographical meta-narrative is less universal than particular. In fact, Vico's ambitious reconstruction is founded on one particular country, his own, Italy, whose wisdom he deems more ancient than that of Greece (Vico thought that Roman concepts had been inspired by an Etruscan culture that was earlier than Greek philosophy and had probably been adapted by Greek translators).[23] Vico insists less on Roman centralism than on the particularism of the Neapolitan South, on specifically idiomatic gods and heroes, and on the regenerative function of local plebeians.

Vico's *New Science* explains the origin of Rome – less archaic as a model than Homer's evocations of kings, heroes, and giants, but the constant paradigm of a universalism that will provide a frame for all subsequent civilizations – as having been due to hospitality, or *philoxenia*. He assumes that the original family units, gathered around one central archaic father, often mutinied and disbanded, because of the endemic violence implied in these rapports. "Thereupon the strong, with a fierceness born of their union in the society of families, slew the violent who had violated their lands, and took under their protection the miserable creatures who had fled from them."[24] This generated the "heroism of virtue" for which Rome became known, the principle being of sparing the submissive fugitives and declaring relentless war on too proud enemies. This virtue allowed for the transition from "the feral state, fierce and untamed" to "human society" and "matrimony" (*SN*, 196). "Thus marriage emerged as the first kind of friendship in the world; whence Homer, to indicate that Jove and Juno lay together, says with heroic gravity that 'they celebrated their friendship.' The Greek word for friendship, *philia*, is from the same root as *phileo*, to love; and from it is derived the latin *filius*, son" (*SN*, 196). This is why the history of early Rome acquires such an importance for Vico; it is there that one can distinguish between the children of the *famuli*, the former refugees, and the *liberi*, sons of the former heroes. All heroic cities were founded as asylums: Cadmus founded Thebes as an asylum, Theseus declared Athens an "altar of the unhappy" (by which, according to Vico, one meant "the impious vagabonds who were without all the divine and human blessings that human society had afforded the pious"). The same obtains of Rome: "Romulus founds Rome by opening an asylum in the clearing; or rather, as founder of new cities, he, with his comrades, founds it on the institution of the asylums from which the ancient cities of Latium had arisen." (*SN*, 200).

According to Vico, a civilization is measured by its capacity to turn strangers into guests:

the asylums were the origins of the cities, whose eternal property it is that men live secure from violence in them. In this way, from the multitude of impious vagabonds who everywhere repaired to the lands of the pious and strong and found safety there, came Jove's gracious title, the hospitable. For the asylums were the first hospices in the world, and those who were there received were the first guests or strangers of the first cities. (*SN*, 200)

Vico is not, however, a sentimentalist like Gabriel, and he never omits a consideration of internal tensions brought about by the arrival of new-comers. He shrewdly notes that in the early Rome, the patricians, who held all the power, considered the plebeians not only as inferiors but as enemies: he explains how, when cities were founded on "orders of nobles and troops of plebeians," two consequences arose: "(1) that the plebeians always wanted to change the form of government, as in fact it is always they who change it, and (2) that the nobles always want to keep it as it is" (*SN*, 225). One can verify here how forcefully Vico anticipates Marx.

Another disjuncture is generated from such an internal strife: a first division opposes the "wise" and the "vulgar," an epithet for the plebe-ians who were considered as foreigners by the nobles. "The second divi-sion was that between citizen and *hostis*, which meant both guest or stranger and enemy, for the first cities were composed of heroes and of those received in their asylums" (*SN*, 225). Vico's philology is correct in this case: Emile Benveniste has also noticed the curious derivations between one sense of *hostis* (a guest, foreigner who has certain rights, similar if not identical to a Roman citizen's) and the other (the enemy), and he adds that it was when the old Roman society became a Nation that the split occured: one would start distinguishing between *Hospes* (he who receives the other, the host) and *Hostis* or *Hostes* (the hostile foreigner).[25]

After a few more philological remarks on the Italian word *ostello* for "inn" – we should not forget that Earwicker is variously described as a publican or an innkeeper – Vico gives a few Homeric examples of what an inhospitable *hostis* could represent:

Thus Paris was the guest, that is to say enemy, of the royal house of Argos, for he kidnapped noble Argive maidens, represented by the character of Helen. Similarly, Theseus was the guest of Ariadne, and Jason of Medea. Both abandoned the women and did not marry them, and their actions were held to be heroic, while to us, with our present feelings, they seem, as indeed they are, the deeds of scoundrels. (*SN*, 226)

Vico grows passionate, as it were and undoubtedly accuses Paris, Theseus, and Jason of being scoundrels. Their adventures provide the seeds of epic poems, but also highlight strong internal tensions within the very values that underwrite culture and civilization.

This is why Joyce invents the rather mystifying character of Hosty – also known as "the Cad" – in order to embody the Viconian idea of a rebellious plebeian, and also of a dangerous guest who may turn out to be an enemy. This fundamental ambivalence has been well analyzed by Hillis Miller in a superb passage of his essay "The Critic as Host," in which he speculates in Viconian fashion on the relationship between guest and host, host and parasite, hotels and hospitals, armies and hostilities.[26] He points out that "Host" has also the meaning of the Eucharist, the consecrated wafer of bread that derives from the notion of *hostia*, sacrificial victim. From Father Flynn's parodic "High Toast" (*D*, 12) or his endless talks about the mysteries of the Eucharist (*D*, 13), to HCE who in *Finnegans Wake* is repeatedly punned into a Christ-figure uttering: "Hoc Est Corpus" to his disciples or pub customers, one might say that Joyce never stopped pondering the intricacies lurking in the overdetermined bond uniting the guest (like the child narrator of "The Sisters," Stephen, the Cad, and Earwicker's sons) with the host or Host. When Guest and Host merge, a sort of superimposed ectoplasm creates the uncanny figure of a paternal Ghost.

Like Rome, Dublin was meant as a refuge, an asylum for persecuted outlaws – a passage of the *Wake* suggests this when dealing with the "lokil calour and lucal odour" of what we have to assume is partly evocative of Dublin: "the southeast bluffs of the stranger stepshore, a *regifugium persecutorum*" (*FW*, 51. 31) – in which a Roman ritual known as *Regifugium* is linked with the Litany of the Virgin (refuge of sinners) to suggest a place that will be a "refuge for the persecuted." The Hosty theme is consistently treated in a Viconian manner by Joyce, especially when he quotes fragments from the Roman Law of the XII Tables such as "*hostis et odor insuper petrofractus*" (*FW*, 41.5) or "*Adversus hostem semper sac!*" (*FW*, 167. 34). The boundaries of the Hosty figure are hard to delineate; he seems at times closer to a Shaunian figure (when he becomes one with Wyndham Lewis, for instance, or Professor Jones) and at other times closer to the revolutionary or anarchist type usually associated with Shem.

Hosty is essentially described as a "parasite" (not unlike Lenehan) who slanders Earwicker, but he is also Buckley, the Irish private who shoots the Russian general, thereby precipitating a socialist revolution. His actions generally limit themselves to the writing and disseminating of a scurrilous ballad accusing Earwicker of all possible misdemeanour. Earwicker appears logically as a "host" in his main role of publican: "That host that hast one on the hoose when backturns when he face-fronts none none in the house his geust has guest." (*FW*, 369. 3–5). The host has a free drink "on the house" but nobody can guess his jest – and he is often in his cups, so much so that his customers occasionally reproach him for his liberality: "who always knew notwithstanding when they had had enough and were rightly indignant at the wretch's hospitality when they found to their horror they could not carry another drop" (*FW*, 171. 20–23).

The Wake endlessly recounts stories revolving around a constant inmixture of otherness into the nation, with the successive waves of assimilation turning Picts, Vikings, Norsemen, Norman invaders, British settlers, Jewish merchants, Chinese traders, and so on, into a restless but predominantly Irish mass that would seethe and erupt at times. Joyce had never forgotten Irish accusations that he had "fouled his own nest" before leaving for Trieste, Zurich, and Paris, and this recurs in *Finnegans Wake*, with the difference that it defines former invaders who later "turned out coats and removed their origins and never learned the first day's lesson and tried to mingle and managed to save and feathered foes' nests and fouled their own" (*FW*, 579.34–580. 1). This is in fact the real "Irish hospitality" favored by Joyce in his mature years – an hospitality he never idealized but that he could praise for its synthetic and absorptive qualities. Joyce did not choose Paris for its hospitality (he could have made a better choice). He never had, like the Trojan hero, to make a choice between a homely place devoted to marriage and domestic life (Trieste), a center of symbolic power (Rome), a crucible of artistic experimentation (Zurich), or a capital devoted to love but also to culture (Paris).

When in the French capital, Joyce acted as much the part of Odysseus, using the ruse of his Trojan horse to conquer Parisian cultural networks one by one (one needs only remember how Joyce dealt with the influential French academician Louis Gillet, who was wooed and won over in just a few years, to understand the success of his strategy), as that of Paris (he often cut a poor figure next to more flamboyant friends such as Pound or Lewis), while clinging to a very private lifestyle in a city whose intellectual seductions he shunned. One could almost say that Paris, perhaps because of its lack of warm hospitality, allowed Joyce to take refuge, to find a shelter, regressing to the stage described by Vico when he explains that Homer's Cyclops provided a model for the archaic father of the original family. He had recreated a relatively limited cell made up of relatives and *famuli* (there were tensions as to who would be the privileged interlocutor, and no one, not even a slavishly devoted friend such as Paul Léon, was immune from sudden reversals of opinion). Beckett learned the hard way that one could not admire Joyce, share ideas with him, without becoming at the same time a private secretary (a role that he gladly embraced) and a future son-in-law (a role to which he objected more strenuously). As his story shows, it was indeed too easy to become the "victim" of Joyce's Irish hospitality!

Once he felt he had conquered Paris, Joyce was rapidly disillusioned with his own victory. Was that a Pyrrhic victory in the sense called up by Stephen's meditation on history? Could Joyce have mused, too: "Another victory like that and we are done for."[27] In the same way as the Punic wars tend to look not even punning but simply puny from the perspective of an Anna Livia when she is about to merge with her oceanic father ("I thought you the great in all things, in guilt and glory. You're but a puny. Home! My people were not their sort out beyond there so far as I can" [*FW*, 627. 23–25]), Joyce's assessment of his "conquest," especially in view of Lucia's troubles, may have been rather bitter in the end. The sentence "and to peer was Parish worth thette mess" (*FW*, 199. 8–9) rephrases more dubitably Henry IV's motto ("*Paris vaut bien une messe*"). Was this parish of the world a "capital city" worth Jacob's mess of pottage or the golden apple of literature?

CHAPTER TEN

Hospitality in the capital city

"Amtsadam, sir, to you! Eternest cittas, heil! Here we are again! I am bubub brought up under a camel act of dynasties long out of print, the first of Shitric Shilkanbeard (or is it Owllaugh MacAuscullpth the Thord?), but, in pontofacts massimust, I am known throughout the world wherever my good Allenglisches Angleslachsen is spoken" (*FW*, 532. 6–11). This chapter will take its point of depature here, in the evo-cation of a city which could be Amsterdam, Paris, or Dublin, at any rate the "capital" needed by Joyce in order to write his universal history. I wish to address the complex manner in which Joyce would rebuild his Dublin so as to enlarge it and promote it to the status of world capital while also denouncing it for the ruthless colonial and capitalist exploita-tion this entailed. Joyce's ambivalence toward his city is therefore iden-tical to his perception of its "hospitality" – a dangerous hospitality for sure, but absolutely central to his linguistic mechanism.

We are thus right at the beginning of the "Haveth Childers Everywhere" section in III, 3, a passage that was published indepen-dently and which has often been studied by Joyceans precisely because the composition method appears clearly[1] even while the author's inten-tions have been variously appreciated. Already in the few lines quoted, we can recognize typical references, from Amsterdam to Adam's "office" (*Amt* in German), and then Dublin and the battle of Clontarf, with Sitric Silkenbeard, chief of the Danes and Ansculph Mac Torcall, the Irish king at the time of the Anglo-Irish wars in the twelfth century. Since the foundation of Dublin sends us back to Genesis, less to Adam than to Cain, killer, sinner, and builder, we may wonder at the presence of the Nazi salute: *Heil!* Joyce added this German phrase in 1929, anticipating with curious prescience a political context that extends beyond Irish limits. Whether it is identified with Rome or New Amsterdam, the "eternal city" can embody all cities only if it carries its onus of guilt, betrayal, and totalitarianism. The question I wish to pose is whether

Joyce intends to denounce the fascism lurking behind any myth of foundation, or whether he condones it in the name of generation and creativity. A closer look at the history of the episode will shed some light on this complex issue: a genesis of urban *Genesis* is thus not only possible but necessary.

As David Hayman has shown, this episode provides a good example of Joyce's "revise and complete" method. Each time, Joyce would rewrite the whole draft and add marginal insertions. The division into two parts as in the final version is thus only a secondary product of the incredibly rapid accretion of levels. Joyce uses the proliferating and disseminating "theme" of cities as an equivalent to the theme of "rivers" in the ALP chapter by relying on a similar type of textual serendipity as the accretion process that made "Anna Livia Plurabelle" a masterpiece. In the context of "Haveth Childers Everywhere," I will use the insights into Joyce's creative process provided by Stuart Gilbert's *Paris Journal*. Gilbert notes on January 31, 1931 that Joyce has started working again on the *Wake*, making extensive use of the *Encyclopedia Britannica*:

At last J.J. has recommenced work on *Work in Progress*. The *de luxe edition* by? soon to come out – about the old lady A.L.P. I think. Another about the city (H.C.E. building Dublin). Five volumes of the *Encyclopedia Britannica* on his sofa. He has made a list of 30 towns, New York, Vienna, Budapest, and Mrs. [Helen] Fleischman has read out the articles on some of these. I "finish" Vienna and read Christiania and Bucharest. Whenever I come to a name (of a street, suburb, park, etc.) I pause. Joyce thinks. If he can Anglicize the word, i.e. make a pun on it, Mrs. F. records the name or its deformation in the notebook. Thus "Slotspark" (I think) at Christiana becomes Sluts' park. He collects all queer names in this way and will soon have a notebook full of them.[2]

This scene will be familiar to any student of Joyce's notebooks, who will immediately recognize Joyce's city-notes culled in notebooks VI.B.24 and VI.B.29. Gilbert's particular example poses a problem, though, since the word "Slotspark" is indeed to be found in the notebooks (VI.B.24.227) and generates "Slutsgartern" in the *Wake* ("in Kissilov's Slutsgartern or Gigglotte's Hill when I would touch her dot" [FW, 532. 22–23]) which adds to "slut" its sly "garters." And "in Slutsgartern" was inserted in MS 4748b–356, a typescript for *transition* no. 15 in a passage dated July–August 1929 by the editors of the James Joyce Archive. The riddle will no doubt have to be solved by a change in the Archive chronology. Let us briefly survey the text's history, going back to its inception. In 1925, Joyce drafted and rewrote the first version of the Yawn inquest with which III, 3 begins. This version, more or less what we find in David

Hayman's *First Draft Version*, does not engage with the theme of cities, and the only city evoked is Dublin. The section beginning with a dash followed by: "Sir, to You! Here we are again. I am bubub brought up" (MS 47484a–114) stays without major changes in the first proofs of *transition* no. 15 dated April 18, 1928 (Princeton – 39). Then, we can see how the typescript for the same proofs (dated December 1928–January 1929) shows the handwritten insertion of city names (MS 47484a–234). Here, "Amsterdam" is the first, followed by "Mannequins Passe" (Brussels) and "Lambeyth and Dolekey" (London coupled with a Dublin suburb) on the following page. The second proofs for the same issue of *transition* add more cities to the list, including in January 1929 "Eternest Cittas, heil!" (MS 47484b–351). In August 1929, or perhaps later, at least if we follow the chronology provided by Gilbert's *Paris Journal*, the draft is typewritten, which allows Joyce and other amanuenses (Paul Léon, Padraic Colum, Stuart Gilbert, Helen Joyce) the opportunity to add various interlinear words. Among them one can distinguish "in Kissilov's Slutsgarten" written in Joyce's own hand, immediately changed into "Slutsgartern" by the addition of an extra "r" (MS 47484b–356). The passage is then typed again as such some time early in 1930, when Joyce prepares the typescript for *Haveth Childers Everywhere* that was to be published in June 1930. There, one can read together the beginning "Amtsadam, Sir, to you! Eternest cittas, heil!" (in which periods have been replaced by handwritten exclamation marks) and on the same page the reference to "Kissilov's Slutsgartern or Giglotte's Hill" (MS 47484b–426). This is of course HCE's defensive speech by which he awkwardly tries to exculpate himself of various sins (here, just "malfeasance trespass against parson with the person of a youthful gigirl") while accusing himself all the more damningly in his stammering half-confession. Other cities than Dublin seem merely to provide a backdrop of universal gossip – concerning which Earwicker's reputation seems to have suffered: "<baad>bahad, nieceless to say, to my reputation on Babbyl <m>Malket for daughter-in-trade being lightly clad" (MS 47484b–426).[3]

What is then the significance of the systematic addition of echoes taken from at least forty (if not more, I have counted in fact forty-two cities) cities of the world chosen from entries in the *Encyclopedia Britannica*? Let us return to Joyce's composition as described by Stuart Gilbert. In this case, his associative and collective method implies enlisting the help of many other people, and induces a mechanical linguistic process. Three persons at least are needed in order to constitute this Atlas of puns, this Baedeker of spoonerisms. Gilbert remains highly critical of a method he finds both too simple and too complicated:

The system seems bad for (1) there is little hope of the reader knowing all these names – most seem new even to Joyce himself, and certainly are to me. And supposing the reader, knowing the fragment dealt with *towns*, took the trouble to look up the Encyclopedia, would he hit on the 30 Joyce has selected? (2) The insertion of these puns is bound to lead the reader away from the basic text, to create divagations and the work is hard enough anyhow! The good method would be to write out a page of plain English and then rejuvenate dull words by injection of new (and appropriate) meanings. What he is doing is too easy to do and too hard to understand. (*PJ*, p. 21)

There is indeed something maddeningly simplistic in this writing method (Joyce always insisted that his ideas were simple and basic). The notebooks bear evidence of endless word-lists, cryptic allusions, half-elaborated portmanteau words, seemingly the weird pastimes of a demented lexicographer who would have, on top of that, thrown overboard all philological probity! However, there is something perverse in imagining that Joyce requires that his readers should be looking around for encyclopedias and travel guides, and grapple in vain after thousands of local names only to find the key to a few dubious puns.

This methodological flippancy triggers Gilbert's scorn as he describes Joyce "curled on his sofa, while I struggle with Danish or Rumanian names, pondering puns. With foreign words it's too easy. The provincial Dubliner. Foreign equals funny" (*PJ*, p. 21). The severity evinced by such a close and often nasty "anti-collaborator" relies on a belief in a different textuality. Why not write in "plain English" first and then only add polyglot and intertextual allusions? "The good method would be to write out a page of plain English and then rejuvenate dull words by injection of new (and appropriate) meaning . . . I think I shall try my hand at the simple method myself" (*PJ*, p. 21). This explains why Gilbert never became a novelist, in spite of real literary gifts (evinced, for instance, in his translation of Dujardin's novel, *Les Lauriers sont coupés*). Gilbert's position corresponds that of the reductive reader who imagines that a "first-draft version" of *Finnegans Wake* written in almost "normal" English, providing a paraphraseable "basic text," would produce a continuous narrative which could be summarized as a plot or skeleton-key. Or it suggests conversely the kind of reductive source-hunting Danis Rose and others have offered as a model. These reductive models seem to be the contrary of Joyce's method, a method which is not just perversely too easy and too difficult, because it supposes an "ideal reader." Joyce's first

ideal reader was thus not Stuart Gilbert, but Miss Weaver, Joyce's bene-
factor and former editor from the *Egoist* days – not only was her very
name a pun, but she was also Joyce's patron, who was asked to "prime
the pump" by ordering specific bits of writing. Miss Weaver distinguished herself from Gilbert above all because she never tried to understand his methods without first playing along with them, without
reducing them to a preconceived notion of "meaning." Finally, she was
rewarded by the gift of Joyce's manuscripts: thus she not only rendered
the writing of the book possible but also provided the paradigm for the
"ideal genetic reader" intended by Joyce.

Joyce's curiously collective compositional practice was indispensable
in order to build the "city words" that loom larger and larger at the end
of III, 3. The questions I would like to pose stem directly from Gilbert's
reservations. Is Joyce's method sound or it is a little crazy? Is there a link,
or rather can one establish a structural homology between this allegedly
mechanistic and collective way of writing and the content or theme –
sketched more or less by the idea of building cities – or should we simply
condemn Joyce's absorption in linguistically complicated but fundamentally simple language games? It is true that Joyce simply "anglicizes" the
words he culls from the encyclopedia in a way that betrays his provincial
chauvinism?

If we take the counter-example of words that are already in English,
as when Joyce (or rather an amanuensis in this case) takes notes on New
York, we can see that the technique is identical to that used for the other
more exotic cities. His aim is always to create puns which are all as "gratuitous" or "necessary" as the Slutspark example. Some puns are quite
obvious (meaning, as we may recall, to be found on the road), as when
he transforms "Bronx" (VI.B.24.205) into "bronxitic" at *FW*, 536.13. or
when "Gramercy Park" is reintroduced as "by gramercy of justness"
(534.13). Others imply the constitution of a dense network that keeps on
adding layers to itself; for instance, the notes: "(Red) Fifth Avenue / (Red)
Avenulceen!" (VI.B.24.206) generate "avenyue" (*FW*, 549.20) with a rich
reinscription of NY, while "(Red) Tombs (city prison)" (VI.B.24.206) is
spliced with Dublin in the final version: "through toombs and deem-
peys" (532.28), that links the acronym for Dublin Metropolitan Police
and the famous New York prison. Joyce's tendency is thus to shake the
drifting signifiers as textual atoms caught up in a new *clinamen*, to use the
Stoician concept of an incline providing a pattern to their whirling descent through the cosmic void. For instance, two discrete items that have
also been crossed in red, "Mulberry Bend Park" and "Coney Island,"

both found in the same "New York Continued" page of vi.B.24 are chiasmically inverted so as to cross their properties: "and I did spread before my Livvy, where Lord street lolls and ladies linger and Cammomile Pass cuts Primrose Rise and Coney Bend bounds Mulbreys Island" (*FW*, 553. 4–6)

Not only do London (with Camomile Street and Primrose Street) and New York overlap, but the very signifiers all allegorize "coupling." On the one hand, geography is not inanimate, but caught up in a spiral of love and carnal desire: we never forget that HCE uses the recitation of cities so as to praise his wife and sing their love. On the other hand, the puns carefully collected from the enormous repertoire provided by the dense entries in the eleventh edition of the *Encyclopedia Britannica* function as so many "passages," to take up Walter Benjamin's concept. What Benjamin attempted to allegorize when he took Paris as the "capital of the nineteenth century" in his voluminous and unfinished *Passagenwerk* turns for Joyce into a dream landscape of a Dublin multiplied by all the cities in the world: hospitality as the utopia of linguistic welcome to all. Since Joyce and Benjamin are aware that they cannot literally reproduce an encyclopedia of the city, the question becomes how to enact it in a dynamic language.

If we look at the notes collected under "Warsaw" in vi.B.24.223–24, the picture becomes even clearer. Interestingly, one can notice that the name of the city first occurs in vi.B.24.190 in a Dublin context, already transformed into "Warshow." Most notes have been left uncrossed, and it is clear that Joyce was not extremely stimulated by the reading of this entry. The notes are in his hand, and it looks as if he was more inclined to capture the sounds than to be accurate. Hence potential puns are produced, stressing negative elements, as with "Muckatucksy Parade," that distorts "Mokotowski parade ground" or "Przedndmessy," from the "Przedmiescie Street" said by the Encyclopedia to be the finest in Warsaw! The notes begin with a few signposts like "Sliwicki," "Luzyenky" for "Lazienki gardens," and "Sasky Ogrot" for "Saski Ogrod" (the Saxon garden) but Joyce gets tired after a short while and stops when he is halfway through the description of the Old Town and then moves on to Madrid on the same page (vi.B.24.224). The uncrossed entries "Wolla" (for the suburb of Wola) and "stare miast" for "Stare Miasto" (the old town) later blend with Prague's own "staremesto" (old town) in the rather poetic coining of "under starrymisty" (*FW*, 539.21).

The Madrid notes are in another hand, probably Helen Fleischman's, and they quickly spill over to Vienna: after two barred entries ("Puerta del Sol" and "Buen Retiro") one reads "Plaza," followed by "Amiens" and "Rastro" in upper case letters, and then "Kaiserlane" and "Kaisersstadt." The top of the following page (VI.B.24.225) also mixes up hints of Madrid (with "Prado") and a list of terms taken from Vienna, all in upper case letters and crossed out: "Ringstress" opens the list, a distortion of "Ringstrasse" that finds its way into the final version as "ringstrsse" (*FW*, 547.32), followed by an illegible entry and then by "Schottenhof," "Freiung," "Rathouse," "Graben," "Stock im Eisen." They are all kept more or less intact in the final version, with "Schottenhof" (*FW*, 538.32), "freiung" (538.27), "ratshause" (535.17), "graben" (545.34), and "my dart to throw" (547.21), developed by "a tritan stock" (547.24) to call up the Viennese grove marked by a stump of a tree with a piece of iron in it. "Alserfound" is after a false start (one can read "A," then "Alse," both crossed out) transformed in the notebook into "Elserground" – found in *FW*, 546.11 as "elserground." It looks as if the relative literality was due to the amanuensis who did his or her best to copy the exact spelling of the Encyclopedia entry, while Joyce himself was taking more liberties. On the whole, most of the entries are not substantially modified once they have generated a pun (or even without a pun) in the notebook. All of this tends to confirm that the description given by Gilbert is faithful: Joyce does work in a team; he does not really know the meaning or references of the names he works from; he is interested in a decorative overlay applied in an almost mechanistic manner.

If this process shows that the notebooks belong entirely to the creative process of the *Wake*, Gilbert is mistaken when he believes that they contain all the plot and substance of the text. When he suggested, as we saw, that a better "method would be to write out a page of plain English and then rejuvenate dull words by injection of new (and appropriate) meanings" (*PJ*, p. 21), he either forgot or did not know that Joyce had in fact another text from which he was working, in this case Yawn's dreamy "polylogue" in which, almost at the end, Yawn's disembodied voice returns as the voice of HCE praising his wife and defending himself from calumny. The new "word-machine" invented by Joyce in the winter of 1930, after a period when he had lost interest in his own "work in progress," was designed to radically alter a previous text. The number of layers piled up on the "first draft version" is staggering: the building materials used to transform the interaction between HCE and ALP into a hymn to all the cities of the world are complex but easily distinguishable. We find, first of all, a rich layer focusing on Dublin, documenting its history and present situation, with notes taken from books such as A.

Peter's *Dublin Fragments: Social and Historic*, D. Cosgrave's *North Dublin – City and Environs*, D. A. Chart's *The Story of Dublin*, and a few others. Then we reach the forty or so cities taken from the *Encyclopedia Britannica*: Amsterdam, Athens, Belfast, Belgrade, Berlin, Bern, Brussels, Bucharest, Budapest, Buenos Aires, Cairo, Christiana, Constantinople, Copenhagen, Delhi, Edinburgh, Kabul, Lisbon, London, Madrid, Mecca, Melbourne, Mexico City, New York, Oslo, Ottawa, Paris, Peking, Philadelphia, Prague, Rangoon, Rio de Janeiro, Saint Petersburg, Sofia, Stockholm, Teheran, Tokyo, Vienna, Warsaw, Washington, Wellington. I have added Philadelphia at least for one entry, "Liberty Bell," on vi.B.29.41.

Another layer is provided by a series of direct quotations carefully copied in the notebooks: the infamous charter by which Henry II granted Dublin to the inhabitants of Bristol; Holinshed's often quoted description of the beauties of Dublin in his *Chronicles*; long passages taken more or less literally from Rowntree's book on *Poverty*, well studied by Atherton in *The Books at the Wake*; all of Ibsen's plays and characters, quoted with a curious equanimity; the list of all the Lord Mayors of Dublin, all bringing something to HCE; the eight main statues of Dublin that one encounters going down from Parnell Square to College Green; the list of the fourteen main architects of Dublin: Cassels, Redmond, Gandon, Deane, Shepperd, Smyth, Neville, Heaton, Stoney, Foley, Farrell, Van Nost, Thorneycroft, and Hogan, all neatly copied in long-hand and added to MS 47484b–455, except for poor John Van Nost whose name was first distorted as "Zmot" and then became just Vnost – as he still survives in the final text on *FW*, 552.12. One is tempted to shout in despair: "Enouch!," as the text has it on 535.22, in a wry allusion to the city built by Cain after his murder and flight "East of Eden."

The main issue is therefore the fact, lamented by Gilbert, that the reader will never know all the names and if she or he looks up the Encyclopedia, would never recognize those selected by Joyce. Or, in another key, this leads to the contention put forward by Danis Rose in his 1978 *Index Manuscript* and then taken up with John O'Hanlon in their *Understanding Finnegans Wake* that all the words in the Wake are easily derivable from some written source mediated by the notebooks. Only when all the sources are provided can the text's meaning be revealed. It seems to me that a category mistake is performed here, or that we are laboring under the illusion that genesis is explication. I would call this the genetic fallacy, and believe that "Haveth Childers Everywhere" is a good passage to work from in order to try to dispel it. Since in this case we have retrieved almost all the sources from which the text is constructed, can we say that the meaning of the text is clear? Does Joyce want to depict Dublin as a universal and eternal city? Probably. But where does he stand concerning the disturbing insertion of "heil!" in 532.6? After all, he did not delete the term introduced at a time when it may have sounded innocuous but that in 1939 would have quite a different ring. Is he poking fun at HCE's sexual hubris hinted at by "since I perpetually kept my ouija ouija wicket up" (*FW*, 532. 17–18), and sees its connection with the imperialism of the English language ("in pontofact massimust, I am known throughout the world wherever my good Allenglisches Angleslachsen is spoken" [532.9–11], or is he condoning the term in the name of some mythical reunification of all and sundry?

In other words, is this picture of a Dublin containing all the other cities in the world a political satire? Or are we to allow Joyce to perform the "eternizing" metaphor of essentialist or Jungian myth-making? One of the keys to these questions seems to lie in the composition indeed, but at the level of the interaction between the "first draft" and its overlays. Or, to narrow down the focus, the issue is what took place between January 1929, when Joyce was revising the proofs for *transition* no. 15 (published in February 1929) and May 1930, when Joyce had finished revising the sixty-four pages of *Haveth Childers Everywhere*. The final version of *Haveth Childers Everywhere* found in *Finnegans Wake* (*FW*, 532.6–554.10) does not significantly differ from the book publication of 1930. The flurry of activity recorded by Gilbert in the early months of 1930 can be explained by the relatively short time Joyce disposed of to alter the meaning of his piece.

A reading of the typescript used for the last pages of III, 3 in *transition* no. 15 (231–38) will reveal all too familiar features: Earwicker betrays himself, as we have seen, through slips, *double entendres*, and stutterings, while he reminisces on his marriage, the foundation of his family, the expansion of his commercial endeavors. His love for a fluvial ALP is embodied in the typical geography of Dublin:

But I was firm with her: and I did take the hand of my delights, my jealousy, and did raft her riverworthily and did lead her overland the pace whimpering by Kevin's port and Hurdlesford and Gardener's mall to Ringsend ferry and there on wavebrink did I uplift my magicianer's puntpole and I bade those polyfizzyboisterous seas to retire with himselves from us (rookwards, thou seasea stammerer!) and I abidged with domfire Norsemanship her maiden race, my baresark bride, and knew her fleshly when with all my bawdy did I her worhsip, min bryllupswipe. (Princeton–43)

The *transition* pages already insist on the prototype of a male dominator who remains in control of his wife ("and I did encompass her about, my vermincelly vinegarette, with all loving kindness as far as in man's might it lay and enfranchised her to liberties of fringes" (*ibid.*) but there is no other voice that could offer a discordant commentary or take a critical distance.

When we reach the same passage in the 1930 version, it is less the insertion of allusions to some cities we can recognize ("whimpering by Kevin's creek and Hurdlesford and Gardener's Mall, long Riverside Drive" [MS 47484b–486v], "and to ringstresse I thumbed her with iern of Erin" [MS 47484b–487] that creates a different atmosphere than the sheer excess of references. Earwicker's jealousy leads him to chain ALP to a chastity belt ("I chained her chastemate to grippe fiuming snugglers, her chambrett I bestank so to spunish furiosos" (MS 47484b–487v) and the very presents he offers sound so dismissive that they become truly ridiculous: "and I gave until my lilienyounger turkeythighs soft goods and hardware (catalogue, *passim*) and ladderproof hosiery lines . . . trancepearances such as women cattle bare" (MS 47484b–488). HCE's unbearable paternalism and vainglorious praise of his prowess appear clearly as the equivalent not only of British imperialism but also of the expansion of commerce identified with capitalism.

Let me quote a passage from *Haveth Childers Everywhere* that clearly indicates a much more critical mode of writing:

Like as my palmer's past policy I have had my best master's lessons as the public he knows, and do you know, homesters, I honestly think if I have failed lamentably by accident benefits through shintoed, spitefired, perplagued and cramkrieged, I am doing my dids bits and have made of my prudentials good. I have been told I own stolenmines or something of that sorth in the sooth of Spainien. Hohohoho! Have I said ogso how I abhor myself vastly (truth to tell) and do repent to my netherheart of <sundry>suntry clothing? The amusin part is I will say, hotelmen, that since I, over the deep drowner athacleeath to seek again Irrlanding, shamed in mind, with three plunges of my ruddertail, yet not a bottlenim, <poisted>vaneed imperial standard by weaponright and platzed mine residenze, taking bourd and burgage under starrimisty and ran and operated my brixtol selection here . . . (MS 47484b–474–474v)

Here, we are closer to an open confession of guilt, denouncing all the "absurd bargains" (*FW*, 538. 19) that have made Dublin what it is, not excluding Henry II's charter giving away Dublin to Bristol. This is why it is not a coincidence to see Joyce insert the text of the charter itself: the typed text ("Wherfor I will and firmly command that they do inhabit it and hold it for me and my heirs firmly and quietly, amply and honestly, and with all the liberties and free customs which the men of Tolbris have at Tolbis, and through whole my land") ends here in the addition, and one can see Joyce's hand adding the more pointed words: "fee for farm, enwreak us wrecks" (MS 47484b–374). They echo the nursery rhyme Stephen sings to himself in "Proteus": "Feefawfum. I zmells de bloodz olds an Iridzman" (*U*, 3:293) and suggest that the "freedom" implied by the charter spells out slavery for the natives of the island. Read in the final version (*FW*, 454. 14–23) the effect is devastating.

It comes as the climax of a long paragraph stretching over six pages, and beginning with a recapitulation of the changes wrought on the city by history. The paragraph is announced by the voice of a guide inviting visitors to discover "*Drumcollogher-la-Belle*" and then takes stock of legal, financial, and political changes: "Things are not as they are. Let me briefly survey . . . The end of aldest mosest ist the beginning of all thisorder so that the mast of their <benbailiffs>hansbailis shall the first in our sheriffsby" (MS 47484b–476). The Dublin motto ("Obeyance from the townsmen spills felixity by the toun" [MS 47484b–477–476v and *FW*, 540. 25–26) is followed by a series of platitudes that debunk their own optimism: "Our bourse and politico-ecomedy are in safe with good Jock Shepherd, our lives are on sure in sorting with Jonathans wild and great. Been so free! Thanks you besters! Hattentats have mindered" (MS 47484b–476v and *FW*, 540.26–28). The mention of the two famous English criminals both hanged for their crimes could leave one skeptical about the future of the Dublin "Bourse" (both Stock Exchange and purse). But this does not seem to embarrass the speaker, because these are precisely the methods he extols: "By fineounce and imposts I got and grew and by grosscruple gat I grown ontreachesly: murage and lestage were my mains for Ouerlord's tithing and my drains for render and prender the doles and the tribute" (MS 47484b–477–477v and *FW*, 541.7–10). This paean to financial exploitation is not of course limited to Dublin ("Bulafest onvied me, Corkcuttas graatched" [MS 47484b–477v and *FW*, 541. 16–17]) but applies to all the new imperialist empires, including the United States:

In the humanity of my heart I sent out heyweywomen to refresh the ballwearied and then, doubling megalopolitan poleetness, my great great greatest of these charities, devaleurised the base fellows for the curtailment of their lower man: with a slog to square leg I sent my boundary to Botany Bay and I ran up a score and four of mes while the Yanks were huckling the Empire (MS 4748b–480 and *FW*, 542.35–543.6)

Once more, the Dublin Metropolitan Police is taken to task and metamorphosed into a megalopolitan expansion that keeps "doubling" all the time while severely punishing the inferiors. The law and economy go hand in hand in this exploitative process, since one hears the name of De Valera in "devaleurised," meaning that base money has been devalued, which calls up Swift's campaign against the devaluation of the pence in Ireland. The cricket terms implying some foul play and the allusions to Huck Finn suggest that the business of empire-building is indeed dirty while the assertion that there are twenty-four cities named Dublin in the US merely sets off the fact that the speaker seems satisfied with a world limited to the quadrangle in Trinity College (Botany Bay).[4]

Then a mention of all those who should be grateful to the display of these good deeds ("in homage all and felony" [*FW*, 543. 21]) ushers in the long insertion of the jumbled notes taken from B. S. Rowntree's book *Poverty, A Study of Town Life*.[5] These notes, culled from the book in notebook VI.B.29, pp. 139–53 and then pp. 164–65, are not all in Joyce's hand and some have been dictated probably by Joyce himself. The litany of "respectable" (three times, p. 139), "fairly respectable" (twice, p. 140) and then "as respectable as respectable can be" (p. 143) is relatively restrained in the notebook entries, while the term "respectable" and its cognates are repeated twenty-one times as early as the long typed insertion in MS 47484b–459–60 more or less identical with the final text (*FW*, 543. 22–545.14). The litany climaxes with "and respected and respectable, as respectable as respectable can respectably be" (*FW*, 545. 11–12), creating what Atherton calls a "sardonic refrain"[6] undermining the bland matter-of-factness of these staccato notations on urban poverty in the North of England. It is a Swiftian Joyce who appears here to denounce not only destitution but the wooden language of state bureaucracy that sees, indeed, children as vermin: "children treacly and verminous have to be separated" (a note in Joyce's hand in VI.B.29, pp. 144–45).

This often hilarious prose simply splices and accelerates a few pages from Rowntree. The text reaches surrealist peaks at times, as when we hear about someone who is "mentally strained from reading work on German physics" or about a "decoration from Uganda chief in locked ivory casket" – but reality is stranger than fiction, for all the details are indeed provided by Rowntree's text. Or to go back to the analogy with Walter Benjamin's *Passagenwerk*, it looks as if confronted with the stark reality of urban decay, Joyce and Benjamin prefer to "remain silent," act like *bricoleurs* who simply salvage trivia. In the theoretical section of his *magnum opus*, Benjamin writes: "Method of this project: literary montage. I need say nothing. Only exhibit. I won't filch anything of value or appropriate any ingenious turns of phrase. Only the trivia, the trash – which I don't want to inventory, but simply allow it to come into its own in the only way possible: by putting it to use."[7] Joyce suggests that the history of Dublin, like that of any capital city, confirms that its formation must indeed have been "dirty." Facing such a mixture of concrete accomplishments (as Lacan would say, civilization begins with sewers), and the underside showing the exploitation of the majority, progress appears indissociable from abjection and subjection, the mere act of quoting suffices. Its bittersweet irony exposes how Stephen's "nightmare of history" (*U*, 2: 377) has left traces in monuments, in its own refuse, and above all in language.

One could strongly oppose this new rhetoric of multilayered denunciation with Bloom's messianic projections in the "Circe" episode of *Ulysses*. The delirious socialism of Bloom is often undercut by parody, and when he sees the new Bloomusalem of the future in the shape of a gigantic kidney . . . In "Haveth Childers Everywhere," the dominant tense is not the future, but the present perfect of a recapitulation ("Lo, I have looked upon my pumpadears in their easancies and my drummers have tattled tall tales of me in the land" [*FW*, 545. 26–25]) in the name of a strong "I" who is glorified or himself glorifies his accomplishments. As the evolution of the text has shown, Dublin originally embodied the love and eternal desire linking HCE and ALP then generates a more fragmented "drama parapolylogic" (474.5) that stresses contradiction. The community of anonymous sufferers offers a poignant counterpoint to the shrill and inflated egotism of HCE.

Joyce nevertheless needs the single voice of one speaker (with a few interpolations from the Four Irish Masters and Historians, pp. 534, 535, 540, 546, 547, 550, and 552) as a rhythmical basis that will now and then modulate toward other inflections undercutting its steady surge forward and upward. A relatively clear passage reflects on this cumulative function occupied by the speaker:

Idle were it, repassing from elserground to the elder disposition, to inquire whether I, draggedasunder, be the forced generation of group marriage, holy-crypotgram, of my essenes, or carried of cloud from land of locust, in ouzel galley borne, I, huddled til summone be the massproduct of teamwork, three surtouts wripped up in itchother's, two twin pritticoaxes lived as one, troubled in trine or dubildin too, for abram nude be I or roberoyed with the faineans, of Freejeean grafted ape on merfish, surrounded by obscurity, by my virtus of creation and by boon of promise, by my natural born freeman's journeymanright and my otherchurch's inher light, in so and such a manner as me it so besitteth, most surely I pretend and reclam to opt for simultaneous. Till daybowbreak and showshadows flee. (*FW*, 546. 11–23)

Earwicker admits here that he sums up in himself if not all of humanity at least his own family. The three soldiers and two tempting girls in the park are known as the main sigla of the Doodles family. Freedom is asserted in such a way that it can connote the *Freeman's Journal*, Fijian mermaids, Sinn Fein inverted or even *les rois fainéants* (the last Merovingian kings). In this context, creativity is confirmed not by the number of children or of satellite plantations but by the simultaneity of a group structure.

Joyce's composite portrait of a man who embodies a city belongs to an unanimistic technique – one can think of Jules Romains or Dos Passos – but here it is more an "Arcimboldo city" that is depicted, made up of all the cities in the world summed up by a few basic names. The link between quotation and the city has never been stronger, as one can still see it in French (*cité – citation*). Quotation implies montage, without losing the idea of a general architectonics – and the limit set by the morning and waking up from obscurity. Benjamin uses Proust to define the general outline of his *Passagenwerk* in a paragraph that might be taken as a description of *Finnegans Wake*: "Just as Proust begins his life story with the moment of awakening, so every historical presentation must begin with awakening and, in fact, should deal with nothing else. This one deals with awakening from the nineteenth century."[8]

Since we are kept waiting for this impossible moment when we wake up from the dream conjured by the book we are even now reading, the effect is a dynamic portrayal of the universal city. The city in III, 3 is not the stable site that can be reconstructed or confirmed with the help of street maps and directories. It is rather an expanding linguistic site that never bypasses real history (for instance the name Ouzel Galley calls up a Dublin ship thought to have disappeared and returned miraculously in 1700) but that "re-pairs" it by a system of grafts, duplications, and additions. Dublin is always compared and paired with other cities; cities tend to be coupled, thus New York goes with Kyoto (*FW*, 534.2), Budapest with Belfast, Cork with Calcutta (541.16), Bucharest with Berlin (540.21), London with Buenos Aires (540.34–35), etc. Less than a theme, the city becomes a way of reading the world, a series of dynamic intertranslations. Naming acquires a tremendous weight, and in fact even if no reader could remember all the streets and squares culled from the Encyclopedia entries, it is surprising to see that many names are familiar to, say, a well-traveled tourist.

The last point I would like to make is linked with my first: the issue of language is crucial, and here it is clear that English provides the basic structure. If indeed one can say that Joyce "anglicizes" foreign names, he does this tongue in cheek, without being duped by the implicit imperialism this could betray: he conversely proves the unique "hospitality" of English when he makes it "accept" the most foreign signifiers. We have seen how much the issue of an international language or of a bilingual Ireland preoccupied him. As Mallarmé wrote in his *Mots Anglais*,[9] English is properly speaking the "language of angels," but in Joyce's celestial and terrestrial cities, angels do laugh: "wherever my good Allenglishes Angles*lachs*en is spoken" (*FW*, 532. 10–11) also suggests the German "*lachen*" meaning laugh, while "Eternest cittas" (532. 6) contains the opposite idea of "*ernst*" (earnest, serious). A "citizen" for Joyce is also someone who can laugh at (and in) his own city.

CHAPTER ELEVEN

Joyce's late Modernism and the birth of the genetic reader

I have suggested how Joyce's sense of responsibility concerning the tragedy of Lucia's psychological troubles led him to turn her into a privileged addressee of his last book, until she became the ideal reader who somehow inhabits the text. Here lies the main effect of Joyce's *Wake*: to change if not its audience, at least its reading habits. We have also seen how the context of the thirties created a polarity between the avant-gardist reader and a basic "plain reader." The revolutionary idea of *Finnegans Wake* aims at modifying usual reading practices. Yet Joyce was not the only Modernist writer who believed in such a transformation: before him, Gertrude Stein had postulated the need to invent a "cubist" reader who could be persuaded to see words as colors or shapes, and Pound had vigorously defended the concept of a revitalization of language through poetry capable of destroying "sloppy thinking" and, perhaps, preparing for the new state. Joyce, however, was wary of such direct influence on the reader, and while keeping high esthetic standards, he remained aware of the ethical responsibility implied by the Modernist wish to create a new public.

The differences between two critical "industries" of Modernism, the Pound and Joyce schools, can exemplify important variations in the emergence of a new genetic Modernism, the discovery of an original type of reading practice linked with a renewed attention to textual materiality. Joyce and Pound appear exemplary in that they enact two aspects of the typically Modernist strategy that forces critics to take the act of reading and writing into account, and to become alert to historical modes of textualization. Their Modernist epics force the reader to become the "hero" of a drama involving the editing and deciphering of texts. In a sweeping survey of epic forms, Moretti's book, *Modern Epic*,[1] could thus not avoid references to the genetic approach when dealing with Joyce – who is the only "epic" writer treated in this fashion. In one detailed reading, Moretti points to Joyce's accretive style, showing how one paragraph printed in the *Little Review* version of "Hades" (from *Ulysses*) doubles its size in the course of several revisions. Bloom's parataxis, while plunging the reader into the recesses of his subconscious, allows for an indefinite expansion of the text. "Every sentence, and almost every word, of the stream of consciousness is a word in itself: complete, independent. Every paragraph, a digression in miniature – which continues to expand . . ."[2] Clearly Moretti has felt the need to become "genetic" without accounting for such an approach: the remarks on Joyce's accretions are followed by statistical investigation of recurrences, which are then justified by Moretti's admitted indulging in "a bit of vulgar materialism."[3] My point is that one cannot just engage in this approach without providing a rationale for its use and applications.

If we agree that the *Cantos* and *Finnegans Wake* include not only "real history" but the history of their language and the history of the production of this language, the reading activity will have to account theoretically for this modification. For instance, in his first Canto, Pound uses the Homeric tradition and its accidents to launch his Odyssey – Odysseus' quest turns into a voyage through seas of manuscripts and translations. This reduces the function of the author to that of a rereader and misquoter of a vast array of texts. Is this enough to give birth to the modern "textual condition"? We enter the textual condition when stylistic parody playing on polyphonic "voices" is replaced by the trope of a "polymechanism" of writing – when the Homeric paradigm is not just that of a "polytropos" man but also of a "polymechanical" textuality (by which I refer to Pound's identification of Odysseus as "Diogenes, Laertiade, polumechan' Odusseu"). This is Calypso's description in *Odyssey* v, 203 and it is used twice in rapid succession (*Odyssey* xi, 60 and 92) in the *Nekuia* episode which became Pound's first Canto.[4] When Pound renders Tiresias' apostrophe as "Man of ill star, why come a second time"[5]) he suggests that Odysseus has already been to Hell and that each voyage of exploration is merely a repetition of a previous textual voyage.

The great change in Modernism occurs when *Finnegans Wake* and the later *Cantos* begin problematizing language as a birthing progress through translations, voices, stylistic polyphony, and intertextual echoes (as adumbrated already in the "Oxen of the Sun" episode of *Ulysses*) while moreover including an entire history of printing and of publishing. As Carol Shloss puts it, *Finnegans Wake* has become "a History of the Book" and Joyce's last text turns into "an encyclopedia of printing history, printing terms, and printing practices."[6] More than Pound's,

Joyce's last works announce a new era, the time of the collective hyper-textual reading, and usher in a new mode of textuality, an original "condition" that Jerome MacGann calls "the textual condition." McGann takes Pound as paradigm of the textual condition when he insists upon the material and social function of writing, but his thesis would entirely apply to the *Wake*. Pound's *Cantos'* centrality in the Modernist canon derives from the fact they demand "radial readings"[7] which involve "decoding one or more of the contexts that interpenetrate the scripted and physical text" and include an entire "sociohistory of the work." As McGann writes, the *Cantos* are not just an epic including history, but a poem including bibliography. Thanks to Garland publishing house, we can now find all the manuscripts of Joyce in print as well as all of Pound's texts arranged in chronological order and in facsmile, however, without the manuscripts. The fact that Garland's policy has been quite different with Pound's works is not a matter of chance, since it suggests that it aims at producing a different "genetic reader": Pound's manuscripts are available only to those scholars who can go to the Beinecke Library, and what has been published is a facsimile, in chronological order, of all of Pound's texts. Indeed, editing the genetic manuscript has become a central issue.[8]

ECO, JOYCE, AND THE NEW READER

Finnegans Wake is a text which aims at giving birth to a new reader, a reader who has to approach the difficult and opaque language less with glosses and annotations than through the material evidence of the note-books, drafts, corrected proofs reproduced by the James Joyce Archive. We have lost the illusion that we might discover a "first-draft version" of *Finnegans Wake* written in almost "normal" English and providing a par-aphraseable narrative that could be summarized by a plot or skeleton-key. This reductive notion is steadily opposed and deconstructed by Joyce's writing method, a method that nevertheless presupposes an "ideal reader." My further contention is that this ideal reader will become a "genetic" reader, or in another sense a generic reader, both engendered by the text and engendering the text.

The function of what might be called a "genreader" is to be a textual agent that actively confronts a new type of materiality and temporality: texts have to be read in the context of an expanding archive that also creates its own sense of pedagogy. Such a reader, like Moretti, will read differently since he or she has had to use the notebooks and the drafts in order to approach the opaque mass of *Finnegans Wake*. This is why the notion of an "ideal reader" is announced by Joyce in a famous passage explaining how the *Wake* has been "sentenced to be nuzzled over a full trillion times for ever and a night till his noddle sink or swim by that ideal reader suffering from an ideal insomnia" (*FW*, 120. 12–14) that is curiously located in a context of critical editing of medieval manuscripts – Joyce had the Book of Kells in mind.

The concept of an "ideal reader" as it has been developed by Umberto Eco, who, indeed, began his academic career as a Joycean, cannot keep its semiologic neutrality and has to confront political or ideological issues. The phrase of "ideal reader" retrieved some of its urgency in a critical debate which took place around Eco under the title of "Interpretation and overinterpretation."[9] In his 1990 Tanner lectures at Cambridge, Eco alludes from time to time to *Finnegans Wake* as a crux for semioticians, but he also postulates the principle of the limitation of interpretation. If there can be no criteria defining what a "good" interpretation of a text may be, there should be criteria telling one what "bad" interpretations are. Eco examines how Geoffrey Hartman over-interprets while "deconstructing" Wordsworth's "Lucy" poem (*IO*, p. 60) and counters this allegedly dangerous tendency by distinguishing between *intentio lectoris* and *intentio operis*. The "intention of the work" serves to prohibit private or fanciful associations, without implying a return to the classical notion of the "author's intentions," or *intentio auctoris*. "My idea of textual interpretation as the discovery of a strategy intended to produce a model reader, conceived as the ideal counterpart of a model author (which appears only as a textual strategy), makes the notion of an empirical author's intention radically useless" (*IO*, p. 66). Similarly, in *The Limits of Interpretation*,[10] Eco explicitly identifies his concept of *intentio lectoris* with Joyce's "ideal reader" and devotes a whole essay to Joyce. There, one expects to find a definitive version of the "ideal reader" theory, coupled with the criteria enabling us to distinguish between "good" and "bad" interpretations of Joyce. In that chapter Eco remarks that most semioticians have been silent about Joyce, perhaps because the punning language of the *Wake* relies too systematically on Pierce's idea of "unlimited semiosis." Eco studies a few Joycean puns (*meanderthaltale*, *scherzarade*), and explores their almost infinite inter-branchings.

Finally, in a tantalizingly short subchapter entitled "The Temptation of Deconstruction," Eco admits that the "ideal reader" of the *Wake* could indeed be described as a "deconstructionist reader" for whom texts are inexhaustible, for whom any true interpretation is a creative misprision, and in short for whom there can only be an "infinite series of original re-creations" (*LI*, p. 148). However, this is a temptation one has to resist, says Eco, who returns to the idea that all interpretations are not equally valid: "It is impossible to say which is the best interpretation of a text, but it is possible to say which ones are wrong. In the process of unlimited semiosis it is certainly possible to go from any one node to every other node, but the passages are controlled by rules of connection that our cultural history has in some way legitimated" (*LI*, p. 148).

The main criteria derive from the way the text projects an "ideal reader" who can produce conjectures about its meaning:

How to prove that a given interpretive conjecture is, if not the only right one, at least an acceptable one? The only way is to check it against the text as a coherent whole: any interpretation of a certain portion of a text can be accepted if it is confirmed, and must be rejected if it is challenged, by another portion of the same text. In this sense the internal textual coherence controls the otherwise uncontrollable drift of the reader. (*LI*, pp. 148–49)

While most critics are ready to agree with this principle of internal coherence, where can one find decisive theoretical rules?

BERIA'S DISAPPEARANCE, AGAIN

In an appendix entitled "Some Final Joycean Gossip," Eco provides a practical example when he evokes the exchange of arguments between Ruth von Phul and Nathan Halper in two issues of the *Wake Newslitter* in 1965. These seasoned Joyceans were engaged in a debate about the latest historical allusion discovered in *Finnegans Wake*. Halper gave the name of Beria, who seems to be present in "berial" (*FW*, 415.31) in a passage of the "Ondt and the Gracehoper" fable which is rife with allusions to Russian Soviets ("So vi et" [414.14]) and socialists ("social list" [415. 31]) but this was in order to show that this was a misreading. The word had been added by Joyce between March 1928 and August 1929, whereas Beria became known to the Western world only in December 1938, when he was named Commissar of Internal Affairs to gain fame in the famous Moscow purges. Following the exchange gleefully, Eco applauds the masterful way seasoned Joyceans could check their interpretive impulses and apply Occam's razor to their own ingenuities:

Beria is thus liquidated – once more after his death. The context privileges the biblical allusion [to Zophah's son, Beri, according to 1 Chronicles 7: 36]. I love that discussion. All the participants proved to be smart enough to invent acrobatic interpretations, but both, in the end, were prudent enough to recognize that their brilliant innuendoes were not supported by context. They won the game because they let *Finnegans Wake* win. (*LI*, pp. 150–51)

We may reach a first conclusion: the context that will determine the principle of "internal cohererence" is determined in a normative and historical way. A "naive" reader who only knows the date of publication might err in thinking that Beria is present in "The Ondt and the Gracehoper" tale. Apparently, then, Eco's principle of coherence calls for a genetic approach, which alone can trace successive additions to a passage. If the example of Beria confirms a definitive limit to possible overinterpretation, it could be useful to examine the issue from the strict historical perspective which we identify with genetic criticism. We discover in notebook VI.B.19 that Joyce had at least jotted down a reference to a book by S. P. Melgunoff, the author of *Red Terror in Russia* published by Dent in 1926. In this book, Melgunoff denounces the atrocities of the Tcheka in the repression of the post-revolutionary years. The reference is to be found in VI.B.19.135, and is followed by "Tcheka" and "Popoff (Philpoff)." The reference to the book was crossed out for use in *FW*, p. 116. 7–8. While Melgunoff does not mention Beria, who was already active as a Tchekist organizer in Georgia and Transcaucasia, he names many of his immediate colleagues. The first version of Melgunoff's book was published in 1924, and he kept on denouncing the Russian secret police from his European exile, not unlike Nabokov's father (who was assassinated by right-wing "white Russians"). Beria had been appointed head of the Communist Party of Transcaucasia in 1931, and he published in 1935 a *History of the Bolshevik Organization in Transcaucasia* whose ambition was to show the overall benign influence of Stalin. An active and prominent member of the Tcheka since 1920 – it was renamed the GPU in 1921 and then the OGPU in 1923 – Beria was already a feared apparatchik who swore fealty only to Stalin.

All these facts bring us closer to the date of August 1929, when "berial" was added to the version printed in *Tales Told of Shem and Shaun*. Now a doubt can be registered: if indeed Joyce was interested in the politics of terror and repression in Stalinist Russia as early as 1926, might he not have come across a stray mention of Beria, or have heard from an informant who could have identified the already sinister name? Even if I am not suggesting that Beria *is* hidden in "berial," my point is that it would be extremely misleading to take this case as an indisputable example of what Joyce did *not* intend. Admittedly, the allusion is rather unlikely, but in this case, in order to rule out the possible historical reference, one needs to reconstruct and identify Joyce's mental process, and start from a theoretical principle and not only a historical one. Since the principle of historical coherence is a minimalist and "bottomline" one, we will need to have recourse to a concept of Joyce's procedures (with a strict hierarchy of his priorities, and a system in which interpretations are classified in relation to their verisimilitude). The main danger of this procedure is that we have again shifted from the *intentio operis* to the *intentio auctoris*, and that if the coherence of the text has to be superseded by that of the "whole work," we are not too far from the old bogey of authorial intentions.

Could the evidence of the archive, in this case the notebooks, yield further information to help us out of this theoretical impasse? If we look more closely at the genetic material, we note that Joyce decides to use the reference to *Red Terror in Russia* when he adds a layer of political overtones to his analysis of the Letter in I, 5 after the passage in which psychoanalytic criticism is mocked. The passage in "The Letter" alludes first to Ezra Pound's right-wing brusque bluntness, then proceeds with: "for we also know, what we have perused from the pages of *I Was A Gemral*, that Showting up of Bulsklivism by 'Schottenboum', that Father Michael about this red time of the white terror equals the old regime and Margaret is the social revolution while cakes mean the party funds and dear thank you signifies national gratitude" (*FW*, 116. 5–10). These political references were all added late to the Galleys, first as handwritten interlinear additions (MS 47476 a–212) then as typed "Corrections for Galley 64" (MS 47476 b–360 v). The same page lists the reference to Ezra Pound, the quote from Melgunoff's book in vi.B.19 ("red time of white terror") and an allusion to Spartacus which neatly splices the German revolutionary movement which failed in 1919 with more classical times and heroes.

"Red Terror" thus does not allude only to the Hungary of 1919 (as McHugh's *Annotations* has it), but primarily to Russia with its famous decree of September 5, 1918 on the "Red Terror" which granted special powers to the Communist secret police. When this network is developed at about the same time in the Fable of the Ondt and the Gracehoper, with the unmistakable "So vi et," the "internal coherence" of the work is not really ascertainable. Are we to read this as a sign of Joyce's growing political equanimity? Is he indulging in a parody of the idiom of left-wing critics while putting the Right and the Left on an equal footing? The question of Joyce's political bias has always fascinated critics, and one can only conclude that the notebooks offer little light on this problem. Notebook vi.B.34 (approximately dated 1933) yields curious allusions: "J.J. pro-german" (p. 121), "fake Juif stories" (p. 154), "Nazi Priers" (p. 156). The last entry is added to what seems a sinister reference to Nazi Germany at the end of ii, 3: "Forwards! One bully son growing the goff and his twinger read by the Nazi Priers," (*FW*, 375. 17–18). Joyce seems to link Earwicker with Nazi politics and the most right-wing elements of Irish nationalism. In Notebook vi.B.31, Earwicker is called "His Crushing Experience" (p. 182), and the next page has: "Nazi" (p. 183).

THE WORK'S AUTHORITY

If the notebooks, unhappily, hardly allow for any reconstruction of the ideological consistency of the text, they all make fun of some type of overinterpretation. In the *Wake*, Joyce repeatedly dramatizes the fact that "critics" may take any word out of context and make it signify what they want – thus "cakes mean the party funds" (*FW*, 116.09). Does this imply that there is an "intention" – be it of the author or of the work – as to what words ought really to mean or just mean what they say, and that we should just know that cakes mean "only" cakes? If the only rule we are left with is that we cannot accept historical events posterior to the publication (such as the famous reference to "coventry" in *FW*, 353.26 – the city was to be partly destroyed by bombs during World War II – in the context of atomic bombing and total destruction, still another proof of Joyce's prophetic powers), then we have not really progressed toward a definition of the *intentio operis*. The methodological problem might be solved if we admit Rorty's refusal (in his response to Eco in *IO*) to consider any intention at all, whether it be that of the text, the author, or the reader. Rorty sees the principle of "internal coherence" as a metaphor which loses any validity as soon as the reader discovers a coherence in a given reading (*IO*, p. 97). If Rorty sides with Derrida against Eco and Paul de Man, his textual pragmatism soon loses any normative criteria of sense-making, and just tells the readers to enjoy the text. For him, one can no more "crack the code" of the *Wake* than one can distinguish between use and interpretation or know the author's actual intentions.

Joyce's publicized "intentions" look indeed quite baffling, at least if we trust the strange letter of May 20, 1927 in which Joyce considers leaving the *Wake* to James Stephens, who would finish it in his place:

As regards that book itself and its future completion I have asked Miss Beach to get into closer relations with James Stephens . . . He is a poet and Dublin born. Of course he would never take a fraction of the time or pains I take but so much the better for him and me and possibly for the book itself. If he consented to maintain three or four points which I consider essential and I showed him the threads he could finish the design. J J and S [the colloquial Irish for John Jameson and Son's Dublin whisky] would be a nice lettering under the title. It would be a great load off my mind. I shall think this over first and wait until the opposition becomes more general and pointed. (*LI*, pp. 253–54)

Joyce's idea that he can explain the book's purpose and texture in just a few lines is mind-boggling. What stands out, however, is not just a total transfer of power, control, intentionality, or authority, but an extension of the author's signature: instead of "J.J." one would find "J.J. and S." This seems also to be the gist of the "Letter" episode, in which Joyce multiplies the precautions as far as agency and meaning are concerned, but clearly states the "authority" of the whole: "but while we in our wee free state . . . may have our irremovable doubts as to the whole sense of the lot, the interpretation of any phrase in the whole, the meaning of every word of a phrase so far deciphered out of it . . . we must vaunt no idle dubiosity as to its genuine authorship and holusbolus authoritativeness" (*FW*, 117.34–118.4). Each local interpretation will have to remain dubious while the whole ("holusbolus" suggesting as much "bogus" as "whole and entire") is "authoritative": this implies that Joyce himself is ready to renounce complete control over a text considered as his property, provided the work's "engine" is perceived by his readers (seen as so many followers, disciples, or devoted annotators).

This would be a rare case of an author capable of renouncing his own intentionality – under the sole condition that the *intentio operis* should be preserved as a consensual principle, upon which any further and different agency could be grafted. The notion of authority has to be accepted as integral to Joyce's view of his own textual machine, a machine from which he can step out, after he has signed it as the prime mover and inventor. Moreover, this concept does not posit an "ideal reader" as adequate to the *intentio operis*. Precisely because a continuous insomnia generates a symptomatology, the "genreader" will have the choice between varieties of error, between typologies of pathological misreadings. One could distinguish between obsessional structures (the work will have to be studied rigorously, with a minimum of help from outside sources), paranoiac delusions (the sense of having found the ultimate key or cracked the code), or hysterical projections (the text will become a master who has to be seduced at any cost, often at the risk of losing "common-sense").

One can understand better why Eco concludes in an aporetic fashion the Joyce chapter of his *Limits of Interpretation*. If we follow his own line of reasoning, even if he has failed to provide a set of decisive criteria for invalidating bad or not very good readings, he can conclude on an optimistic note, precisely because he has described how a "community of interpreters" has reached by and in itself a common ground, has agreed "internally" on a principal of minimal coherence. A pragmatic approach would be closer to Joyce's insight into an *auctoritas operis* which can be developed for its own sake. It would thus recommend not a semiotic interpretation, but only a semantic interpretation, developed when we learn to play with the text. The reading process becomes indeed a learning process, with its own specific pedagogy, in the way one learns (first making all sorts of errors) to play games such as bridge, scrabble, or interactive video-programs. If we agree to see the embodiment of the principle of the "ideal genetic reader" in actual Joycean "interpretive communities," we will have at least reached two points of agreement: a radical historicization of all the possible interpretive strategies, doubled with a no less historical material history of textual production.

TEXTUAL TRANSMISSION

To begin thinking the inscription of the "genreader" in the text, it seems important to evoke the actual context in which Joyce started writing his *Work in Progress*. David Hayman and others have shown that the first systematic model for the composition of *Finnegans Wake* was the Tristan and Isolde legends. The 1924 republication of Bédier's *Le Roman de Tristan et Iseult* (Paris, 1900) must have been interpreted as a good omen by Joyce, who had already used Bédier's books in 1922–23, when he started the very strange compilation of all his previous works in the "Scribbledehobble" notebook. There, the Tristan material was concentrated under the heading of "Exiles I and II." As Hayman notes, "Joyce began the second phase of his notetaking after he had read Bédier's attempt to reconstitute the ur-text's noble tone and savage content."[11] Joyce could not ignore the fact that Bédier's version implied certain choices among the manuscripts that were available, since his notes also refer to Bédier's scholarly two-volume book on *Le Roman de Tristan par*

Thomas (Paris, 1902 and 1905). Joyce used the second volume in his notes on VI.A.302 in order to contrast the original twelfth-century tale and the later thirteenth-century prose versions. In fact, out of twenty or so extant versions of the prose *Tristan*, Bédier chose one manuscript as the best, the manuscript MS. 103 at the Bibliothèque Nationale. However, this manuscript dates from the fifteenth century, and the decision has been questioned by many specialists.

How could this later version – an abridged version, with numerous variants and departures from the other manuscripts which survive from the thirteenth century – be taken by Bédier as the ur-text of the prose *Tristan*? Some interesting differences are to be found, since the MS. 103 version is the only manuscript of the prose version in which Tristan changes his name to Tantris (a point which, thanks perhaps to Ezra Pound, had attracted Joyce's attention: "Tantris is shadow of Tristan [E.P.]" in VI.A.301, *JJA*, 95). This feature belongs to the verse tradition. In this version alone, Tristan disguises himself as Tantris during his stay in Ireland, where he falls in love with Iseult. Their love happens thus previous to the love philtre. If we go beyond the thematic network of associations culled by Joyce with his usual ant-like industry, we can understand how his embryonic writing in progress was caught up in one of the most exciting philological controversies of the twenties, a controversy whose outcome was to lead to the foundation of modern textual genetics.

Bédier's seemingly gratuitous choice derived from his belief that the later version was somehow more "original" than all other prose versions because it contained all these narrative jewels culled from an earlier line of texts, and was a direct refusal of the more "scientific" but also more "German" method used by Gaston Paris, who had applied Lachmann's methods to the editing of medieval texts as early as 1872.[12] Cerquiglini's *Eloge de la Variante* asserts that Bédier forces medieval texts into a pattern defined by modernity: "Bédier's anti-methodology brings the medieval text closer to the stable, fixed and authorized text of modernity" (*EV*, p. 101). In other words, the thrust of Modernism lies precisely in a return to a "medieval" instability, which will eventually question a pseudo-stability wrongly indentified with typographical reproduction and authorial certainty. Indeed, Modernism will contradict Modernity in this respect.

At the time Joyce was researching the Tristan legends and all its variants, Bédier's decision to prefer a stable text to what was obviously a series of variants was questioned by a Benedectine monk, whose work signals a return to a brand of "advanced Lachmannism" in textual matters.[13] Dom Quentin had established himself as an authority on textual questions when he published in 1922 his *Mémoire sur l'établissement du texte de la Vulgate* and applied his method to various textual issues in his *Essais de critique textuelle (ecdotique).*[14] In one of the chapters of this book, Dom Quentin contrasts Bédier's procedure to his own method and shows how Bédier's subjective and incoherent reconstruction of the text derives from his belief in a "faulty copy of a lost original from which the actual seven manuscripts we have derive" (*ECT*, p. 162). Despite his opposition to Lachmann, Bédier still thinks in terms of "common mistakes" (*fautes communes*), a concept which suggests that some versions are less authoritative than others. Quentin can demonstrate that Bédier's earlier edition of *Le Lai de l'ombre*, published in 1890, relied only upon one family of manuscripts, while his more recent version uses exclusively another family, whereas one should compare *three* families of manuscripts. What passes as Bédier's "taste" is thus just an implicit critical decision that takes one stemma as more authoritative than the other. For Quentin, a rigorous edition has to take all families into account and study their divergences systematically, without being afraid of reproducing "faulty" versions. In fact, he suggests that all versions are somehow faulty.

Quentin's method aims at founding what he calls an "ecdotics." "*L'ecdotique*," deriving from the Greek '*Ekdoxη* (meaning "reception" and "succession," as in "receiving by succession"), implies a systematic comparison of all extant manuscript versions in order to reconstruct not an "original" version but an "archetype." Whereas Bédier believes that, when the "original" version is lacking, one must take whichever version appears satisfactory, provided one supplements it with passages from other versions which look better or are simply missing from the first one, Quentin invents a system of comparison of variants by triads and "families" in order to provide a general tabulation of all actual manuscripts and not rely upon a strictly dichotomic system of classification. Instead of reconstructing an "original" text which would have been copied with numerous "mistakes," he replaces the term of "error" by that of "variant": "our method is a criticism of the archetype: it aims at reconstituting the archetype with the help of the manuscript tradition deriving from it; it rejects the notion of 'mistake' [*faute*] which derives from the conception one has of the 'original'; it knows only the various forms available in different manuscripts" (*ECT*, p. 65).

The "archetype" is thus a hypothetical construct, a model which derives from the "stemma" corresponding to families of texts which can be separated and collated through a systematic contrastive analysis. "Nothing is more important than the task of clearly distinguishing between criticism based on the original and criticism based on the archetype" (*ECT*, p. 43). In some cases, the archetype of actual manuscripts can be different from the original, which will never be known. Quentin attempts to be faithful to the spirit of certain textual traditions that are "alive" and not "dead" and names two ecdotic traditions, the multiple versions of troubadour songs and the apparently endless corrections of Biblical manuscripts, which for centuries kept producing interesting echoes and distortions. As Shaun notes in the right hand margin of II, 2, we have moved "FROM CENOGENETIC DICHOTOMY THROUGH DIAGONISTIC CONCILIANCE TO DYNASTIC CONTINUITY" (*FW*, 275, R 1). "Kainogenesis" is "cenogenesis" or a new birth, linking Joyce's little family to Pound's old principle of "making it new." This provides then "PROBAPOSSIBLE PROLEGOMENA TO IDEAREAL HISTORY" (262, R 1).

Thus, what we take to be the *Wake*'s radical departures in the handling of story-line, plot, and language have precise theoretical counterparts in the contemporary debate opposing Bédier, Paris, and Dom Quentin. *Finnegans Wake* is both historical and trans-historical in the way it exploits current debates about the nature of textuality and transforms them into the text itself. As we have seen, the "Letter" episode (I, 5) uses Sullivan's edition of *The Book of Kells* as a point of departure for a praise of textual instability and the multiplicity of variants. Pages 119 to 123 of *Finnegans Wake* do precisely what the *Scribbledehobble* notebook had set out to enact: they gloss the doubts and uncertainties of textual editions, and while they pretend to be commenting on a medieval manuscript, they describe both the 732 pages of the original edition of *Ulysses* (*FW*, 123.6, with an allusion to the printer, Maurice Darantiere) and the forthcoming, never-ending "Work in Progress."

Joyce was acutely and painfully aware of the faulty nature of the printed edition of *Ulysses*, and he subsequently applied this very idea to his new book, perhaps because it was to be founded on the concept of theological sin or *faute*. In the *Wake*, indeed, the world becomes a sort of felicitous misprint or a masturbatory slip of God's pen, with the qualification that this "mistake" immediately generates countless variants which reproduce themselves in more or less anarchic fashion. The multiple variants always hesitate between the status of a hypothetically reconstructed "family" or "stemma" (the "archetype" of Dom Quentin) and the status of trivialized repetitions of repetitions without any available "original" (the stereotypes of a language which keeps quoting and distorting itself, always guilty of a logical *hysteron proteron*). This also corresponds to the systematic hesitation between the oral status of the book – with the numerous references to an epic and oral tradition – and its reflexive description as the "Letter" of literature. To go back to Lacan's terminology, it looks as if Joyce had been aware of the "knot" his egoistic writings would produce in his family – and in the extended family of his subsequent readers.

Although the "genreader" of *Finnegans Wake* appears obsessed by a pervasive sense of sin or *faute*, these mistakes are ineluctable. Sin may just be a misquotation from the Book of Good, but in Joyce's book we keep misreading, missing meanings, producing forced interpretations, seeing things which are not there. This contradicts Eco's idea that there are no rules that could say what a "better" reading would be, only rules that dismiss "bad" readings. I would suggest on the contrary that we can only tell whether readings are better or worse (they will please us better) but that we cannot ever condemn "bad" readings. We shall simply not use them if they do not accord with our priorities. The "genreader" should not be afraid of misreadings: because all the variants return as kaleidoscopic stereotypes, the "genreader" starts learning a textual process (as Pound's *Cantos*, which are supposed to embody a lifetime for which there is "no substitute"). Contrarily to Eco's "ideal reader," the "genreader" cannot become the counterpart of an "ideal text" whose *intentio operis* could be ascertained with mathematical, philological, or theological precision. Facing an expanding archive, the "genreader" progresses through an excess of intentions and meanings that never adequately match each other. Therefore the "genreader" will be *genetic* in that (s)he (like the she-hen viewing literature as a mound of rubbish from which meaning will be finally extracted) is always becoming, and transforming the text whose intentions are to be ascribed to a whole unstable archive, and *generic* because always poised in some sort of textual and sexual undecidability.

This comes as the consequence of the hypertextual and collective corpus generated by *Finnegans Wake*. What is meant by this corpus? A collection of texts, including everything available, letters, notebooks, drafts, critical glosses, annotations, introductions, commentaries, with a surplus of emotional meaning often found in musicalization or lyricism. One could take the example of the last monologue to show that the notebooks contain real "jazzy" improvisations, that are then incorporated into the machine. Here again, one could show how the "genreader" is addressed emotionally beyond gender. The notebooks finally reduce James Joyce to one of the book's characters (through the system of sigla). In VI.B.15. 146, Joyce's role is evoked: "J.J. putting actions / to sleep / sending night over / world." In VI.B.149, he sees himself as having "abolished preface, dedication, / notes, letter to press, / interviews, chapter titles, / capitals, inverted commas." In VI.B.8, he opposes his method to Flaubert's: "Flaub.[ert's] treatment of language is a kind of despair / JJ contrary." In VI.B.21.22 he writes: "JJ's not hell open / to christians but/ English open to/ Europeans." Joyce could deprecate his work, as in: "W i P – a French letter which does not succeed in coming off, never quite" (VI.B.35.67), but more often keeps faith with his unshakeable belief that the work's impact ought to be tremendous. What matters for him is less to bury Beria a second time than to revolutionize the old world by destroying "old sense." This is why the notebooks pay Jolas a last homage:

> X revolution of word
> manage – –
> burial of old sense (VI.B.32.210)

CHAPTER TWELVE

Stewardship, Parnellism, and egotism

The birth of a new reader may not be as momentous as the birth of a new nation, but Joyce's hope is that in the end the two notions will merge. We have seen how he moved from an early anarchistic and esthetic egoism to a broader conception of hospitality understood as the ability of one language to welcome all the other languages (which entails generalizing "bilinguism" to include the whole world). The issue evolves from an egoistic refusal to serve any master or cause to a concern with "owning" the new language. The issue of ownership should also – and here is the difficult transition – attack the ideological veils that perpetuate oppression. Religion will no doubt have its role to play in that context, since already for Marx, religion provided the main theoretical model with which one could understand (and therefore criticize) the very nature of ideology. For Marx and Engels, thinkers like Hegel, Bruno Bauer, Feuerbach and Max Stirner all performed a religious trick by which the economic basis of society was misread and mystified, veiled in the name of pseudo-transcendent entities such as Man, the Spirit, or the Ego. For Stirner, however, Marx and Engels merely replaced one system of domination with another.

In Stirner's view, egoism does not stem from simple "self-interest" but aims at "ownness" that is "self-mastery," a form of individual autonomy. Patriotism and nationalism no less than the "cause of the proletariat" thus become for Stirner so many alienating "ghosts." We have seen how Stephen's "ineradicable egoism" produces a systematic delusion, by which he imagines in the early "Portrait of the Artist" that "the deeds and thoughts of the microcosm" constantly "converge to him" (*APA*, 259). It will take Bloom's counterweight to introduce a forcefully original parallactic vision. In an age marked by the three "masters of suspicion" who have relentlessly dethroned the old ego, Marx, Nietzsche, and Freud, we may smile at such Joyce's juvenile delusions of grandeur. Yet, as we have seen, the ego's centrality is heuristic and enabling in that it provides a practical and theoretical impetus for a rethinking of all the economies of desire upon which a culture of liberation can be founded.

This is why it might be useful to have another look at the parable of the dishonest steward that marks the culmination of the satire of debased and perverted Catholicism in *Dubliners*. At the end of "Grace," Father Purdon's sermon in the Jesuit church of Gardiner street epitomizes the moral complacency and spiritual simony always associated in the collection with degraded *petit bourgeois* values. Dublin is presented as the capital of simony: spiritual values have been reduced to commodities, while commercial interest still needs a religious sponsor to disguise its cynicism.[1] The preacher (whose name calls up a then famous street in the red-light district of Dublin while evoking a Jesuitical "pardon" all too easily granted to sinners) concludes his sermon with these words:

"For the children of this world are wiser in their generation than the children of light. Wherefore make unto yourselves friends out of the mammon of iniquity so that when you die they may receive you into everlasting dwellings."

Father Purdon developed the text with resonant assurance. It was one of the most difficult texts in all the Scriptures, he said, to interpret properly. It was a text which might seem to the casual observer at variance with the lofty morality elsewhere preached by Jesus Christ.[2]

The modernized text of Luke 16 used by Father Purdon is at variance with either the King James Version or the Catholic Bible, where one does not find "when you die" but "when you fail." The basic story is well-known: a master, a lord (*adon*) who is also a "rich man," has heard rumors that his *oikonomos* (or *villicus* in the Vulgate) has "wasted his goods." The master tells him two things that are slightly contradictory: first that he has to "give an account of [his] stewardship," then that he will be dismissed ("for now thou canst be steward no longer"). The steward is aware that he has very little time before being actually dismissed, and chooses not to "give an account," that is not to defend himself. He calls in all the debtors of his master and invents an ingenious a trick "so that they may receive (him) into their houses": when a debtor owes a hundred barrels of oil, he changes the debt to fifty barrels; another debtor owes a hundred quarters of wheat, he changes the debt to eighty quarters. This frantic moment of falsification is also a scene of writing and dictation: "And he said to him: Take thy bill [*gramma*] and sit down quickly and write [*grapson*] fifty . . . He said to him: Take thy bill and write eighty" (Luke, 16: 6–7). He does not write anything himself, a point to which I will have to return, but just orders the "iniquitous" reductions of debts.

The story of the Steward of Iniquity offers a parable linking debt, sin, writing, and hospitality. The steward's model, insofar as it is a model – its exemplarity is given by default, since Luke deplores a lack of natural wisdom in religious matters, whereas ruse and cleverness are often applied for practical or financial "human" issues – teaches how to steal from a debt and how to bet on hospitality. Because the *oikonomos* has been asked to give an account of his stewardship, he suddenly launches into systematic anti-economy: the *oikonomos*, who would have been called an "accountant" in modern language, and has so far mediated between a rich owner and a crowd of debtors, now starts perverting this relationship. There is a certain degree of haphazard anarchy in the rapid reductions he authorizes, from a hundred to fifty in one case, from a hundred to eighty in another, which may be ascribed to pure improvisation. The debtors will only profit marginally, for, indeed, the steward does not erase their debts, even though he might have been tempted to do so by simply destroying the tell-tale tablets altogether as another irate Moses back from the Mount.

This would undermine the force of the parable whose meaning hinges on a particular respect for written deeds. As I have already noted, the steward does not write himself, he merely dictates to happily surprised debtors. He looks a lot like Mr. Bloom who, according to his fellow Dubliners at least, is reluctant to sign his name to the new document: "Nothing in black and white" (*U*, 8: 988). In the parable, these rewritten tablets are partly deliberate falsification and forgery, partly chance miscalculation. Any writing is shown here to be mere rewriting, keeping the trace of a previous pact that cannot be erased but only written over, tampered with or partially canceled.

One of the ironies of the parable's outcome is that the master, instead of being furious about the added injury, praises the ruse of his accountant as if he knew, in a Hegelian fashion, that history only progresses through cunning and makes good use of betrayal ("And the lord commended the unjust steward, forasmuch as he had done wisely," Luke 16: 8). In fact, whether he knew it or not, the steward's tactic was the best plan to be rehired on the spot. However, his astute strategy aimed at being invited by the master's debtors, who no doubt will later show some measure of gratitude. Since he expects to be without money or job, and is above begging or working with his hands ("To dig I am not able; to beg I am ashamed") he will have to depend upon the others: this is the steward's irrefutable syllogism. The context of this potentially scandalous commendation of an "unjust" man whose "iniquity" is highly praised gives it another twist: Luke, writing in the name of Jesus, means to attack the Pharisees who, as we know, were with the Scribes the staunchest defenders of the old dispensation, and the guardians of the Mosaic faith after the destruction of the Temple by the Romans. Luke's story questions the Pharisees' aristocratic self-righteousness, their denial of debt and their damaging blindness in front of an impending catastrophe.

The steward who gives by reducing debts which are not his own, in the hope of future charity and hospitality, is aware that somehow his accounts, like those of everybody, will never tally. Since no one can pay back fully, debt remains, and it is far wiser to gain new accomplices than to bet on one's purity facing the Law. The righteous and "just" Pharisees are on the other hand described as "covetous" (Luke 16: 14), which suggests that they already embody what Max Weber denounced as the "Protestant spirit" of early capitalism. They identify material possessions with divine election; but they are misers above all because they feel too secure. They labor under the delusion that they are the elect, the *ariston*, the chosen ones; their riches, both in an economic and spiritual sense, that should prove their moral distinction, are in fact spurious – precisely because they believe mistakenly that they have no debt to account for. They are the "sentimentalists" denounced by Meredith, Renan, and Stephen, for they wish to abolish time in a misguided assumption of static ethical transparency.

The steward's predicament can be universalized to all humanity: we are all going to "account" for our lives, and we are all going to be found wanting. The catastrophe of death and judgment is near, we are thinking in times of urgency and panic. The only way we may postpone its terrible effects seems to be by a more cunning calculation: if we cannot make our accounts look right, at least we can redirect a former prevarication into the direction of the others. We will add to our wrongdoing in one sense (instead of justifying the past – but there is no time for that, this would be really wasting one's time) and risk a faster dilapidation of the master's fortune. Lending the money we do not have should at least gain for us the friendship of people whose complicity we may try to buy in advance. Luke's wager stresses human community by betting on a sense of social reciprocity, not on divine pardon. It looks to the others and not to a vertical or transcendent relationship.

This parable supposes an economy of debt gambling on a future underpinned by reciprocal sociability. The *adon* is no doubt pleased to have discovered that if his steward steals, at least he is not stupid; if he loses some money with him, it will only be a fraction of what the latter's clever transactions will bring him. An anagogical reading of the parable suggests that the steward acts like Jesus in Christian doctrine. Jesus will takes away from men's sins, and these sins appear as a sort of collective debt, a debt which can be diminished but never fully canceled; moreover, he also takes something away from the old Jewish Law that he distorts. The steward facing the master is in the same position as Jesus the Son facing his divine Father or as Moses facing God. Both steal from the debt of sin, lessening it in order to reduce the burden of humanity. Hospitality acquires the ethical dimension of a dynamic replacement, of a yet unwritten substitute for the trace left by sin.

The appeal of this parable must have been great indeed for Jesuit casuists; however, in "Grace," Father Purdon tellingly omits the ideological counterweight provided by the following verse: "No servant can serve two masters . . . You cannot serve God and Mammon" (Luke 16: 13) that we found to be so momentous for Joyce's critical analysis of Ireland. By this clear admonition, Jesus refuses the Pharisaic equation between money and election. Money is seen less as a true "general equivalent" measuring future exchange than as an unstable token of iniquity, and this is essential to the parable, since it explains how it can be read as a sort of negative Pascalian "wager" argument. It makes more sense to bet on the future outcome of one's actions than to justify past deeds.

Precisely because one cannot serve two masters, money should not be mistaken for a sign of election; being a debased sign, it can only play a role as a tool to gain friends. A rapid evaluation of chances with the others all in debt can prepare for a new start in life, since a half-clean slate looks safer than the uncertain outcome of a trial. It is thus not necessary to justify oneself in front of the law. A prudential judgment implying one's egoistic interest (that is putting one's interest first and foremost) is to be preferred to an evidential judgment that will go through all the motions of finding proofs, evidence, testimonies, all of which are of no avail in a time of haste. There is simply no time for the endless deferral of a Kafkaian trial. As *Finnegans Wake* demonstrates at some length, the very time of dreams and the night of history already contains all the postponements of an indefinite trial such as the one in which the Earwicker family is caught. Guilt and sin are the stuff these dreams are made of, one can only wake up in the morning – but not settle the issue once and for all.

Such a prudential grammatology in which a stroke of the pen can reduce a debt without abolishing it points to the function of Christ as a Redeemer who buys humanity out of original sin but on the installment plan, as it were. Failure can be positive, we can live with an interminable debt, provided we have been wise enough to bet on a future entirely circumscribed by the arc of hospitality. The verticality of transcendence experienced as one's subjective link to the law has been replaced by a horizontal principle of personal interest, mutual help, and social responsibility. Hospitality, by virtue of its ethical and interactive nature, replaces a symbolic economy of sin as debt by a social economy of sin as shame, thereby pushing the model away from a Protestant view and closer to an "Oriental" model. We have thus unwittingly moved from an assertion of "Myself Alone!" to a wider claim such as: "Ourselves Alone!" If we wish to situate the parable in an Irish context (or in any post-colonial context, for that matter), we see how egoistic calculations can generate a sense of reciprocity and responsibility.

There is also an anagogic level of reading in the parable: thanks to an overlapping between earthly hospitality (the steward has optimistically calculated that his remissions of debt will grant him automatic offers of hospitality and that the others will "receive him into their houses") and heavenly hospitality (the mansions of Heaven that will welcome the blessed), the parable retains a trace of messianic meaning. The event that has already occurred (the birth of Christ) will be duplicated as the second coming, provided the newcomer is "welcome" among people who can forget wrongdoing in exchange for personal interaction.

How far then can one calculate or buy hospitality in advance? Isn't Jesus caught here red-handed in advocating some kind of moral simony? Is Joyce merely denouncing him, or following in his steps? For it looks as if Joyce's calculated politics of egoism had been underwritten by such an assumption that is almost identical to the steward's: if he was able to recreate the "conscience of his race" in writing, or if he could "do better" than, say, Dante and Shakespeare together, then he and his family would always find people willing to receive them into their houses. And if one decides to read this parable with a stress on writing as an intransitive process and not merely as an instrument, then its morality is that messianism will sooner or later be replaced by Maecenatism – or simply put, literary patronage. Miss Weaver's generosity will function clearly as one of the "houses" into which our Modernist steward will be received.

In his life-long identification with a "joking Jaysus," Joyce's cunning appears quite similar to the ruse of the steward praised by Jesus in Luke's text. The paradox here is that the most egoistic motivation (fighting for mere economic survival while refusing too degrading tasks or anything that would deflect from the chosen route) turns into a praise of hospitality and conviviality. But, unlike Father Purdon, Joyce never forgets that "No servant can serve two masters" (Luke 16: 13). As we have seen, the Italian article on "Fenianism" denounced the fact that "Ireland, weighed down by multiple duties, has fulfilled what has hitherto been considered an impossible task – serving both God and mammon, letting herself be milked by England and yet increasing Peter's pence" (*CW*, 190), while Stephen bitterly refers to himself as "the servant of two masters . . . an English and an Italian" (*U*, 1: 638), adding as we have seen: "And a third . . . there is who wants me for odd jobs" (*U*, 1: 641). The third master is obviously an Irish nationalism that found its authentic voice with the Sinn Fein movement of Arthur Griffith, after having been launched by Parnell's Home Rule movement. Joyce who had been described by Yeats in 1923 as "the son of a small Parnellite organizer,"[3] briefly traversed the violent and anarchist phase of "Neither God nor a Master!" before rethinking the links that connect religion and mastery; that is, getting an insight into the complementarity (despite their antagonism) of traditional Catholicism used as a site of popular resistance to colonialist oppression and of a local capitalism that will need vital exchanges with main economical centers such as imperial London.

One of the ironies of history, not missed by Joyce, is that the signifier "steward" adheres as an echo at least and with a letter's difference to the middle name of his main political hero, Charles Stewart Parnell. The Catholic bishops of the end of the nineteenth century would probably have agreed to see Parnell as a "Steward of Iniquity" for the Irish people. Parnell's untimely demise had nevertheless heralded a brighter future for Ireland, for as he stated in the often quoted Cork speech: "No man has the right to fix the boundary of the march of a nation." This network of entangled motives reappears in the *Wake* when the popular ballad-composer Hosty is presented as HCE's enemy or *hostis* (*FW*, 41.5). The Dublin crowd is as eagerly waiting for the ballad that will be heard a few pages later and is compared to the first performance of Handel's *Messiah* in Dublin:

with their priggish mouths all open for the larger appraisiation of this longawated Messiagh of roaratorios, were only halfpast atsweeeep and after a brisk pause at a pawnbroking establishment for the prothetic purpose of redeeming the songster's truly admirable false teeth and a prolonged visit to a house of call at Cujas Place, fizz, the Old Sots' Hole in the parish of Saint Cecily within the liberty of Ceolmore not a thousand or one national leagues, that was, by Griffith's valuation, from the site of the statue of Primewer Glasstone setting a match to the march of a maker (last of the stewards peut-être) . . . the rascals came out of the licensed premises . . . wiping their laughleaking lipes on their sleeves, how the bouckaleens shout their roscan generally (seinn fion, seinn fion's araun.) and the rhymer's world was with reason the richer for a wouldbe ballad . . . (*FW*, 41.27–42. 13)

Griffith seems to keep up Parnell's cause, even if the latter is ironically conflated with James II, the last reigning Stuart king (or perhaps Joyce also alludes mockingly to his "friend" Stuart Gilbert) in deciding that the Irish nationalist slogan of *Sinn Féin Amhain* ("Ourselves Alone") will offer a proper response to Gladstone. But radical independence is impossible: Parnell's "march of a nation" hesitates here between a much less isolationist game of "match-making" and the revolutionary conflagration of "setting a match to." It is clear from this passage at any rate, as from many others, that Joyce is no more endorsing Griffith's program than he is frozen in a Parnellite limbo that would blend an old-fashioned liberalism with a reluctance to take into account the revolutionary turmoil of Ireland, the fight for independence, the partition and the civil war of 1922.[4] Like the steward of Luke's parable, Joyce has to bet on the future, he bets on his literary fame and on the future of the Book – not only by requesting of others that they should help him in time of need, but by staking everything on the production of a new type of writing that remains halfway between oral dictation and faulty transcription, between hurried improvisation mimicking a father's voice and scribbled notes or tablets misrepresenting the higher values of culture.

I have quoted earlier Manfred Pütz's view that *Finnegans Wake* belongs entirely to the atmosphere of the late thirties, is a typical product of a belated avant-garde or of what Miller has called "late Modernism." I would like to stress an opposite idea here, namely that the text can only live up to its claims (if we agree to take them seriously) by staying ahead of its time and heralding a future that looks a little like the vision Joyce had of a more or less unified Europe in a time of globalization, using English as a common vehicular language while retaining many of the old particularist features defined by nationality, ethnicity, and creed. When the world looks more and more like a global village, the *Wake* relentlessly insists on its futurity, as when it "invents" television and the atomic bomb at a time when these were only projects, mere possibilities, and scientific blueprints, and sees the future determined by the creation of a new multiethnic, multilinguistic, and multiracial humanity. The main issue nevertheless lies with language, and Joyce foresaw that Ireland would have a lot to gain from its bilingual status, both a major asset in forging new links with the American continent and in reaching a reunification through an integration with an expanding European community. By replaying the comedy or tragedy of conquest and resistance as a dream of universal history, Joyce intends to stay away both from sectarian violence and from sentimentalism, that is, the tendency to romance over one's failures (a tendency that he found so fascinating and revolting in his own father) or to essentialize "natures" taken in isolation from historical processes of production.

This is why I would like to conclude with two vignettes linking Joyce's concern for the "music of the future" with conflicting views of an "egoism" that paradoxically but inevitably transforms itself into ethical altruism. They come from this precious witness, Arthur Power, who befriended Joyce in the twenties. Just after the publication of *Ulysses*, Joyce surprised Power by confiding that he still believed in realism. This is what he told the younger Irish friend:

> What makes most people's lives unhappy is some disappointed romanticism, some unrealizable or misconceived ideal. In fact you may say that idealism is the ruin of man . . . Nature is quite unromantic. It is we who put romance into her, which is a false attitude, an egotism, absurd like all egotisms. In *Ulysses* I have tried to keep close to fact . . . (*CJJ*, 98)

Realism, or the wish to remain close to "fact," destroys an "egotism" that would encompass idealism, sentimentalism, and Romanticism. Primitive man is taken as a model because he would, one assumes, think first of his own survival facing nature, and only then would slowly elaborate his "supreme fictions," as Wallace Stevens would say. Let us take good note that Joyce has attacked "egotism," and not "egoism." If there was any confusion, it should be blamed on Power himself.

For in 1931, Arthur Power felt that the old intimacy with Joyce was harder to resume. He invited a reluctant Joyce to dinner while they were both in London and documents a growing feeling of estrangement. This happened precisely at a crucial turning point for Joyce, at the time of the birth of Stephen Joyce. As Power had driven them to a very far and bad restaurant that Joyce did not like, the mood grew tense, until, in an effort to relieve the tension, Joyce announced the big news. The dialogue is worth quoting in full:

> – I have just received very important news.
> – What is it? I asked, thinking it must be something of literary importance.
> – A son has been born to Georgio and Helen in Paris.
> In truth I am not a family man who dotes on children . . .
> – Is that all? I replied.

– It is the most important thing there is, said Joyce firmly, his voice charged with meaning.
A sudden suspicion crossed my mind; "the most important thing there is" meant that another Joyce had been born into the world. Even to this day I am still in doubt; for Joyce's estimation of his merit would on occasion suddenly flare up to a point of madness.
Anyway, at the mere suspicion of it – for egotism has its limit – my bad temper rose up again and I said:
– I cannot see that it is so important. It is something which happens all the time, everywhere, and with everyone.
A tense silence fell between us as I drove up Kensington High Street. (*CJJ*, 110)

It would be hard on Power to stress the awkward irony of his self-defeating formulation. His brutally insensitive deflation was couched in universalizing terms that the Joyce of *Finnegans Wake* might have used in another context, while completely missing the "non-literary" and quite personal sense of joy and completion in the Irish writer. Nothing indeed could be less "egotistic" than to rejoice over the birth of a grandson!

In fact, if one wants to stick to purely literary issues of egoism and egotism, it looks as if Joyce's heir was not his own grandson, but another Irish writer, Samuel Beckett – although this may be quite another story. In his French novels particularly, especially *The Unnamable* and *Texts for Nothing*, we can see how the problematic of endless "egologies" returns with a vengeance to haunt the text and all its "accomplices" (readers, writer, characters, and all the intermediary "pronouns" by which they negotiate an increasingly difficult interaction). Beckett had to start again at the beginning in order to be sure on a different track, by questioning the literary trick of a voice that can say "I" when it is not identical to this "I." One example will suffice, and will provide a fitting conclusion:

Perhaps it is time I paid a little attention to myself, for a change. I shall be reduced to it sooner or later. At first sight it seems impossible. Me, utter me, in the same foul breath as my creatures? Say of me that I see this, feel that, fear, hope, know and do not know? Yes, I will say it, and of me alone. Impassible, still and mute, Malone revolves, a stranger forever to my infirmities, one who is not as I can never not be. I am motionless in vain, he is the god. And the other? I have assigned him eyes that implore me, offerings for me, need of succour. He does not look at me, does not know of me, wants for nothing. I alone am man, all the rest is divine.[5]

Notes

1 *APRÈS MOT, LE DÉLUGE* : THE EGO AS SYMPTOM

The chapter title refers to the last line of the limerick written by Joyce for his friend Eugène Jolas to celebrate the publication of *Mots-Déluge*:

> VERSAILLES 1933
> There's a genial young poetriarch Euge
> Who hollers with heartiness huge:
>   Let sick souls sob for solace
>   So the jeunes joy with Jolas
> Book your berths: Après mot, le déluge!

I reproduce the text as quoted in Eugène Jolas, *Man from Babel* (Yale: Yale University Press, 1998), p. 112. Jolas mentions that, according to a critic, his neological poems were "halfway between madness and genius" (*ibid.*). The limerick is also reproduced by Richard Ellmann in *James Joyce*, 2nd revised edn, p. 587.

1 Paul Gray, "The Writer James Joyce," *Time*, June 8, 1998, p. 105. One can notice that in the *Time* issue of August 3, 1998, Joyce is heralded as a "Winner" in the section "Winners and Losers." See the short comment p. 23: "His *Ulysses* is named century's best novel. Is Joyce somewhere gloating? yes I said yes!"

2 See Sigmund Freud and William C. Bullitt, *Thomas Woodrow Wilson: A Psychological Study* (Boston: Houghton Mifflin, 1966). Hereafter *TWW*, and page number.

3 See Tyrus Miller, *Late Modernism: Politics, Fiction and the Arts Between the World Wars* (Stanford: Stanford University Press, 1999).

4 Eugène Jolas, *Man from Babel*, p. 99.

5 I have done this in detail in the last chapter of my *Jacques Lacan* (London: Palgrave, 2001), pp. 154–82. Here, I simply highlight elements concerning the issue of egoism.

6 *James Joyce, Oeuvres II*, ed. Jacques Aubert (Paris: Gallimard, Bibliothèque de la Pléiade, 1996).

7 Lacan's memory is probably more accurate when he speaks of being twenty at the famous reading and lecture devoted to *Ulysses* on December 7, 1921

(Lacan, born in 1901, was indeed twenty) than meeting Joyce at *La Maison des Amis des Livres* when he was seventeen: in 1918, Joyce had not yet moved to Paris. See *Joyce avec Lacan*, ed. Jacques Aubert (Paris: Navarin, 1987), p. 22. Hereafter *JAL*, and page number.

8 See for useful close readings of these seminars Roberto Harari, *Como se llama James Joyce? A partir de "El Sinthoma" de Lacan* (Buenos Aires: Amorrortu editores, 1996). A very useful summary is provided by Ellie Ragland-Sullivan, "Lacan's Seminars on James Joyce: Writing as Symptom and 'Singular Solution'", in *Psychoanalysis and . . .*, ed. R. Feldstein and Henry Sussman (New York: Routledge, 1990), pp. 76–86. Néstor Braunstein has been the first Lacanian analyst to take the "return of the ego" in Lacan's seminar seriously. See his very lucid essays: "La clínica en el nombre propio," in *El Laberinto de las Estructuras*, ed. Helí Morales Asencio (Mexico: Siglo 21, 1997), pp. 70–96 and "El ego lacaniano," in *En Las Suplencias del Nombre del Padre*, ed. Helí Morales and Daniel Gerber (Mexico: Siglo 21, 1998), pp. 53–74.

9 "So Lacan had invented a Joycean portmanteau word (*sinthome*) to suggest the idea of redemption through literature. The word evoked several other terms that according to Lacan could be regarded as 'signifiers' in the Joycean universe: these included 'home,' as in Home Rule, the slogan calling for Irish independence of Britain; and *St. Thomas*. So *sinthome* could also be written *sinthome* rule or *sinthomas aquinas*." Elisabeth Roudinesco, *Jacques Lacan*, trans. Barbara Bray (New York: Columbia University Press, 1997), p. 373. See the entire account pp. 371–74.

10 See Jung's pronouncements on Joyce and Lucia in *JJII*, pp. 679–80.

11 Jacques Lacan, "Le Sinthome," *Ornicar?*, 9 (April 1977), p. 38.

12 Jacques Lacan, "Le Sinthome," *Ornicar?*, 11 (September 1977), p. 8.

13 It was first given as a lecture in London in 1951, then published two years later in *The International Journal of Psychoanalysis*. See Jacques Lacan, "Some Reflections on the Ego," *International Journal of Psychoanalysis*, 34 (1953).

14 Jacques Lacan, *Ecrits: A Selection*, trans. A. Sheridan (New York: W. W. Norton, 1977), p. 231.

15 *Joyce & Paris*, ed. Jacques Aubert (Lille and Paris: CNRS, 1979).

16 "Le Sinthome," *Ornicar?*, 8 (1976), p. 6.

17 Jacques Lacan, "Ecrits Inspirés," in *De la psychose paranoïaque dans ses rapports avec la personnalité, suivi de premiers écrits sur la paranoia* (Paris: Seuil, 1975), pp. 379–80.

18 Roger Vitrac, *transition* 18 (1929), pp. 176–90.

19 *Ibid.*, p. 180.

20 See Néstor Braunstein's excellent survey in *La Jouissance, un concept lacanien* (Paris: Point Hors Ligne, 1992). Forthcoming in English from Verso.

21 Jacques-Alain Miller, "A Reading of Some Details in *Television* in Dialogue with the Audience," *Letters from the Freudian Field*, 4, 1/2 (Spring-Fall 1990), p. 26.

22 Sigmund Freud, *The Interpretation of Dreams*, trans. James Strachey (New York: Avon Books, 1965), p. 157. Hereafter, *ID*, and page number.

23 See *ID*, 304, n. 2. Ernest Jones, who is quoted here, concludes a paper on "A Forgotten Dream" by the remark that "Most of the individual features of Freud's dream theory are also illustrated in the analysis, the almost grotesque egocentricity of the dream-thoughts . . ." "A Forgotten Dream," in *Papers on Psycho-Analysis* (Boston: Beacon, 1967), p. 241.

24 It is interesting to see that a recent translation of the first version of *The Interpretation of Dreams* has systematically downplayed the theme of egoism. Thus when Freud writes extremely explicitly: "Träume sind absolut egoistisch" (Sigmund Freud, *Die Traumdeutung* [Frankfurt: Fischer Verlag, 1972], p. 320), Joyce Crick translates: "Dreams are absolutely self-centred." See Sigmund Freud, *The Interpretation of Dreams* (Oxford: Oxford University Press, 1999), p. 246 – as if this "egoism" was still felt to be in bad taste.

25 Sigmund Freud, "A Child is Being Beaten," in *Sexuality and the Psychology of Love* (New York: Collier, 1978), pp. 107–32.

26 Sigmund Freud, "The Poet and Day-Dreaming," in *On Creativity and the Unconscious*, ed. B. Nelson (New York: Harper and Row, 1958), p. 50. Hereafter *PDD*, and page number.

27 I am quoting in parentheses the German original of "Der Dichter und das Phantasieren" from Sigmund Freud, *Bildende Kunst und Literatur* (Frankfurt: Fischer, 1970), p. 179.

28 Mary Gaitskill, *Two Girls, Fat and Thin* (New York: Poseidon, 1991). See also Jeff Walker, *The Ayn Rand Cult* (Chicago: Open Court, 1999), pp. 327–29.

29 Barbara Branden, *The Passion of Ayn Rand* (New York, Doubleday, 1986), pp. 158–67.

30 Ayn Rand, *The Fountainhead* (New York: Signet, 1993), p. 709. Hereafter *F*, and page number.

31 Quoted by Barbara Branden, *The Passion of Ayn Rand*, p. 133.

32 Ayn Rand and Nathaniel Branden, *The Virtue of Selfishness* (New York: Signet, 1964), p. 13.

33 Slavoj Zizek, "The Lesbian Session," *Lacanian Ink*, 12 (Fall 1997), p. 59.

34 Ayn Rand, *The Virtue of Selfishness*, p. 37.

35 James Joyce, *Poems and Exiles*, ed. J. C. C. Mays (London, Penguin, 1992), pp. 163–64.

36 Stuart Gilbert, *Reflections on James Joyce. Stuart Gilbert's Paris Journal*, ed. T. F. Staley and R. Lewis (Austin: University Press of Texas, 1993), p. 46. This diary entry is dated May 6, 1932. Gilbert acrimoniously calls James Joyce "a spoilt god" (p. 6) and notes that if Lucia "worked for the glory of God, not her own, would make a name in the world of missals, evangelaries and the like" (p. 58).

37 *Stuart Gilbert's Paris Journal*, p. 48. Dated May 24, 1932.

38 See Jacques Lacan's doctoral thesis, *De la psychose paranoïaque dans ses rapports avec la personnalité* (Paris: Seuil, 1975).

39 Alain Manier, *Le Jour où l'espace a coupé le temps: Etiologie et clinique de la psychose* (Plancoët: Editions La Tempérance, 1995).

40 Here one might quote Stuart Gilbert's bitter gibe: "One afternoon Joyce

described a domestic battle – about Lucia's eyes and scar: the woman in tears (she is going to have her eyes straightened); walking with me, Joyce became quite human and complained of his daughter not being 'normal,' and her incapacity to stick to anything! Joyce in quest of normality in his family is comic." *Stuart Gilbert's Paris Journal*, p. 19 (dated January 29, 1930).

2 THE EGO, THE NATION, AND DEGENERATION

1 The most literal translation would be: "The Unique One and His Propriety" – with an unmistakable masculine possessor. See the useful remarks by David Leopold in his edition of Max Stirner, *The Ego and Its Own* (Cambridge, Cambridge University Press), 1995, pp. xxxix–xl. He notes that it was the American anarchist Benjamin Tucker who chose the English title.
2 Michael Levenson, *A Genealogy of Modernism* (Cambridge: Cambridge University Press, 1984), pp. 63–68.
3 David Weir, *Anarchy and Culture: The Aesthetic Politics of Anarchism* (Amherst: University of Massachusetts Press, 1997), pp. 213–27.
4 *Ibid.*, p. 158.
5 Terry Eagleton, "Nationalism: Irony and Commitment," in *Nationalism, Colonialism and Literature* (Minneapolis: University of Minnesota Press, 1990), p. 33.
6 Vincent Cheng, *Joyce, Race and Empire* (Cambridge: Cambridge University Press, 1995).
7 *Ibid.*, pp. 34–45.
8 Eagleton, "Nationalism: Irony and Commitment," p. 36.
9 G. W. H. Hegel, "Foreword" to *The Phenomenology of Spirit*, trans. A. V. Miller (Oxford: Oxford University Press, 1977), p. 9.
10 Max Nordau, *Degeneration* (New York: Appleton and Co., 1895). Hereafter *D*, and page number.
11 William Greenslade, *Degeneration, Culture and the Novel 1880–1940* (Cambridge: Cambridge University Press, 1994). See particularly the chapter devoted to Nordau, pp. 120–33.
12 *The Egoist*, 3, 9 (September 1916), pp. 129–31.
13 See Liah Greenfeld, *Nationalism: Five Roads to Modernity* (Cambridge, MA: Harvard University Press, 1992).
14 See Alain Finkielkraut's useful book *The Defeat of the Mind* (New York: Columbia University Press, 1995).
15 Ernest Renan, "What is a Nation?," in *The Poetry of Celtic Races and Other Studies*, W. E. Hutchinson (London: Walter Scott, 1896), p. 81.
16 About this ambivalence of memory, see the excellent article by Jacques Mailhos, "The Art of Memory: Joyce and Perec," in *Transcultural Joyce*, ed. Karen Lawrence (Cambridge: Cambridge University Press, 1998), pp. 151–69.
17 Benedict Anderson, *Imagined Communities* (New York: Verso, 1991). Anderson quotes Renan about "forgetting," p. 6, and develops this in "Memory and Forgetting," pp. 199–206.

18 Padraic Colum, *Ourselves Alone!* (New York: Crown, 1959), p. 78.

19 See the interesting assessment by Brian Maye in his section: "Griffith an Anti-Semite?," in *Arthur Griffith* (Dublin: Griffith College Publications, 1997), pp. 362–72.

20 Quoted and translated by Padraic Colum in *Ourselves Alone!*, p. 32.

21 Seamus Deane, *Celtic Revivals: Essays in Modern Irish Literature 1885–1980* (London: Faber, 1985), p. 92.

22 Trevor Williams, *Reading Joyce Politically* (Gainesville: University Press of Florida, 1997), pp. 14 and 28.

23 Emer Nolan, *James Joyce and Nationalism* (New York: Routledge, 1995).

24 Tyrus Miller, *Late Modernism: Politics, Fiction and the Arts Between the World Wars* (Stanford, Stanford University Press, 1999).

25 *The Gender of Modernism: A Critical Anthology*, ed., Bonnie Kime Scott (Bloomington: Indiana University Press, 1990).

26 Jean-Paul Sartre, *Saint Genet: Actor & Martyr*, trans. Bernard Frechtman (London: Heinemann, 1988).

27 This is at least the thesis of the very stimulating reading of Heidegger by Reiner Schürmann, in *Heidegger on Being and Acting: from Principles to Anarchy*, trans. Christine-Marie Gros and the author (Bloomington: Indiana University Press, 1987).

28 Martin Heidegger, "The Way to Language" in *Basic Writings*, ed. David Farrell Krell (New York: Harper and Collins, 1993), p. 414.

29 Max Stirner, *The Ego and Its Own*, p. 324. I have modified the translation of the last sentence.

30 Here, I have substantially modified the translation of "The Way to Language" in *Basic Writings*, pp. 419–20, to be closer to the text. See Martin Heidegger, *Unterwegs zur Sprache* (Pfullingen: Günther Neske, 1959), p. 262. See *Splinters of Experience* by Kryzstof Ziarek (Evanston: Northwestern University Press, forthcoming).

31 T. S. Eliot, "Marina," *Collected Poems 1909–1962* (London: Faber, 1963), p. 116.

3 JOYCE THE EGOIST

1 *L'Egoïste* is an expensive, very large-sized luxurious fashion magazine based in Paris which publishes exclusive photographs by famous photographers. It appears irregularly in two bulky sections, and costs 200 francs (US$ 40). As an excellent omen, the thirteenth issue was published in June 1996 (Paris).

2 Launched by Caron Perfumes, Paris in the spring of 2000. This means: "It is in the darkness (or in black) that one recognizes the anarchist."

3 Jacques Derrida, *Ulysses Gramophone*, in *Acts of Literature*, ed. Derek Attridge (New York and London: Routledge, 1992), pp. 297 and 300.

4 The full title is more revealing: *Le Parfum de la femme et le sens olfactif dans l'amour: étude psycho-physiologique* (Paris: E. Dentu, Librairie de la Société des Gens de Lettres, 1889). I translate literally: "Woman's perfume and the olfactory sense in love: a psycho-physiologiocal study." Joyce apparently

bought it in Zurich; see Richard Ellmann, *The Consciousness of Joyce* (London: Faber, 1977), p. 109.

5 Dora Marsden, "Authority: Conscience and the Offences," *The Egoist*, 15 (August 1, 1914), p. 283.

6 Bruce Clarke, *Dora Marsden and Early Modernism: Gender, Individuality, Science* (Ann Arbor: University of Michigan Press, 1995). See also Robert von Hallberg, "Libertarian Imagism," *Modernism/Modernity*, 2, 2 (April 1995), pp. 63–79.

7 "Views and Comments," *The New Freewoman* (December 15, 1913), p. 244.

8 Rachel Blau Du Plessis, *The Pink Guitar: Writing as Feminist Practice* (New York: Routledge, 1990), p. 45.

9 *The New Freewoman*, 1 (June 15, 1913), p. 1.

10 Max Stirner, *The Ego and His Own*, trans. S. T. Byington, ed. J. J. Martin (New York: Dover, 1973), p. 3.

11 Dora Marsden, "The Lean Kind," *The New Freewoman* (June 15, 1913), p. 3.

12 *Ibid.*, p. 5.

13 Max Stirner, *The Ego and His Own*, trans. S. T. Byington (New York: Benjamin Tucker, 1907), pp. 43–44. Hereafter, *EO*, and page number.

14 Karl Marx and Friedrich Engels, *The German Ideology*, *Collected Works*, vol. V (New York: International Publishers, 1976), p. 152. Hereafter, *GI*, and page number.

15 Jacques Derrida, *Specters of Marx*, trans. P. Kamuf (New York: Routledge, 1994). I had covered a similar ground in my work *La Pénultimème est morte* (Seyssel: Champ Vallon, 1993). See also *The Ghosts of Modernity* (Gainesville: University Press of Florida, 1996), pp. 223–27.

16 I use here the revised but incomplete translation of Max Stirner's *The Ego and His Own*, ed. John Carroll (London: Jonathan Cape, 1971), p. 261, and have changed "affair" into "cause" (*Sache*).

17 Stanislaus Joyce, *The Complete Dublin Diary*, ed. George H. Healey, p. 3.

18 Dominic Manganiello, *Joyce's Politics* (London, Routledge, 1980), pp. 67–72.

19 Quoted in Karl Marx and Friedrich Engels, *Ireland and the Irish Question* (Moscow, Progress Publishers, 1971), p. 151. Hereafter *IIQ*, and page number.

20 Michael Levenson, *A Genealogy of Modernism* (Cambridge: Cambridge University Press, 1984), p. 68.

21 Weldon Thornton, *The Antimodernism of Joyce's Portrait of the Artist as a Young Man* (Syracuse, NY: Syracuse University Press, 1994). Hereafter *TAJ*, and page number.

22 James Joyce, *Dubliners*, ed. Terence Brown (London: Penguin, 1992), p. 107.

23 George Meredith, *The Egoist* (1879, revised 1897), ed. R. M. Adams (New York: Norton, 1979), p. 71. Hereafter *E*, and page number.

24 Jenni Calder, "The Insurrection of Women," in *E*, pp. 472–80.

25 George Meredith, *The Ordeal of Richard Feverel* (1858, revised 1878; New York: Signet, 1961), p. 196. Ironically, one may find this saying attributed to Oscar Wilde. For instance, in Jonathan Green's *Cassell Dictionary of Cynical Quotations* (London: Cassell, 1994), under the heading "Sentimentality" one finds the following maxim: "A sentimentalist is simply one who desires to have the

luxury of an emotion without paying for it." Oscar Wilde. (p. 256). "Cribbed out of Meredith," indeed!

26 See *Dora Marsden and Early Modernism*, p. 123.

27 *Ibid.*, p. 66.

28 Charles Olson, "Mayan Letters," in *Selected Writings*, ed. Robert Creeley (New York: New Directions, 1976), pp. 81–82.

29 Stendhal (Henry Beyle), "Souvenirs d'Egotisme," in *Oeuvres Intimes* (Paris: Gallimard, 1966), pp. 1393–483. "Le génie poétique est mort, mais le génie du *soupçon* est venu au monde. Je suis profondément convaincu que le seul antidote qui puisse faire oublier au lecteur les éternels *Je* que l'auteur va écrire, c'est une parfaite sincérité" (p. 1394). Pound admired this passage.

30 Arthur Power, *Conversations with James Joyce* (London, Millington, 1974), p. 98.

31 This is a point that has been well developed by Slavoj Zizek in *Enjoy Your Symptom!* (New York: Routledge, 1992).

32 Adrienne Monnier, "L' 'Ulysse' de Joyce et le public français," in *Les Gazettes, 1923–1945* (Paris: Gallimard, 1996), p. 248.

33 "Un égoïste, c'est quelqu'un qui ne pense pas à moi." *Egoïste*, 13, 1 (1996), p. 59.

34 At the opening of Bill Copley's paintings in Paris, Marcel Duchamp had inscribed these words on the wrapping paper of distributed candies: "A guest + a Host = a Ghost." In Marcel Duchamp; *Duchamp du signe: Ecrits* (Paris: Flammarion, 1975), p. 162.

4 THE ESTHETIC PARADOXES OF EGOISM: FROM NEGOISM TO THE THEORETIC

1 I have touched upon this issue in the conclusion to *Joyce Upon the Void* (London: Macmillan, 1991), pp. 217–22.

2 I am borrowing the idea of successive "paradoxes" in order to describe conceptual tensions from Antoine Compagnon's insightful *Les Cinq Paradoxes de la modernité* (Paris: Seuil, 1990).

3 James Joyce, *Critical Writings*, ed. Ellsworth Mason and Richard Ellman, p. 145.

4 James Joyce, *A Portrait of the Artist as a Young Man*, ed. Chester Anderson. When I quote the 1904 "Portrait of the Artist," I refer to this edition.

5 Bernard Bosanquet, *Three Lectures on Aesthetics* (London: Macmillan, 1923), p. 30. Henceforth, *TLA*, and page number.

6 As quoted by Wlad Godzich in his Preface to Paul de Man's *The Resistance to Theory* (Minneapolis: University of Minnesota Press, 1986), p. xiv.

7 For a subtle analysis of this tension, see Vicki Mahaffey's brilliant *Reauthorizing Joyce* (new edn, Gainesville: University Press of Florida, 1995).

8 See Slavoj Zizek, *The Sublime Object of Ideology* (London: Verso, 1989), pp. 201–31. See also Immanuel Kant, *The Critique of Judgement*, trans. J. C. Meredith (Oxford: Oxford University Press, 1952), pp. 90–203.

9 See Ginette Verstraete, *Fragments of the Feminine Sublime in Friedrich Schlegel and James Joyce* (New York: Suny Press, 1998).

10 Jacques Lacan, *Television*, ed. Joan Copjec, trans. D. Hollier, R. Krauss, and A. Michelson (New York: Norton, 1990), p. 15–16:

> A saint's business, to put it clearly, is not *caritas*. Rather, he acts as trash; his business being *trashitas*. So as to embody what the structure entails, namely allowing the subject, the subject of the unconscious, to take him as the cause of the subject's desire.
>
> In fact it is through the abjection of this cause that the subject in question has a chance to be aware of his position, at least within the structure . . .
>
> That produces an effect of *jouissance* – who doesn't "get" the meaning along with the pleasure? The saint alone stays mum; fat chance of getting anything out of him. That is really the most amazing thing in the whole business. Amazing for those who approach it without illusions: that saint is the refuse of *jouissance*.

11 Arthur Rimbaud, "A Season in Hell" in *Collected Poems*, trans. Oliver Bernard (London: Penguin, 1986), p. 315.

12 *Ibid.*, p. 335.

13 I will return to this issue in the last chapters.

14 Edmund Burke, *A Philosophical Enquiry into the Origin of our Ideas of the Sublime and the Beautiful* (Oxford: Oxford University Press, 1990), p. 71.

15 Colleen Jaurretsche, *The Sensual Philosophy: Joyce and the Aesthetics of Mysticism* (Madison: University of Wisconsin Press, 1997).

16 Cf. Terry Eagleton, *The Ideology of the Aesthetic* (Oxford: Blackwell, 1990), and Ginette Verstraete, *Fragments of the Feminine Sublime in Friedrich Schlegel and James Joyce*, pp. 190–93.

17 I have dealt with this theme in *The Ghosts of Modernity* pp. 210–15.

18 James Joyce, *Letters*, III, p. 361. The Italian original has: "Ho gli occhi stanchi. Da più di mezzo secolo scrutano nel nulla dove hanno trovato un bellissimo niente." (*Letters*, III, p. 359).

19 See *The Ghosts of Modernity*, pp. 102–23.

5 THEORY'S SLICE OF LIFE

1 The translation is mine. Lautréamont, *Oeuvres complètes d'Isidore Ducasse, Les Chants de Maldoror* (Paris: Livre de Poche, 1964), p. 132.

2 *The Egoist*, 2, 1 (January 1, 1915), p. 13.

3 Remy de Gourmont, "Lautréamont," in *The Egoist*, 1, 16 (August 15, 1914), p. 309, footnote.

4 *Ibid.*, p. 309.

5 *The Ghosts of Modernity*.

6 *Georges de La Tour and his World*, ed. Philip Conisbee (Washington: National Gallery of Art), 1996, p. 96.

7 James Joyce, "Paris Notebook," *Critical Writings*, p. 146.

8 Aristotle, *Problems*, trans. W. S. Hett (London: Heinemann, 1926), pp. 47–63. I am quoting from Book II, "Problems connected with sweat."

9 *Ibid.*, pp. 13–15.

10 Aristotle, *History of Animals*, trans. W. S. Hett (London: Heinemann, 1926),

Book 5, p. xxxi (556 b 25). A little earlier, Aristotle has allowed that lice do indeed copulate, but that the result of this copulation is imperfect:

> But whenever we find creatures spontaneously generated in living animals or in the earth or in plants, or in the parts of these . . . then when these copulate a product results which is never the same as the parents, but imperfect . . . Thus, when lice copulate, they produce nits, flies produce larvae, fleas produce egg-like grubs; and from these the parent kind is never produced, nor indeed any animal at all, but simply the sort of thing I have mentioned. (539 b 5–13)

11 *Les Présocratiques*, ed. J.-P. Dumont, D. Delattre, and J.-L. Poirier (Paris: Gallimard, Pléiade, 1988), pp. 158–59.

12 See Ezra Pound, *The Cantos* (London: Faber, 1989), pp. 24–25.

13 My translation. In attempting to remain as literal as possible, I have been helped by Roger Munier's commentary in "Héraclite, Les fragments," *La Nouvelle Revue Française*, 436 (May 1989), pp. 14–30.

14 James Joyce, *Letters* II, p. 160.

15 The best treatment of Most is to be found in Dominic Manganiello's *Joyce's Politics*, pp. 101–02.

16 Ezra Pound, *The Cantos*, p. 63.

17 Vladimir Nabokov, *Lectures on Literature* (London: Picador, 1983), p. 259.

18 William Empson, *Seven Types of Ambiguity* (London: Penguin, 1995), p. 46. I am very grateful to Victor Sage for having pointed out the reference to Empson.

19 Robert Burns, *Poems in Scots and English* (London: Everyman, 1993), p. 103.

20 James Joyce, *Oeuvres* II, ed. Jacques Aubert, p. 244.

21 Aristotle, *History of Animals*, Book 5, p. xxxii (557 b 6–9).

22 Blaise Pascal, *Pensées*, trans. A. J. Krailsheimer (London: Penguin, 1966), p. 90.

23 "Did he like elms? Did he know Joyce's poem about the two washerwomen? He did, indeed. Did he like it? He did. In fact he was beginning to like very much arbors and ardors and Adas. They rhymed." Vladimir Nabokov, *Ada* (Harmondsworth, Penguin, 1970), p. 48.

24 See Rodolphe Gasché, "On Reading Responsibly," in *Inventions of Difference* (Cambridge, MA: Harvard University Press, 1994), pp. 237–50, and also pp. 278–79 for a reply to Zizek.

25 Jacques Lacan, seminar on "The Purloined Letter," in *The Purloined Poe, Lacan, Derrida and Psychoanalytic Reading*, ed. J. P. Muller and William Richardson (Baltimore: Johns Hopkins University Press, 1988), pp. 39 and 53.

26 *Ibid.*, p. 40.

6 THE EGOIST VS. THE KING

1 In *The Workshop of Daedalus*, ed. Robert Scholes and Richard M. Kain (Evanston, IL: Northwestern University Press, 1965), p. 100.

2 Quoted in Forrest Read's edition of *Pound/Joyce* (London: Faber, 1968), pp.

17–18. Pound's slightly garbled French may be construed as saying either: "Very few men contribute" or "For fear that men contribute to it."

3 *The Egoist*, January 15, 1914, pp. 26–27.

4 *Ibid.*, p. 27.

5 James Joyce, *Ulysses*, ed. H. W. Gabler.

6 See Peter Costello, *James Joyce: The Years of Growth 1882–1915* (London: Kyle Cathie, 1992), pp. 214–16.

7 James Joyce, *Critical Writings*, ed. Ellsworth Mason and Richard Ellmann, pp. 190–91.

8 Ezra Pound, "James Joyce: At Last the Novel Appears," in *The Egoist*, February 1917, p. 21.

9 Joseph Kelly, *Our Joyce: From Outcast to Icon* (Austin: University of Texas Press, 1998), p. 77.

10 *The Egoist*, February 1917, p. 30.

11 *The Egoist*, October 1916, p. 159.

12 *The Egoist*, February 1917, p. 22.

13 *Our Joyce: From Outcast to Icon*, p. 79.

14 A good illustration is given by Vladimir Nabokov: "*other men die; but I / Am not another; therefore I'll not die.*" See *Pale Fire* (New York: Berkley Medallion, 1969), p. 28.

15 "Mr. Bennet and Mrs. Brown" (1924), in *A Woman's Essays*, ed. Rachel Bowlby (London: Penguin, 1992), p. 70. See also Peter Stansky's *On or About December 1910* (Cambridge, MA: Harvard University Press, 1996).

16 Jonathan Rose, *The Edwardian Temperament 1895–1919* (Athens: Ohio University Press, 1986), pp. xiii–xiv.

17 Andreas Huyssen, *After the Great Divide: Modernism, Mass Culture, Postmodernism* (Bloomington: Indiana University Press, 1986).

18 Wyndham Lewis, *Time and Western Man*, ed. Paul Edwards (Santa Rosa, CA: Black Sparrow Press, 1993), p. 90.

19 Ezra Pound, "Hugh Selwyn Mauberley," in *Selected Poems* (London: Faber, 1968), p. 178.

20 Ezra Pound, *Literary Essays*, ed. T. S. Eliot (London: Faber, 1964), p. 403.

21 Cheryl Herr, *Joyce's Anatomy of Culture* (Urbana: University of Illinois Press, 1986).

22 I quote Anthony Suter's translation of *Les Lauriers sont coupés* by Edouard Dujardin, *The Bays are Sere*, followed by *Interior Monologue* (London: Libris, 1991), p. 3. Hereafter, *Bays* and page number.

23 "The grey warm evening of August had descended upon the city and a mild warm air, a memory of summer, circulated in the streets. The streets, shuttered for the repose of Sunday, swarmed with a gaily coloured crowd. Like illumined pearls the lamps shone from the summits of their tall poles upon the living texture below which, changing shape and hue unceasingly, sent up into the warm grey evening air an unchanging unceasing murmur." James Joyce, *Dubliners*, ed. Terence Brown, p. 43. I shall return to the issue of Joyce's depiction of Irish landscapes, with their emotionally charged overtones, in chapter 9.

24 Dorothy Richardson, *Pointed Roofs*, in *Pilgrimage*, vol. I (Urbana: University of Illinois Press, 1979), p. 171.

25 This letter is quoted by Dujardin in *Interior Monologue*. See *Bays*, p. 22.

26 Virgina Woolf, *Mrs. Dalloway*, ed. E. Showalter (London: Penguin 1992), p. 62.

27 Marcel Proust, *Remembrance of Things Past*, vol. I, trans. C. K. Scott Moncrieff and Terence Kilmartin (New York: Randon House, 1982), p. 3.

28 Dorothy Richardson, "Women and the Future," in *The Gender of Modernism*, ed. Bonnie Kime Scott (Bloomington: Indiana University Press, 1990), p. 412.

29 *Ibid.*, p. 413.

30 *Ibid.*

31 *Mrs. Dalloway*, p. 49.

32 *Ibid.*, p. 143.

33 *Ibid.*, p. 188. This is repeated a few pages later, p. 205.

34 Virginia Woolf, *A Room of One's Own* (Harmondsworth: Penguin, 1970), p. 102.

35 Virginia Woolf, "Modern Novels (Joyce)," in *The Gender of Modernism*, ed. Scott, pp. 642–43.

36 Virginia Woolf, *A Woman's Essays*, p. 85.

37 See Ellmann, *JJII*, p. 679.

38 H. G. Wells, "James Joyce," from *The New Republic* March 10, 1917, repr. in James Joyce, *A Portrait of the Artist as a Young Man*, ed. Chester Anderson, p. 332.

39 James Joyce, *LIV*, p. 329. Originally written in French. I have modified the translation of *"qui, du reste, se règlent très bien sans son aide."*

40 *Time and Western Man*, p. 88.

41 Letter from January 9, 1940, in *LIV*, p. 403.

42 Pound published this essay in *The New Age* of July 12, 1917. See Ezra Pound, *Selected Prose 1909–1965* (London: Faber, 1973), pp. 159–73. Pound begins with Flaubert's famous statement: "If they had read my 'Education Sentimentale' these things would not have happened" (p. 159).

7 THE CONQUEST OF PARIS

1 Giambattista Vico, *The New Science*, trans. Thomas Goddard Bergin and Max Harold Fisch (Ithaca, NY: Cornell University Press, 1984), § 800. One customarily refers to the *New Science* by paragraph numbers, which I do, using always the same edition. I will develop this analysis in chapter 9.

2 I am alluding to my essay on "Joyce the Parisian," in *The Cambridge Companion to James Joyce*, ed. Derek Attridge (Cambridge: Cambridge University Press, 1990), pp. 83–102.

3 Among many other critics, Richard Ellmann has noted that the evocation of Triestine sexual activities ("Belluomo rises from the bed of his wife's lover's wife") had been transferred without modifications to the evocation of Paris in "Proteus," in a paragraph to which I will return, which concludes

with: "Faces of Paris men go by, their wellpleased pleasers, curled *conquista-dores*" (*U*, 3: 215). See Richard Ellmann, *JJII*, p. 344.

4 Stuart Gilbert, *James Joyce's Ulysses: A Study* (New York: Vintage Books, 1955), p. 72, footnote 1.

5 *Ibid.*, p. 124, footnote 1.

6 Vico, *The New Science*, § 611.

7 *Ibid.*, § 708.

8 Quoted from *The Divine Comedy of Dante Aligheri, Inferno*, trans. Allen Mandelbaum (New York: Bantam, 1982), p. 43.

9 *Ibid.*, p. 245.

10 *Odyssey*, XVIII, 270–71. I am quoting Albert Cook's translation of the *Odyssey* (New York: Norton, 1967), p. 252.

11 *Ibid.*, XIX, 530–33.

12 One will find an easily available reproduction in Ellmann's *JJII*, p. xxxvii.

13 See *ibid.*, p. 397.

14 This portrait has been reproduced in *Revue du Littoral*, 36 (October 1992), p. 232. It is accompanied by a commentary in German by Paul Federn, also translated in the same issue pp. 234–35.

15 Lytton Strachey, "Ought the Father to Grow a Beard?," in *The Shorter Strachey*, ed. Michael Holroyd and Paul Levy (Oxford: Oxford University Press, 1980), pp. 19–20.

16 Quoted by Francis Wheen, *Karl Marx: A Life* (New York: Norton, 1999), p. 380.

17 See *ibid.*, pp. 349–83.

18 See Bob Cato's and Greg Vitiello's *Joyce Images* (New York: W. W. Norton, 1994), p. 31. Hereafter *JI* and page number.

8 JOYCE'S TRANSITIONAL REVOLUTION

1 See Blake's "The Marriage of Heaven and Hell" (1793). Stuart Gilbert claims that he added these quotes to the proclamation at the last minute.

2 Quoted in H. S. Harris, *Hegel's Development: Toward the Sunlight (1770–1801)* (Oxford: Oxford University Press, 1972), p. 511. Harris reproduces the "Earliest System-Programme of German Idealism" in an appendix, pp. 510–12.

3 See for instance Joyce's unequivocal condemnation of Romanticism in his conversations with Arthur Power: Arthur Power, *Conversations with James Joyce* pp. 98–99.

4 Samuel Beckett and others, *Our Exagmination Round His Factification for Incamination of Work in Progress* (1929; reprinted London: Faber, 1972), pp. 142–43. Henceforth *Our Exagmination . . .* and page number.

5 C. K. Ogden and I. A. Richards, *The Meaning of Meaning* (1923) (New York: Harcourt and Brace, 1968), pp. 5–6. Henceforth *MM*, and page number.

6 Suzette Henke, "Exagmining Beckett & Company," in *Re-Viewing Classics of Joyce Criticism*, ed. Janet Egleson Dunleavy (Urbana and Chicago: University of Chicago Press, 1991), pp. 60–81.

7 See my discussion of Ginette Verstraete's *Fragments of the Feminine Sublime in Friedrich Schlegel and James Joyce* in chapter 4.

8 I have tried to show how the collaboration between Graves and Riding provided the English-speaking world with a clear definition of Modernism in "Uncoupling Modernism," in *The Ghosts of Modernity*, pp. 205–10.

9 Published on the first page of *transition* no. 16–17, June 1929.

10 Charles Duff, *James Joyce and the Plain Reader* (London: Desmond Harmsworth, 1932.) The essay is prefaced by Herbert Read, who has people like Graves and Riding in mind when he states at the beginning of his introductory letter that "Joyce is, of course, primarily a poet" (p. 8). Henceforth *JJPR*, and page number.

11 C. K. Ogden, "Work in Progress by James Joyce," *transition*, 21 (March 1932), reproduced in *In Transition: A Paris Anthology*, ed. by N. R. Fitch (New York: Doubleday, 1990), p. 135.

12 C. K. Ogden, *Debabelization* (London: Kegan Paul, 1931). Henceforth, *D*, and page number.

13 Manfred Pütz, "The Identity of the Reader in *Finnegans Wake*," *James Joyce Quarterly*, 11, 4 (Summer 1974), pp. 387–93.

14 Sigmund Freud, *The Question of Lay Analysis, An Introduction to Psychoanalysis*, trans. Nancy Procter-Gregg (New York: Norton, 1950).

9 HOSPITALITY AND SODOMY

1 Terry Eagleton, "Nationalism: Irony and Commitment," in *Nationalism, Colonialism and Literature*, ed. Seamus Deane (Minneapolis: University of Minnesota Press, 1990), p. 36.

2 *LII*, 166.

3 See Walter Benjamin, *Das Passagenwerk* (Frankfurt: Suhrkampf, 1983), vol. I, pp. 52–55 and 70–73.

4 Flann O'Brien, *The Dalkey Archive* (London, Flamingo, 1993), pp. 170–71.

5 Richard Ellmann, *James Joyce*, p. 245.

6 See Jacques Derrida and Anne Dufourmantelle, *De L'hospitalité* (Paris: Calmann-Lévy, 1997).

7 They have been republished together under the title of *Les Lois de l'hospitalité* (Paris: Gallimard, 1965).

8 Pierre Klossowski, *Roberte ce soir* (Paris: Editions de Minuit, 1953), p. 13.

9 Fritz Senn, "Protean Inglossabilities," in *Inductive Scrutinies* (Dublin: Lilliput Press, 1995), p. 151.

10 See Richard Ellman's biography of Wilde for the use of this phrase during the trial. Essentially, the "Love that dare not speak its name" is the chaste love between an older man and a younger man. Richard Ellmann, *Oscar Wilde* (New York: A. A. Knopf, 1988), p. 463.

11 In that sense, Joyce would be at the opposite of a Pound who still castigates Usura as Sodomy in his *Cantos*, both being "contra naturam" – as Aquinas and most medieval theologians had it.

12 I owe a lot to Joseph Peguigney's excellent article, "Sodomy in Dante's

Inferno and *Purgatorio*," *Representations*, 36 (Fall 1991), pp. 22–42. As he notes on p. 23, sodomy was indeed one of the "sins against nature" for most medieval theologians, but for Aquinas it was only halfway between bestiality and masturbation.

13 "*Quia amare est velle alicui bonum*:," Aquinas, *Summa Theologica 1*, art. 2, par. 1, in *Summa Sancti Thomae*, ed. E. C.-R. Billuart (Paris and Rome, 1872), 2:397.

14 "The Portrait of Mr. W. H.," in *The Works of Oscar Wilde*, 941.

15 Lawrence Danson, "Oscar Wilde, W. H., and the Unspoken Name of Love," *ELH*, 58, 4 (1991), p. 980.

16 *Ibid.*, p. 981.

17 See the reproduction of Queensbury's visiting card in H. Montgomery Hyde, *The Trials of Oscar Wilde* (London: William Hodge, 1948), p. 98.

18 One will have recognized André Pézard's controversial thesis in *Dante sous la pluie de feu* (Paris: Vrin, 1950). See also J. Peguigney's "Sodomy," for a clear contextualization of this interpretation. I am alluding to Dante's *Inferno, The Divine Comedy of Dante Alighieri*, trans. Allen Mandelbaum, pp. 135–37.

19 The Marquess of Queensbury took pains to focus on Wilde's appearance only. The following exchange is typical: "Then I asked: 'Lord Queensbury, do you seriously accuse your son and me of improper conduct?' He said, 'I do not say you are it, but you look it.' (Laughter)" (Hyde, *Trials of Oscar Wilde* p. 119). Wilde's appeal for "seriousness" is debarred by the upsurge of laughter triggered by Queensbury's reply. After an admonition by the judge, Queensbury reasserts: "But you look it, and you pose as it, which is just as bad." Joyce took the hint: what matters is not the "matter" or substance of the indicted perversion but its appearance. The crux of such alleged "perversion" is that no one can possibly distinguish between seriousness and laughter, "posing" and sexual "facts," transgressing and pretending to transgress. This is an insight that has been later developed by Jean Genet, as I have tried to show in "Jean Genet: La Position du Franc-Tireur," *L'Esprit Createur*, 35, 1 (Spring 1995), pp. 30–39.

20 Hyde, *Trials of Oscar Wilde*, p. 120.

21 Sam Slote, "Wilde Thing," paper read at the 1992 Dublin Joyce Symposium. See David Hayman, *The Wake in Transit* (Ithaca, NY: Cornell University Press, 1990), pp. 130–38, for links between the Tristan–Isolde–Mark configuration, incest, and Wilde's "sin."

22 Vyvyan Holland, *Son of Oscar Wilde* (London: Rupert Hart-Davis, 1954), p. 14.

23 For all these points, see Bruno Pinchard, *La Raison dédoublée* (Paris: Aubier, 1992) and his excellent introduction to Vico's *De l'antique sagesse de l'Italie*, trans. Jules Michelet in 1835 (Paris: Garnier-Flammarion, 1993).

24 *The New Science of Giambattista Vico*, trans. Bergin and Fisch, p. 196. Henceforth *SN*, and page number.

25 Emile Benveniste, *Le Vocabulaire des institutions Indo-Européennes*, vol. 1, *Economie, parenté, société* (Paris: Editions de Minuit, 1969), pp. 92–101, pp. 341, pp. 360–61.

26 J. Hillis Miller, "The Critic as Host," in *Deconstruction and Criticism* (London: Routledge, 1979), pp. 220–22.

27 See Don Gifford and Robert J. Seidman, *Ulysses Annotated* (Berkeley: University of California Press, 1988), p. 30, for Joyce's sources.

10 HOSPITALITY IN THE CAPITAL CITY

1 See the important appendix in Danis Rose and John O'Hanlon, *Understanding Finnegans Wake* (New York: Garland, 1982), pp. 331–40.
2 *Reflections on James Joyce. Stuart Gilbert's Paris Journal*, pp. 20–21. Hereafter *PJ*, and page number.
3 Small angular brackets mean "deleted word."
4 See Roland McHugh, *Annotations to Finnegans Wake* (Baltimore: Johns Hopkins University Press, 1991), p. 543. McHugh refers to Dillon Cosgrave's book on *North Dublin* for this piece of information.
5 Benjamin Seebohm Rowntree, *Poverty, a Study of Town Life* (London: Macmillan, 1902).
6 James Atherton, *The Books at the Wake* (New York: Viking, 1960), p. 76.
7 Walter Benjamin, "N. Re The Theory of Knowledge, Theory of Progress," trans. Leigh Hafrey and Richard Sieburth, in *Benjamin, Philosphy, Aesthetics, History*, ed. Gary Smith (Chicago: University of Chicago Press, 1989), p. 47. The original is to be found in Walter Benjamin, *Das Passagenwerk*, vol. 1 (Frankfurt: Suhrkamp, 1983), p. 574.
8 Walter Benjamin "N. Re The Theory of Knowledge, Theory of Progress," p. 52 (modified) and *Das Passagenwerk*, vol. 1, p. 580.
9 Stéphane Mallarmé wrote: "Who were the Saxons? Angles: Angles, just as they called themselves." *Les Mots Anglais*, in *Oeuvres Complètes*, ed. Henri Mondor (Paris: Gallimard, 1961), p. 905.

11 JOYCE'S LATE MODERNISM AND THE BIRTH OF THE GENETIC READER

1 Franco Moretti, *Modern Epic: The World System from Goethe to Garcia Marquez* (London: Verso, 1996), pp. 123–229.
2 *Ibid.*, pp. 151–52.
3 *Ibid.*, p. 155.
4 I have analyzed the function of textual repetition in my *Language, Sexuality and Ideology in Ezra Pound's Cantos* (London: Macmillan, 1986), pp. 67–69.
5 I refer to Pound's quotation of Divus's version in his article "Early Translator of Homer," in *Literary Essays*, pp. 261 and 262. See also Pietro Pucci's fascinating comments in *Odysseus Polutropos: Intertextual Readings in the Odyssey and the Iliad* (Ithaca, NY: Cornell University Press, 1987, pp. 33–49. I refer to Ezra Pound, *The Cantos*.
6 Carol Shloss, "*Finnegans Wake* as a History of the Book," in *James Joyce: The Centennial Symposium*, ed. Maurice Beja, P. Herring, M. Harmon, D. Norris (Urbana: University of Illinois Press, 1986), p. 110.
7 Jerome McGann, *The Textual Condition* (Princeton: Princeton University Press, 1991), p. 119. Hereafter *TC*, and page number.

8 See Ronald Bush, "Excavating the Ideological Faultlines of Modernism," in *Representing Modernist Texts: Editing as Interpretation*, ed. George Bornstein (Ann Arbor: University of Michigan Press, 1991), p. 80. See also the excellent piece by Vicki Mahaffey on *Ulysses* in the same volume.

9 Umberto Eco, Richard Rorty, Jonathan Culler, and Christine Brooke-Rose, *Interpretation and Overinterpretation* (Cambridge: Cambridge University Press, 1992). Hereafter *IO*, and page number.

10 Umberto Eco, *The Limits of Interpretation* (Bloomington and Indianapolis: Indiana University Press, 1990). Hereafter *LI*, and page number.

11 David Hayman, *The Wake in Transit*, p. 74.

12 For a brief but illuminating account of the opposition between Paris and Bédier, see Bernard Cerquiglini, *Eloge de la variante* (Paris: Seuil, 1989), pp. 73–101. Hereafter *EV*, and page number.

13 I borrow this expression from Cerquiglini, *ibid.*, p. 122, n. 43.

14 Dom Henri Quentin, *Essais de critique textuelle (ecdotique)* (Paris: Picard, 1926). Hereafter *ECT*, and page number.

12 STEWARDSHIP, PARNELLISM, AND EGOTISM

1 For a spirited reading of the parable, see Margot Norris: "Setting Critical Accounts Right: Tom Kernan, Usury and Unjust Stewardship" in *A Collideorscape of Joyce: Festschrift for Fritz Senn*, ed. Ruth Frehner and Ursula Zeller (Dublin: Lilliput Press, 1998), pp. 51–67.

2 James Joyce, *Dubliners*, ed. R. Scholes and A. W. Litz (New York and London: Penguin and Viking, 1976), p. 173.

3 Quoted by Ellmann in *JJII*, p. 693, footnote.

4 See Charles Ford, "Dante's Other Brush: Ulysses and the Irish Revolution," *James Joyce Quarterly*, 29, 4 (Summer 1992), pp. 751–61.

5 Samuel Beckett, *The Unnamable*, in *Three Novels* (New York: Grove Press, 1991), p. 300. For an excellent analysis of the paradoxes of egologic subjectivity in Beckett, see Daniel Katz, *Saying I No More: Subjectivity and Consciousness in the Prose of Samuel Beckett* (Evanston, IL: Northwestern University Press, 1999).

Bibliography

Anderson, Benedict, *Imagined Communities* (New York: Verso, 1991).

Aquinas, *Summa Sancti Thomae*, ed. E. C.-R. Billuart (Paris and Rome, 1872).

Aristotle, *Problems*, and *History of Animals*, trans. W. S. Hett (London: Heinemann, 1926).

Atherton, James, *The Books at the Wake* (New York: Viking, 1960).

Attridge, Derek, ed., *The Cambridge Companion to James Joyce* (Cambridge: Cambridge University Press, 1990).

Aubert, Jacques, editor *Joyce & Paris* (Lille and Paris: CNRS, 1979).

Joyce avec Lacan (Paris: Navarin, 1987).

James Joyce, Oeuvres II (Paris: Gallimard, Bibliothèque de la Pléiade, 1996).

Beckett, Samuel, *Three Novels* (New York: Grove Press, 1991).

Beja, Maurice, P. Herring, M. Harmon, D. Norris, eds., *James Joyce: The Centennial Symposium* (Urbana: University of Illinois Press, 1986).

Benjamin, Walter, *Das Passagenwerk* (Frankfurt: Suhrkamp, 1983).

Benveniste, Emile, *Le Vocabulaire des institutions indo-européennes*, vol. 1, *Economie, parenté, société* (Paris: Editions de Minuit, 1969).

Blau Du Plessis, Rachel, *The Pink Guitar: Writing as Feminist Practice* (New York: Routledge, 1990).

Bornstein, George, ed., *Representing Modernist Texts: Editing as Interpretation* (Ann Arbor: University of Michigan Press, 1991).

Bosanquet, Bernard, *Three Lectures on Aesthetics* (London: Macmillan, 1923).

Branden, Barbara, *The Passion of Ayn Rand* (New York: Doubleday, 1986).

Brannigan, John, Geoff Ward, and Julian Wolfreys, eds., *Re:Joyce. Text, Culture, Politics* (London: Macmillan, 1998).

Braunstein, Néstor, *La Jouissance, un concept lacanien* (Paris: Point Hors Ligne, 1992).

"La clínica en el nombre propio," in *El Laberinto de las Estructuras*, ed. Helí Morales Asencio (Mexico: Siglo 21, 1997) pp. 70–96.

"El ego lacaniano," in *En Las Suplencias del Nombre del Padre*, ed. Helí Morales and Daniel Gerber (Mexico: Siglo 21, 1998), pp. 53–74.

Burke, Edmund, *A Philosophical Enquiry into the Origin of our Ideas of the Sublime and the Beautiful* (Oxford: Oxford University Press, 1990).

Burns, Robert, *Poems in Scots and English* (London: Everyman, 1993).

Cato, Bob and Greg Vitiello, *Joyce Images* (New York: W. W. Norton, 1994).

Cerquiglini, Bernard, *Eloge de la variante* (Paris: Seuil, 1989).

Cheng, Vincent, *Joyce, Race and Empire* (Cambridge: Cambridge University Press, 1995).

Clarke, Bruce, *Dora Marsden and Early Modernism: Gender, Individuality, Science*, (Ann Arbor: University of Michigan Press, 1995).

Colum, Padraic, *Ourselves Alone!* (New York: Crown, 1959).

Compagnon, Antoine, *Les Cinq Paradoxes de la modernité* (Paris: Seuil, 1990).

Conisbee, Philip, ed., *Georges de La Tour and his World* (Washington: National Gallery of Art, 1996).

Costello, Peter, *James Joyce: The Years of Growth 1882–1915* (London: Kyle Cathie, 1992).

Danson, Lawrence, "Oscar Wilde, W. H., and the Unspoken Name of Love," *ELH*, 58, 4 (1991) pp. 979–1000.

Dante (Alighieri), *The Divine Comedy*, trans. Allen Mandelbaum (New York: Bantam, 1982).

Davies, Malcolm and Jeyaraney Kathirithamby, *Greek Insects* (New York: Oxford University Press, 1986).

Davis, Robert Con, *The Fictional Father* (Amherst: University of Massachusetts Press, 1981).

Deane, Seamus, *Celtic Revivals: Essays in Modern Irish Literature 1885–1980* (London: Faber, 1985).

Deane, Seamus, ed., *Nationalism, Colonialism and Literature* (Minneapolis: University of Minnesota Press, 1990).

Derrida, Jacques, *Specters of Marx*, trans. P. Kamuf (New York: Routledge, 1994).

Derrida, Jacques, in Anne Dufourmantelle, ed., *De l'hospitalité* (Paris: Calmann-Lévy, 1997).

Duchamp, Marcel, *Duchamp du signe: écrits* (Paris: Flammarion, 1975).

Duff, Charles, *James Joyce and the Plain Reader* (London: Desmond Harmsworth, 1932).

Dumont, Jean-Paul, *et al.*, eds., *Les Présocratiques* (Paris: Gallimard, Pléiade, 1988).

Dunleavy, Janet Egleson, *Re-Viewing Classics of Joyce Criticism* (Urbana and Chicago: University of Chicago Press, 1991).

Eagleton, Terry, *The Ideology of the Aesthetic* (Oxford: Blackwell, 1990).

Eco, Umberto, *The Limits of Interpretation* (Bloomington and Indianapolis: Indiana University Press, 1990).

Eco, Umberto, with Richard Rorty, Jonathan Culler, and Christine Brooke-Rose, *Interpretation and Overinterpretation*, ed. S. Collini (Cambridge: Cambridge University Press, 1992).

Eliot, Thomas Stearns, *Collected Poems 1909–1962* (London: Faber, 1963).

Ellmann, Richard, *The Consciousness of Joyce* (London, Faber, 1977).
   James Joyce, 2nd revised edn, (Oxford: Oxford University Press, 1983).

Empson, William, *Seven Types of Ambiguity* (London: Penguin, 1995).

Finkielkraut, Alain, *The Defeat of the Mind*, trans. Judith Friedlander (New York: Columbia University Press, 1995).

Fitch, Noel Riley, ed., *In Transition: A Paris Anthology* (New York: Doubleday, 1990).

Ford, Charles, "Dante's Other Brush: Ulysses and the Irish Revolution," *James Joyce Quarterly*, 29, 4 (Summer 1992), pp. 751–61.

Frehner, Ruth, and Ursula, Zeller, eds., *A Collideorscape of Joyce: Festschrift for Fritz Senn* (Dublin: Lilliput Press, 1998).

Freud, Sigmund, *The Interpretation of Dreams*, trans. James Strachey (New York: Avon Books, 1965).

Die Traumdeutung (Frankfurt: Fischer Verlag, 1972).

The Interpretation of Dreams, trans. Joyce Crick (Oxford: Oxford University Press, 1999).

"A Child is Being Beaten," in *Sexuality and the Psychology of Love* (New York: Collier, 1978) pp. 107–32.

On Creativity and the Unconscious, ed. B. Nelson (New York: Harper and Row, 1958).

Bildende Kunst und Literatur (Frankfurt: Fischer, 1970).

The Question of Lay Analysis, An Introduction to Psychoanalysis, trans. Nancy Procter-Gregg (New York: Norton, 1950).

Freud, Sigmund, and William C. Bullitt, *Thomas Woodrow Wilson: A Psychological Study* (Boston: Houghton Mifflin, 1966).

Gaitskill, Mary, *Two Girls, Fat and Thin* (New York: Poseidon, 1991).

Galopin, Augustin, *Le Parfum de la femme et le sens olfactif dans l'amour: étude psycho-physiologique* (Paris: E. Dentu, Librairie de la Société des Gens de Lettres, 1889).

Gasché, Rodolphe, "On Reading Responsibly," in *Inventions of Difference* (Cambridge, MA: Harvard University Press, 1994).

Gifford, Don and Robert J. Seidman, *Ulysses Annotated* (Berkeley: University of California Press, 1988).

Gilbert, Stuart, *James Joyce's Ulysses: A Study* (New York: Vintage Books, 1955).

Reflections on James Joyce. Stuart Gilbert's Paris Journal, ed. T. F. Staley and R. Lewis (Austin: University Press of Texas, 1993).

Godzich, Wlad, ed., *Paul de Man, The Resistance to Theory* (Minneapolis: University of Minnesota Press, 1986).

Green, Jonathan, *Cassell Dictionary of Cynical Quotations* (London: Cassell, 1994).

Greenfeld, Liah, *Nationalism: Five Roads to Modernity* (Cambridge, MA: Harvard University Press, 1992).

Greenslade, William, *Degeneration, Culture and the Novel 1880–1940* (Cambridge: Cambridge University Press, 1994).

Harari, Roberto, *Como se llama James Joyce? A partir de "El Sinthoma" de Lacan* (Buenos Aires: Amorrortu editores, 1996).

Harris, H. S., *Hegel's Development: Toward the Sunlight (1770–1801)* (Oxford: Oxford University Press, 1972).

Hayman, David, *The Wake in Transit* (Ithaca, NY: Cornell University Press, 1990).

Hayman, David, ed., *European James Joyce Studies, Genetic Probes* (Rodolpi, Amsterdam, 1996).

Hegel, G. W. H., *The Phenomenology of Spirit*, trans. A. V. Miller, (Oxford: Oxford University Press, 1977).

Heidegger, Martin, *Basic Writings*, ed. David Farrell Krell (New York: Harper and Collins, 1993).

Unterwegs zur Sprache (Pfullingen: Günther Neske, 1959).

Herr, Cheryl, *Joyce's Anatomy of Culture* (Urbana: University of Illinois Press, 1986).

Holland, Vyvyan, *Son of Oscar Wilde* (London: Rupert Hart-Davis, 1954).

Homer, *Odyssey*, trans. Albert Cook (New York: Norton, 1967).

Huyssen, Andreas, *After the Great Divide: Modernism, Mass Culture, Postmodernism* (Bloomington: Indiana University Press, 1986).

Hyde, H. Montgomery, ed., *The Three Trials of Oscar Wilde* (London: William Hodge, 1948).

Jaurretsche, Colleen, *The Sensual Philosophy: Joyce and the Aesthetics of Mysticism* (Madison: University of Wisconsin Press, 1997).

Jolas, Eugène, *Man from Babel* (Yale: Yale University Press, 1998).

Jones, Ernest, *Papers on Psycho-Analysis* (Boston: Beacon, 1967).

Joyce, James, *Finnegans Wake* (London: Faber, 1939).

Critical Writings, ed. Ellsworth Mason and Richard Ellmann (New York: Viking, 1964).

A Portrait of the Artist as a Young Man, ed. Chester Anderson (New York: Viking, 1968).

Selected Letters, ed. Richard Ellmann (London: Faber, 1975).

Ulysses, ed. H. W. Gabler (London: Penguin, 1986).

Dubliners, ed. Terence Brown (London: Penguin, 1992).

Poems and Exiles, ed. J. C. C. Mays (London, Penguin, 1992).

Joyce, Stanislaus, *The Complete Dublin Diary*, ed. George H. Healey (Ithaca, NY: Cornell UniversityPress, 1971).

Kant, Immanuel, *The Critique of Judgement*, trans. J. C. Meredith (Oxford: Oxford University Press, 1952).

Kaplan, Carola M. and Anne B. Simpson, eds., *Seeing Double: Revisioning Edwardian and Modernist Literature* (New York: Saint Martin's Press, 1996).

Katz, Daniel, *Saying I No More: Subjectivity and Consciousness in the Prose of Samuel Beckett* (Evanston, IL: Northwestern University Press, 1999).

Kelly, Joseph, *Our Joyce: From Outcast to Icon* (Austin: University of Texas Press, 1998).

Lacan, Jacques, "Some Reflections on the Ego," *International Journal of Pyschoanalysis*, 34 (1953).

De la psychose paranoïaque dans ses rapports avec la personnalité, suivi de premiers écrits sur la paranoia (Paris: Seuil, 1975).

"Conférences et entretiens dans des universités nord-américaines," in *Scilicet* nos. 6/7 (Paris: Seuil, 1976) pp. 7–63.

"Le Sinthome," *Ornicar?*, 9 (April 1977), pp. 32–40, 10 (July 1977), pp. 5–12, and 11 (September 1977), pp. 2–9.

Lacan, Jacques, seminar on "The Purloined Letter," in *The Purloined Poe, Lacan, Derrida and Psychoanalytic Reading*, ed. J. P. Muller and William Richardson (Baltimore: Johns Hopkins University Press, 1988).

Lacan, Jacques, *Television*, ed. Joan Copjec, trans. D. Hollier, R. Krauss, and A. Michelson (New York: Norton, 1990).

Lautréamont (Isidore Ducasse), *Oeuvres Complètes d'Isidore Ducasse, Les Chants de Maldoror* (Paris: Livre de Poche, 1964).

Levenson, Michael, *A Genealogy of Modernism* (Cambridge: Cambridge University Press 1984).

Lewis, Wyndham, *Time and Western Man*, ed. Paul Edwards (Santa Rosa, CA: Black Sparrow Press, 1993).

MacCabe, Colin, *James Joyce and the Revolution of the Word* (London: Macmillan, 1978).

Mahaffey, Vicki, *Reauthorizing Joyce*, new edn (Gainesville: University Press of Florida, 1995).

Mailhos, Jacques, "The Art of Memory: Joyce and Perec" in *Transcultural Joyce*, ed. Karen Lawrence (Cambridge: Cambridge University Press, 1998) pp. 151–69.

Mallarmé, Stéphane, *Oeuvres complètes*, ed. Henri Mondor (Paris: Gallimard, 1961).

Manganiello, Dominic, *Joyce's Politics* (London: Routledge, 1980).

Manier, Alain, *Le Jour où l'espace a coupé le temps: Etiologie et clinique de la psychose* (Plancoët: Editions La Tempérance, 1995).

Marsden, Dora, ed., *The New Freewoman* and *The Egoist*, London 1913–19.

Marx, Karl, and Friedrich, Engels, *The German Ideology, Collected Works*, vol. v (New York: International Publishers, 1976).

Ireland and the Irish Question (Moscow: Progress Publishers, 1971).

Maye, Brian, *Arthur Griffith* (Dublin: Griffith College Publications, 1997).

McGann, Jerome, *The Textual Condition* (Princeton: Princeton University Press, 1991),

McHugh, Roland, *Annotations to Finnegans Wake*, 2nd revised edn (Baltimore: Johns Hopkins University Press, 1991).

Meredith, George, *The Ordeal of Richard Feverel* (New York: Signet, 1961).

The Egoist, ed. Robert M. Adams (New York: Norton, 1979).

Miller, Jacques-Alain, "A Reading of Some Details in *Television* in Dialogue with the Audience," *Letters from the Freudian Field*, 4, 1/2 (Spring-Fall 1990).

Miller, J. Hillis, "The Critic as Host," in *Deconstruction and Criticism* (London: Routledge, 1979), pp. 217–53.

Miller, Tyrus, *Late Modernism: Politics, Fiction and the Arts Between the World Wars* (Stanford, CA: Stanford University Press, 1999).

Monnier, Adrienne, *Les Gazettes, 1923–1945* (Paris: Gallimard, 1996).

Moretti, Franco, *Modern Epic: The World System from Goethe to Garcia Marquez* (London: Verso, 1996).

Munier, Roger, "Héraclite, Les fragments," *La Nouvelle Revue Française*, 436, (May 1989), pp. 14–30.

Nabokov, Vladimir, *Lectures on Literature* (London: Picador, 1983).

Ada (Harmondworth, Penguin, 1970).

Nolan, Emer, *James Joyce and Nationalism* (New York: Routledge, 1995).

Nordau, Max, *Degeneration* (New York: Appleton and Co., 1895).

O'Brien, Flann, *The Dalkey Archive* (London: Flamingo, 1993).

Ogden, C. K., *Debabelization* (London: Kegan Paul, 1931).

Ogden, C. K. and I. A. Richards, *The Meaning of Meaning* (New York: Harcourt and Brace, 1968).

Olson, Charles, *Selected Writings*, ed. Robert Creeley (New York: New Directions, 1976).

Pascal, Blaise, *Pensées*, trans. A. J. Krailsheimer (London: Penguin, 1966).

Peguigney, Joseph, "Sodomy in Dante's *Inferno* and *Purgatorio*," *Representations*, 36 (Fall 1991), pp. 22–42.

Pézard, André, *Dante sous la pluie de feu* (Paris: Vrin, 1950).

Pinchard, Bruno, *La Raison dédoublée* (Paris: Aubier, 1992).

Pound, Ezra, *Literary Essays*, ed. T. S. Eliot (London: Faber, 1964).
  Selected Prose 1909–1965 (London: Faber, 1973).
  Selected Poems (London: Faber, 1968).
  The Cantos (London: Faber, 1989).

Power, Arthur, *Conversations with James Joyce* (London: Millington, 1974).

Proust, Marcel, *Remembrance of Things Past*, vol. I, trans. C. K. Scott Moncrieff and Terence Kilmartin (New York: Randon House, 1982).

Pucci, Pietro, *Odysseus Polutropos: Intertextual Readings in the Odyssey and the Iliad* (Ithaca, NY: Cornell University Press, 1987).

Pütz, Manfred, "The Identity of the Reader in *Finnegans Wake*," *James Joyce Quarterly*, 11, 4 (Summer 1974), pp. 387–93.

Quentin, Dom Henri, *Essais de critique textuelle (ecdotique)* (Paris: Picard, 1926).

Rabaté, Jean-Michel, *Joyce Upon the Void* (London: Macmillan, 1991).
  La Pénultième est morte (Seyssel: Champ Vallon, 1993).
  James Joyce, Authorized Reader (Baltimore: Johns Hopkins University Press, 1991).
  The Ghosts of Modernity (Gainesville: University Press of Florida, 1996).

Ragland-Sullivan, Ellie, "Lacan's Seminars on James Joyce: Writing as Symptom and 'Singular Solution'," in *Psychoanalysis and . . .*, ed. R. Feldstein and Henry Sussman (New York: Routledge, 1990) pp. 76–86.

Rand, Ayn, *Atlas Shrugged* (New York: Signet, 1992).
  The Fountainhead (New York: Signet, 1993).

Rand, Ayn and Nathaniel Branden, *The Virtue of Selfishness* (New York: Signet, 1964).

Renan, Ernest, *The Poetry of Celtic Races and Other Studies*, trans. W. E. Hutchinson (London: Walter Scott, 1896).

Richardson, Dorothy, *Pointed Roofs* (*Pilgrimage* vol. I) (Urbana: University of Illinois Press, 1979).

Rimbaud, Arthur, *Collected Poems*, trans. Oliver Bernard (London: Penguin, 1986).

Rose, Danis, and John O'Hanlon, *Understanding Finnegans Wake* (New York: Garland, 1982).

Rose, Jonathan, *The Edwardian Temperament 1895–1919* (Athens: Ohio University Press, 1986).

Roudinesco, Elisabeth, *Jacques Lacan*, trans. Barbara Bray (New York: Columbia University Press, 1997).

Sartre, Jean-Paul, *Saint Genet: Actor & Martyr*, trans. Bernard Frechtman (London: Heinemann, 1988).

Scholes, Robert, and Kain, Richard M, eds., *The Workshop of Daedalus*, (Evanston, IL: Northwestern University Press, 1965).

Schürmann, Reiner, *Heidegger on Being and Acting: from Principles to Anarchy*, trans. Christine-Marie Gros and the author (Bloomington: Indiana University Press, 1987).

Scott, Bonnie Kime, ed., *The Gender of Modernism* (Bloomington: Indiana University Press, 1990).

Senn, Fritz, *Inductive Scrutinies* (Dublin: Lilliput Press, 1995).

Slote, Sam, "Wilde Thing," unpublished paper read at the 1992 Dublin Joyce Symposium.

Smith, Gary, *Benjamin, Philosophy, Aesthetics, History* (Chicago: University of Chicago Press, 1989).

Stansky, Peter, *On or About December 1910* (Cambridge, MA: Harvard University Press, 1996).

Stendhal (Henry Beyle), "Souvenirs d'Egotisme," in *Oeuvres Intimes* (Paris: Gallimard, 1966).

Stirner, Max, *The Ego and His Own*, trans. S. T. Byington (New York: Benjamin Tucker, 1907).

    The Ego and His Own, trans. S. T. Byington, ed. J. J. Martin, (New York: Dover, 1973).

    The Ego and Its Own, ed. David Leopold (Cambridge: Cambridge University Press, 1995).

Strachey, Lytton, *The Shorter Strachey*, ed. Michael Holroyd and Paul Levy (Oxford: Oxford University Press, 1980).

Thornton, Weldon, *The Antimodernism of Joyce's Portrait of the Artist as a Young Man* (Syracuse, NY: Syracuse University Press, 1994).

Valente, Joseph, ed., *Quare Joyce* (Ann Arbor: Michigan University Press, 1999).

Verstraete, Ginette, *Fragments of the Feminine Sublime in Friedrich Schlegel and James Joyce* (New York: Suny Press, 1998).

Vico, Giambattista, *The New Science*, trans. Thomas Goddard Bergin and Max Harold Fisch (Ithaca, NY: Cornell University Press, 1984).

    De l'Antique Sagesse de l'Italie, trans. Jules Michelet (1835), ed. Bruno Pinchard (Paris: Garnier-Flammarion, 1993).

Von Hallberg, Robert, "Libertarian Imagism," *Modernism/Modernity*, 2 (April 1995), pp. 63–79.

Walker, Jeff, *The Ayn Rand Cult* (Chicago: Open Court, 1999).

Weir, David, *Anarchy and Culture: The Aesthetic Politics of Anarchism* (Amherst: University of Massachusetts Press, 1997).

Wheen, Francis, *Karl Marx: A Life* (New York: Norton, 1999).

Wilde, Oscar, *The Works of Oscar Wilde* (London: Spring Books, 1963).

Williams, Trevor, *Reading Joyce Politically* (Gainesville: University Press of Florida, 1997).

Woolf, Virginia, *A Woman's Essays*, ed. Rachel Bowlby (London: Penguin, 1992).

    Mrs. Dalloway, ed. E. Showalter (London: Penguin 1992).

    A Room of One's Own (Harmondsworth: Penguin, 1970).

Ziarek, Kryzstof, *The Splinters of Experience* (Evanston, IL: Northwestern University Press, forthcoming).

Zizek, Slavoj, *The Sublime Object of Ideology* (London: Verso, 1989).

    Enjoy Your Symptom! (New York: Routledge, 1992).

    "The Lesbian Session," *Lacanian Ink*, 12 (Fall 1997), pp. 59–69.

Index